excellence in

Procurement Strategy

How to strategically align corporate and procurement objectives

excellence in
Procurement Strategy

How to strategically align corporate and procurement objectives

Stuart Emmett & Barry Crocker

Contents

About this book

We covered in *Excellence in Procurement* (Emmett and Crocker, 2008) the tactical side of procurement, for example, the procurement cycle or the Procure to Pay (P2P) process. This starts with the initial customer need, through the sourcing and placing of orders, to the subsequent delivery and payment, and finally to reviewing the complete cyclical process.

We also looked in this book at the best practice for pricing, relationships, global sourcing, outsourcing, information communication technology (ICT), corporate social responsibility (CSR) and supplier development.

Since 2008, we amplified some of these best practices in other *Excellence in...* titles, for example, *Supplier Management* (2009), *Services Procurement* (2009) and *Global Supply Chain Management* (2010).

In *Excellence in Procurement*, we also gave our outline of a vision for procurement. Therefore, in this Procurement Strategy book, we will now take this vision forward, and show how to align an organisational corporate strategy with an organisation's procurement objectives.

In doing this, we will take the view that the design and implementation of a Procurement Strategy must consider demand (and the customers), the organisation's processes and the supply (and the suppliers); accordingly, in this book, the vision is viewed as follows:

Demand side (this comes first, as everything else follows on from satisfying a need from customers):

- Procurement will champion involvement with customers and be proactive to meet anticipated customer requirements.
- Procurement will provide customers with by delivering a quality product at the right time and at the right price.

Procurement organisation (the structure and process needs to be "right" and in alignment with enabling policies)

- Procurement will join with the rest of the organisation in recognising:
- ✓ Profit and success only comes from satisfaction
- ✓ People working with other people run the organisation and its supply chain, therefore people relations is the key to success.
- Procurement will recognise that the supply chain is a series of internal and external cross-functional processes and procurement will be an active and willing member of the internal cross-functional structure that connects to all of the external supply processes.
- Procurement will actively encourage and embrace as the norm:
- ✓ Selective use of technology, for example, E-Commerce, is used as appropriate for the organisation.
- ✓ Education and training and professional standing with professional

certification will be a requirement, (as is found with accountancy, legal professions etc).

✓ Measuring of lead-time, their improvement and the removal of all supply lead-time variability by negotiating fixed, known and reliable supply lead times with both internal and external parties.

✓ Outsourcing of all noncore activity, including where required, part or all, of tactical procurement.

✓ Continuously review its own activities and practice improvement including searching for procurement best practices from all sectors.

Supply side (the third "heartbeat" of a procurement strategy providing the supply for customers), therefore:

- Suppliers will recognise that they are critically important in the provision of new ideas, innovation and value that can increase the performance of the organisation.
- Procurement will share with suppliers a joint common agenda; to meet customer requirements.
- Procurement will be committed to its key suppliers for mutual benefit and gain over the medium to long term, and will work together for continuous improvements year on year.
- Procurement will ensure that "fit for purpose," supplier selection and evaluation is undertaken and that this key activity is not rule bound or covered by restrictive bureaucratic procedures that are now out of date.
- Procurement will be the sponsors of and ethical dealing within their organisation.
- Procurement will not be seen as "the free lunch guys" or will be involved in any corrupt practices and "under the table deals" that denigrate personal morality, an organisation and society.

The above topics are the essential parts of this book, along with a discussion on aligning corporate strategy with procurement strategy. We would of course acknowledge that such a breaking down into parts is artificial, as it can then ignore the reality of the cross-functional interrelationships between the parts.

Here, meeting demand in any organisation and arranging for the supply is a holistic system, that involves process dependencies and variabilities across the many functional interfaces.

Indeed, as we have noted above, a Procurement Strategy must recognise and enable all of the appropriate supply chain cross-functional aspects.

We would also clarify the words Procurement and Purchasing. We use the words interchangeably as we see them as being the same thing, and commonly find this is the view used by most practioneers. We do, however, recognise that for some people, Procurement is strategic, with Purchasing as the tactical operational outworking of that strategy covering the procurement cycle or P2P process. For others, procurement and purchasing are two sides of the same coin, and this coin is called supply. We will not pursue this semantic discussion further, beyond noting that we will need an agreed plan, that must be properly implemented for it to work (strategy) and the plan must enable operations to be effectively carried out (operations).

Finally, we have endeavoured not to include anything in the book that if used, would be injurious or cause financial loss to the user. The user is, however, strongly recommended before applying or using any of the contents, to check and verify for themselves with their own organisation's policies and requirements. No liability will be accepted by the authors for any of the contents.

Author Introduction

Stuart Emmett

My journey to today, whilst an individual one, did not happen without the involvement of other people. On this journey of lifelong learning and meeting people, the original source of an idea or information may have been forgotten. If I have omitted in this book to give anyone credit they are due, I apologise and hope they will contact me so we can correct the omission in a future edition.

To all those who had contact with me please be assured you will have contributed to my learning, growing and developing. If you ask me how, then I will tell you! Whilst thanking you all, my hope is that I have given something positive back to you. I am pleased to acknowledge that my learning still continues; indeed writing this book has certainly contributed to my learning and development.

I have a background in freight, warehousing, shipping, and international trade and have resided in both the UK and in Nigeria. Since 1998 I have been an independent mentor/coach, trainer and consultant trading under the name of Learn and Change Limited. I currently enjoy working all over the UK and on four other continents, principally in Africa and the Middle East, but also in the Far East and South America.

Additional to undertaking training, I have been involved with one to one coaching/ mentoring, consulting, writing, and assessing along with examining for professional institutes' qualifications and as an external MSc examiner.

I'm married to the lovely Christine, and have two adult children, Jill and James; James is married to Mairead. We are additionally the grandparents of three girls (the totally gorgeous Megan, Molly and Niamh).
More about me can always be found out by visiting my web site: www.learnandchange. com. I welcome any comments.

Barry Crocker

I was a lecturer in the Salford Business School at the University of Salford and latterly was the Programme Leader for the MSc Procurement, Logistics and MSc Supply Chain Management. Previously, I had many years industrial experience in various management positions in the field of transport, warehousing and physical distribution.

I have also been an assistant chief examiner for the professional stage of the CIPS Diploma and an external examiner for several universities.

Currently I am an independent trainer and consultant and I have conducted many training sessions for multi-nationals in Africa, the Middle East, the Far East and Russia in the field of Procurement, Logistics and Supply Chain Management. Some of these training sessions have been undertaken with my co-author, Stuart. I would like to give special thanks to my lady, Rosalind, without whom this book would not have been possible.

Other titles

By Barry Crocker
- *Procurement Principles and Management* (2008)with Bailey, Farmer, Jessop and Jones
- *Inbound Logistics Management* (2012) with Jessop and Morrison

By Stuart Emmett
- *The Discipline Pocketbook* (2001)
- *Improving Learning for Individuals and Organisations* (2002)
- *How to Mentor and Support Learning* (2003)
- *Stores & Distribution Management* (2004), with Ray Carter and Peter Price
- *The Supply Chain in 90 minutes* (2005)
- *Excellence in Warehouse Management* (2005)
- *Logistics Freight Transport: Domestic and International* (2006)
- *Excellence in Inventory Management* (2007), with David Granville
- *Excellence in Supply Chain Management* (2008)
- *The Leadership Gospels* (2008)
- *The Learning Toolkit* (2008)
- *The Personal Development Toolkit* (2008)
- *The Team Building Toolkit* (2008)
- *The Customer Service Toolkit* (2008)
- *The Communication Toolkit* (2008)
- *The Motivation Toolkit* (2008)
- *The Systems Thinking Toolkit* (2008)
- *Excellence in Freight Transport* (2009)
- *Green Supply Chains; An Action Manifesto* (2010), with Vivek Sood
- *Excellence in Leadership and Management* (2011), with Nigel Wyatt
- *Excellence in Maintenance Management* (2011), with Paul Wheelhouse
- *Excellence in Public sector Procurement* (2011), with Paul Wright
- *Quick Guide: Supplier Relationship Management in the supply chain* (2012)
- *Quick Guide: A Systems view of the Supply Chain* (2012)

Joint Author Stuart Emmett/Barry Crocker:
- *The Relationship Driven Supply Chain; creating a culture of collaboration throughout the chain* (2006)
- *Excellence in Procurement* (2008)
- *Excellence in Supplier Management* (2009)
- *Excellence in Services Procurement* (2010), with David Moore
- *Excellence in Global Supply Chain Management* (2010)

1: Strategic alignment of Corporate and Procurement Strategies

Much of the literature about the changing nature of procurement takes the view that procurement can move away from a narrow focus on buying products and services, in order to integrate strategic planning, improve inter-organisation relations (cross-functional teams) and invest more time in identifying market opportunities.

In this view, procurement has the potential to become an important contributor to organisation-wide goals and an organisations' strategic direction. In the first part of the book, we look at strategy and its fit with procurement, during which we will consider the following:

- Traditional and new roles within Procurement
- Strategic thinking within an organisation
- Four aspects of strategy
- Can procurement be strategic?
- Alignment of objectives
- Corporate objectives and strategy
- Tactical sourcing
- Strategic sourcing
- Procurement and added value
- Integrating procurement with other corporate functions
- Strategy and implementation
- Strategy will always evolve

Traditional and new roles within Procurement

As mentioned above, there is a view that procurement has the potential to become an important contributor to organisation wide goals and the strategic direction of the organisation. This view embraces a changed view of procurement, as shown overleaf:

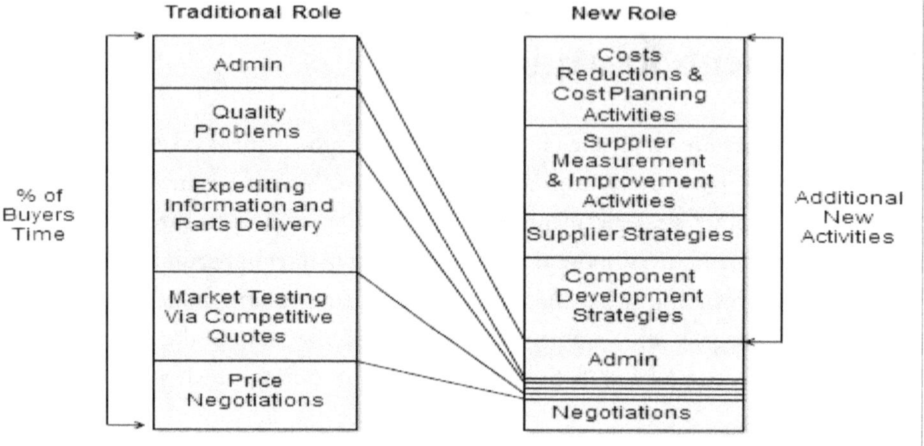

(Source: Adapted from Smith, G (1995) "Gower Handbook of Purchasing")

It is first useful to discuss the idea of being strategic and the concept of strategic management. Although specific definitions can vary, they all relate strategy to the overarching goals of the organisation. For instance, "strategy is the pattern of organisational moves and management approaches used to achieve organisational objectives and to pursue the organisation's mission".

Strategic management has been defined as:

"A system of corporate values, planning capabilities, or organisational responsibilities, that couple strategic thinking with operational decision making at all levels and across the functional lines of authority". **(Source: Gluck, F.W., Kaufman, S.P., Walleck, A.S. (1980) Strategic management for competitive advantage. Harvard Business Review 80404, pp154 – 61)**

In this sense, strategy and strategic management incorporate a number of different concerns or levels of activity within an organisation, and the strategic management process is one of setting goals, establishing strategies, analysing the environment and evaluating different strategies as well as implementing and managing them.

This strategic focus is therefore a broader one, where an understanding of an organisation's overall aims has to be considered, such as its positioning within wider market environments and the potential opportunities and threats that it faces. These elements need to be aligned in order to allow the highest levels of organisational strategy to be consistent and complementary.

Strategic Thinking within an organisation

External environment   Internal environment

Corporate plans and
Strategic missions

Business Unit Strategies
and Goals

Functional Strategies and Goals

Short term decisions and Daily activities

(Source: Carr and Smeltzer, 1997)

This reinforces the view that strategy must go beyond a narrow focus and contribute to the competitiveness of the organisation as a whole.

Porter's well-known "Diamond" (shown overleaf) is a representation of the different elements of competition. Here, demand conditions involves the anticipation of future or potential demand, as well as understanding the different markets and niches that might be exploited. Related and supporting industries include suppliers or localised clusters of organisations, as well as access to them with inter-organisational relations.

These all influence the contexts of organisation level strategy, structure and the patterning of competition and rivalry. We can see from Porter's "Diamond" the potential spaces for purchasing to contribute to the overall strategic manoeuvring of an organisation. The access of both hard resources (such as materials and components), and softer ones (such as different supply chains or supplier networks), and different sets of skills and competencies, is a significant element within the contexts of being strategic and competitive.

Porter's "Diamond"

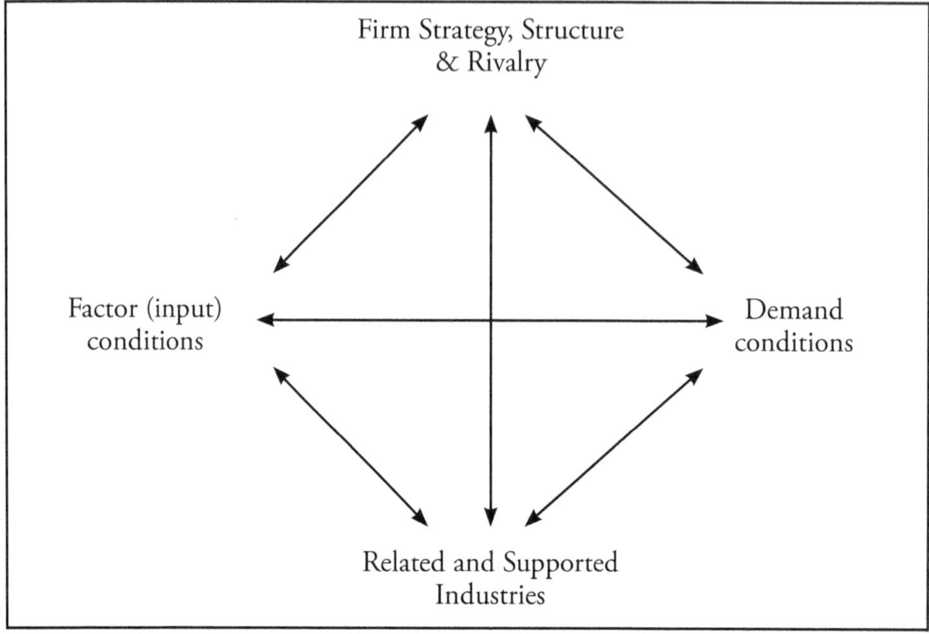

Four aspects of strategy

Another view of strategy can be seen in the following four different aspects for strategy to cover:

1) Corporate-based strategies

Identify and strengthen the key functions to support customer strategies; the secret here is the improvement in functional competence, for example to improve cost effectiveness by:

- cost reduction
- greater selectivity in products, markets etc
- share key functions

2) Customer-based strategies

Identify one or more categories of customers within the total market and concentrate efforts on meeting their needs; for example, how are customers segmented:

- by product/service offered
- by market share/volume etc
- by profit

This is similar to Kraljic's supplier categorisations and will be discussed later.

3) Technology-based strategies

Known for using latest equipment and using appropriate information communication technology with customer connectivity; such a strategy will capitalise on keeping up to date:

- safety
- costs
- productivity
- image

4) Competitor-based strategies

Exploit tangible advantages, capitalize on profit and on cost structure differences by exploiting differences in the:

- sources of profit
- ratio of fixed to variable costs

In terms of competing, Michael Porter (1996) has noted that:

- Strategy is creating fit among an organisation's activities. The success of a strategy depends on doing many things well and integrating them.
- Competitive strategy is about being different. It means deliberately choosing a different set of activities to deliver a unique mix of value.
- Competitive advantage means deciding to be a cost leader or a service/value leader; such characteristics are shown below:

This can be seen as a choice between being a cost leader, for example, food at Aldi, or as a product or service leader, for example, food at Marks and Spencer. Moreover, just to show the tension behind such categorizations, then Aldi would more than likely comment they are both cost and value leaders.

Meanwhile, the following shows the broad differences between these two categories:

"Do it cheaper" and being a Cost leader

- Give same standard products/service at a lower price
- Standard products
- Standard offering
- Production push
- Flow and mass volume production, with high mechanisation
- Low inventory levels
- Focus on productivity and efficiency
- Stable planning
- Lowest possible costs with service a constraint
- Lead time reduction
- Minimise waste

"Do it better" and being a Product or Service Leader

- Give products/services that cannot be found anywhere else
- Customer designed product/services
- Value added bespoke offering
- Market pull
- Job shop production, low mechanisation
- Flexible inventory
- Focus on creativity and innovation
- Flexible planning
- Maximises innovation responses/service with cost a constraint
- Short lead times/quick responses
- Maximise service

Porter's Five Forces Model of Competition

A key aspect here is how to view competition – Porter has the following Five Forces view:

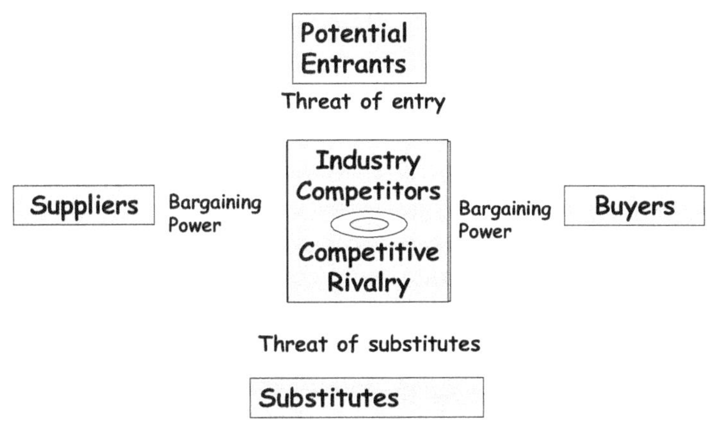

The 'Five Threats', or 'Forces' are from substitutes, entry of new players, the intensity of existing competitors and the bargaining power of suppliers and of buyers. These can be considered as follows:

1) The threat of substitutes

The existence of close substitute products increases the chances of customers switching to alternatives, perhaps in response/opposition to price increases, meaning:

- Buyers have the chance to substitute
- The relative price performance of substitutes
- Buyers switching costs
- Perceived level of product differentiation

2) The threat of the entry of new competitors

Profitable markets that yield high returns will draw in new organisations. The results are many new entrants, which will effectively decrease profitability. Unless the entry of new organisations can be blocked by the current suppliers, the profit rate will fall towards a competitive level. Responses may be from:

- Existence of barriers to entry (patents, rights, etc.)
- Economies of product differences
- Brand equity
- Access to distribution channels
- Absolute cost advantages
- Expected retaliation by incumbents
- Government policies

3) The intensity of competitive rivalry

With most industries, competitive rivalry is the major determinant of the competitiveness of the industry. Sometimes rivals compete aggressively and sometimes rivals compete in non-price dimensions such as innovation, marketing, etc. The following is involved:

- Number of competitors
- Rate of industry growth
- Intermittent industry overcapacity
- Exit barriers
- Diversity of competitors
- Fixed cost allocation per value added
- Level of advertising expense
- Economies of scale

4) The bargaining power of customers

The bargaining power and ability of customers to apply pressure, is described as the market of outputs. It also affects the customer's sensitivity to price changes and involves the following:

- Buyer to suppliers market position
- Bargaining leverage, particularly in industries with high fixed costs
- Buyer voume
- Buyer switching costs relative to suppliers switching costs
- Buyer information availability
- Ability to backward integrate
- Availability of existing substitute products
- Buyer price sensitivity
- Differential advantage (uniqueness) of industry products

5) The bargaining power of suppliers

This is described as the market of inputs. Suppliers of raw materials, components, and services (such as expertise) can be a source of supplier power over the organisation, for example, ink jet printer cartridges, OEM spare parts. Suppliers may refuse to work with the organisation, or charge excessively high prices for unique resources and covers the following:

- Supplier switching costs relative to buyers switching costs
- Degree of differentiation of inputs
- Presence of substitute inputs
- Supplier concentration to buyer concentration ratio

- Threat of forward integration by suppliers relative to the threat of backward integration by organisations
- Cost of inputs relative to selling price of the product

Many find it useful to rate each of the five forces on a 1 to 5 scale so that this will focus attention of the relative strengths of the forces.

Can Purchasing be Strategic?

Some academic research now considers procurement as an important element of the strategic management of organisations. Monczka and Morgan (2000) outlined the following six specific strategic issues for procurement that are critical in achieving competitive advantage and success.

1) **Procurement and sourcing** must be linked to the financial planning and the economic value-added construction of the business. Implementation of new processes and practices must demonstrate the adding of value in some way. The organisation, therefore, also needs to develop the ability to measure the effects of sourcing and procurement strategy.

2) **E-business could become a driving force**, therefore, organisations, which do not exploit the use of e-tools, may lose their competitive edge. This is not just in service sectors with their use of electronic call handling or with the online buying/order processing, but also with inter-organisational collaboration and sharing of information.

3) **Organisations must think and act on a global scale**, not just in terms of expanding import/buying supply chains, but with global markets giving opportunities to work with other organisations.

4) **The use of resources and the decision to retain competencies** within the organisation, or, to outsource those capabilities, cannot be made on purely single financial terms, as this can seriously hamper the ability of organisations to grow and prosper. A strategic and wider view must be taken, which considers the overall goals of the organisation and the long-term development of the organisation as a whole. This involves taking into account all of the resources that an organisation possesses (such as money but also the people, plant/machinery, products/materials etc), and examine what activities and outputs it is aiming to improve upon, extend or add within the context of an overall strategic plan.

5) **The implications for cost management** is to take a more critical view of assessing where the heaviest costs lie within organisational and inter-organisational activities. This involves moving to a total cost of ownership (TCO) approach that will include total acquisition costs (TAC) and for capex, the whole life costs (WLC).

6) Assess how the organisation and its activities differentiate itself from others, and how it provides unique or competitive solutions for customers. Mapping how such different service or product functions respond to customer needs is crucial. Certain products or services may stand out as significantly contributing to the positioning and competitiveness of the organisation, whilst others may provide less advantage, or have higher costs, or be less competitive. The key is to focus on the former, and perhaps to consider outsourcing or reducing commitment to those others.

Alignment of objectives

In order to be able to maximise the effectiveness of the procurement operation, it is important for procurement professionals to understand the links between procurement, the chosen supply strategy and the overall corporate strategy. They need to appreciate the importance of developing procurement strategies for the success of the organisation, so that the common procurement objectives and strategies, recognise common techniques used in procurement strategies. They need also to understand different strategies for buying different products and services

As mentioned above, the strategic character of procurement and supply management has been widely recognised in the literature. Procurement is increasingly viewed as a powerful competitive weapon for improving profitability and strengthening competitive advantage. However, this competitive potential critically depends on whether its decisions and activities are aligned with the organisation's overall strategic objectives. Specifically, procurement strategy and practices must be designed to optimally support the requirements of business strategy in order to positively affect performance. Two concepts of alignment come into view:

- strategic alignment; the fit between business strategy and procurement
- procurement strategy efficacy; the fit between procurement strategy and practices

Procurement competence is the "capability to structure the supply base in alignment with the business priorities of the organisation". According to this view, the procurement function is competent and can effectively act as a contributor to competitive advantage, providing it be integrated by linking procurement plans, policies and actions to the overall strategic business objectives.

The authors propose that procurement's contribution to business performance depends on the degree to which procurement capabilities fit and support the business strategy. This highlights the importance of procurement strategy as an intermediate element between business strategy and procurement capabilities.

Procurement effectiveness is the fit between procurement strategic objectives and procurement activities. It reflects the capability of the human and technological resources and practices of the procurement function to achieve its functional objectives. Strategic alignment and procurement effectiveness are now necessary contributors to competitive advantage and business success.

The general and "top" objectives of organisations must cascade down to the more specific objectives of the business units, functions and individuals; this being clearly depicted in the diagram below:

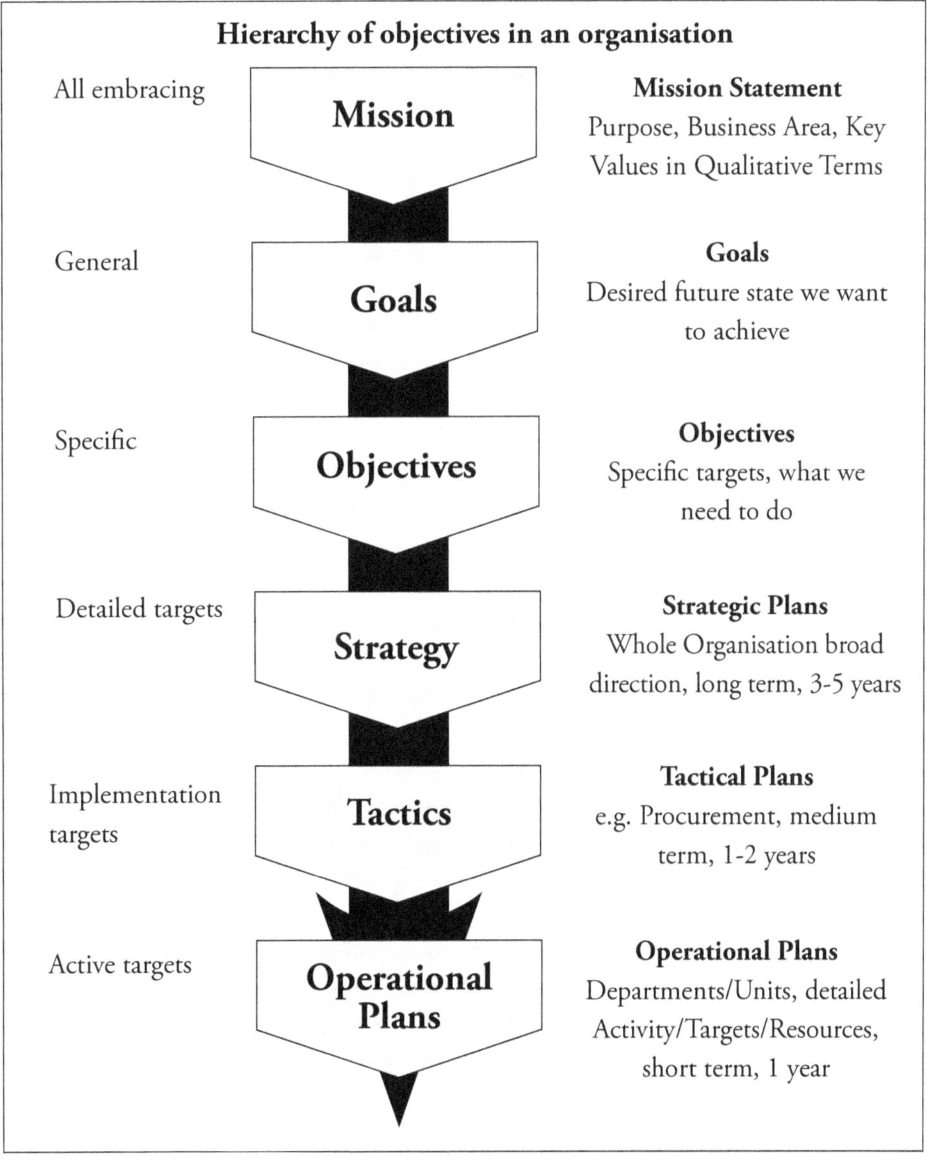

Before the mission, we may use vision statements, as shown in the following relationship:

Vision incorporates those timeless values and beliefs that are intended to move an organisation to its required future. They are an image of what it is trying to do; they represent the future required reality. They should come from the inside of people and when they do not, the vision statement will be a superficial and mere hollow statement of hopes and desires. Visions must therefore contain and reflect values and principles. The outcome here is usually in the form of a substantial but short **Mission** statement, which will encapsulate both the direction and associated guidance that incorporates the purpose and leads into the Goals with policies and power structures that are needed to achieve the task.

Goals are therefore the overall targets to be met that will roll into the objectives and the **Strategic, Tactical and Operational objectives** and go right down to, people's individual roles and responsibilities, polices, plans and schedules.

Strategy can therefore be seen as an organisation's view on how to accomplish their vision by making competitive moves and business approaches. Strategy is therefore the "game plan" for the future by determining how to:

- Position the organisation into its chosen market
- Compete successfully
- Achieve the required good performance

Fundamentally, therefore, strategy proactively shapes how an organisation's business will be conducted, and moulds the independent actions and decisions of managers and employees into a coordinated, organisation-wide game plan.

The following hierarchy shows the relationships involved between Strategy, Tactics and Operations:

We can also see here that strategy uses broad objectives and converts them into policies; Tactics converts these into forecasts and plans, which Operations then in turn convert into schedules and controls. This happens for the total organisation and is often called "The Corporate Strategy". Each of the functional process (like Procurement) will then plan, implement and control their processes (for example by using a Procurement Strategy) so that each functional process will meet the overall corporate strategy.

Corporate Objectives and Strategy

Corporate is concerned with deciding which markets and activities the business should involved in; where it wants to be; and how it is going to get there. Strategy is about making high-level decisions and forms the management game plan for:

- Satisfying customers (meeting customer needs)
- Running the business (organising resources in the most efficient and effective way)
- Beating the competition (strategies and tactics to gain competitive advantage)
- Achieving corporate objectives

Corporate objectives are set at the high level and are quite distinct from any more detailed functional objectives set for the functional areas of a business. Examples of corporate objectives would include targets for:

- Sales revenue; a traditional measure of the size and strength of a business, if revenue is growing then the business is growing
- Profit; both the absolute level of profit and the profit margin, such as the return on sales
- Return on investment (ROCE, ROI); particularly important for capital intensive businesses
- Growth; sales volume, revenue, profit, earnings per share
- Market share; the proportion of markets and industries owned by the business or its products
- Cash flow; this can be similar to a profit objective, but with the focus on maximising the net cash inflow of the business
- Shareholder value; particularly important for publicly quoted businesses where senior management are tasked with growing the value of the business
- Corporate image and reputation; increasingly important and links here with corporate social responsibility, product and customer service quality, and business ethics

Many factors will influence the corporate objectives that are set. Precisely which factors depends on the nature of the business and its markets, and the business ownership.

Some examples of those factors that influence corporate objectives include:

- Age of the business
- Size and legal status
- Ownership (e.g. privately owned; stock exchange quoted)
- Views of owners and managers
- Market conditions
- Legislation
- State of the economy
- Competition
- Risk and attitude to risk
- Corporate culture
- Political factors
- Social attitudes

Drucker has suggested corporate objectives in these key areas:

Area	Examples
Market standing	Market share, customer satisfaction, product range
Innovation	New products, better processes, using technology
Productivity	Optimum use of resources, focus on core activities
Physical & Financial resources	Factories, business locations, finance, supplies
Profitability	Level of profit, rates of return on investment
Management	Management structure; promotion & development
Employees	Organisational structure; employee relations
Public responsibility	Compliance with laws; social & ethical behaviour (CSR)

SMART Objectives

Many business textbooks suggest that both corporate and functional objectives need to conform to a set of criteria referred to as an acronym SMART.

The SMART criteria are summarised opposite:

Specific or simple	The objective should state exactly what is to be achieved
Measurable	An objective should be capable of measurement so that it is possible to determine whether (or how far) it has been achieved
Achievable or attainable	The objective should be one that can be achieved given the circumstances in which it is set and the resources available to the business
Relevant or realistic	Objectives should be relevant to the people responsible for achieving them
Time Bound	Objectives should be set with a period in mind. These deadlines also need to be realistic

Another classification of objectives is as follows:

1) Primary Objectives:

The ultimate, long-term goals of the business (3-10 years typically) and these are the key strategic objectives such as profit growth or shareholder returns

2) Secondary Objectives:

These make a direct contribution to meeting primary objectives. For example, sales growth will help business achieve profit target. Also known as tactical objectives, they are usually focused on the short or medium term of up to 1 year.

A similar distinction can also be made between strategic (corporate) and tactical (functional) objectives.

Strategic	Tactical
Focused on long term	Focused on the short term
Set by the main board	Set by the functional line management
Involve higher risk and uncertainty	Relatively low risk
Likely to involve significant investment/ business resources	Limited resources invested
Difficult to change in the short term	Relatively easy to change
Stretching and challenging	Realistic and achievable

Procurement Strategies

Recent research by the Hackett Group, a leading global strategy and operations consulting organisation, found Chief Procurement Officers (CPOs) reporting procurement strategy priorities that focused on cost and risk reduction, strategic alignment and transformation. Particular procurement strategy priorities most often cited were:

- Sustaining cost reductions achieved in previous periods
- Reducing price and risks of non availability
- Improving the alignment between procurement strategy and the corporate business strategy
- Leveraging supplier relationship management
- Better managing knowledge and information in order to support procurement transformation
- Better understanding of the organisational characteristics of other top performing procurement organisations

If Procurement is sub-optimal, costs can escalate, the business can be exposed to unnecessary risk and customers can be let down through lack of supply. This concept of risk becomes increasingly important in long supply chains (which many actually are), and limiting views to only the one external supplier, the one we are buying from (called often, the tier 1 supplier), whilst ignoring the suppliers suppliers (at tier 2, 3, 4, etc) can be itself a risky approach.

Specific issues and questions to ask here include the following:

- Is a **supply strategy** in place in the organisation? Is this widely known and understood? If not, it needs to be devised and agreed with everyone and all agree to abide by it.
- Addressing the **financial implications/risk involved**, including the level of investment in stock.
- Critically reviewing the **planning estimates** given by each function to guard against demand being inflated at each stage. (This is linked to the supply lead-time, something we consider later in the book).
- How **dependent** is the organisation on **particular key suppliers**; are they single sourced/dual sourced/multi-sourced? This must be critically reviewed and changes implemented as necessary.
- How **dependent** are the suppliers on the **organisation's business**? While it might be of some comfort to learn that the buyer's organisation is a supplier's biggest customer, this is not necessarily an ideal position. Also the buyer's business with suppliers, while profitable to suppliers, may not provide them with a sufficient margin to fund new technology or product developments.
- Have the **supplier's capacity and development plans** been reviewed? What are their production facilities like? Are their quality control procedures satisfactory? Is their production facility flexible enough to meet both anticipated

and unforeseen requirements? Do they have efficient processes? Have we checked the compliances for ethical sourcing, corporate social responsibility etc?

- What **contingency plans** do the suppliers have (as well as their suppliers and their supplier's supplier) in the event that they have a problem, for example, labour difficulties?
- The **supplier's suppliers,** and the supply chain as a whole, should also be kept under **constant review** to ensure there are no weak links; a chain is as long as its weakest link; do we actually know how long the chain is?.
- **Contracts** with suppliers should be kept under review, ensuring that the buyer's interests are clearly represented. All contractual clauses need to be examined; for example is there a service level and supplier lead time agreement with consequences for non-performance. Can quantities be varied and by how much, how often and is there a cost for doing so? Can the buyer suspend or cancel the agreement and in such cases does a penalty apply?
- **How are suppliers selected?** What is the formal procedure and is there a set procedure for regular reviews? Has the suppliers' financial position been reviewed? Is the suppliers environmental and ethical policy acceptable, and does it align with that of the buyers organisation? Is the suppliers' management team easy to work with? Are there cross relationships at senior levels to resolve problems should they arise?

The purchasing professional should also remember they are the link between their own organisation and the supplier; therefore, demand planning should be been done at a senior or corporate level with input from purchasing and others.

Changes or fluctuations in the suppliers' capability levels should also be monitored as these can assume key significance.

Procurement should always be much more than chasing simple cost savings; as the benefits of good procurement include many other aspects:

- Security of supply
- Lower total cost
- Reduced risk
- Improved quality
- More added value
- Greater efficiency
- New innovations

Procurement strategies

Research undertaken by the Aberdeen Group in the USA *(The CPO's Agenda, March, 2005)* identified five primary strategies that procurement leaders were adopting to move from a focus on cost containment to one of value generation. These strategies were:

- Improve supplier development and collaboration
- Enhance and integrate procurement automation infrastructure
- Adopt low cost country supply initiatives
- Transition to a centre-led procurement organisation
- Increase the amount of spend under management while improving spend compliance

Research undertaken by the Future Purchasing Alliance a team made up from leaders in research, education and professional practice, and published in a briefing entitled *Connecting Purchasing & Supplier Strategies to Shareholder Value*, found that whether or not purchasing is significantly aligned with overall business requirements appears to be the critical factor for purchasing future progress and development.

This was more important than organisation type, organisational structures or the level in the business into which procurement reports.

Tactical Sourcing

An example of tactical sourcing is working with colleagues in Marketing and Sales to provide a bid support activity within fast moving technological areas.

Tactical sourcing is therefore to some extent reactive, as it covers those business requirements that cannot be planned in the long term and needs to be proactively managed, so that resources and processes are set aside to manage it within the procurement strategy.

Notwithstanding the above, CIPS suggests that there should be no unplanned or unexpected capital expenditure, as all organisations need to have capital investment plans, which procurement management can then incorporate in their strategic sourcing strategy.

If an unexpected requirement is ad hoc, low risk and low value, procurement professionals should not be involved with obtaining the requirement anyway. All low value requirements should have already been aggregated into call off contracts for use by end users. Such low-value, non-high-risk items, are precisely those that require strategic sourcing plans.

Strategic Sourcing

Strategic sourcing is a core activity in procurement. It is a complex commercial process requiring extensive knowledge and competence and can be defined as "satisfying business needs from markets via the proactive and planned analysis of supply markets and the selection of suppliers with the objective of delivering solutions to meet pre-determined and agreed business needs."

The strategic sourcing activity should form one part of the overall procurement strategy.

1. Positioning

The first stage is the positioning of the procurement function within the organisation at the appropriate level (senior) within an organisation. It should report directly to the Board (or via an appropriate Board representative, Finance is a common one) and it must possess suitable human resources. An Aberdeen Group report showed the following "report to" of the Chief Procurement Officer (CPO):

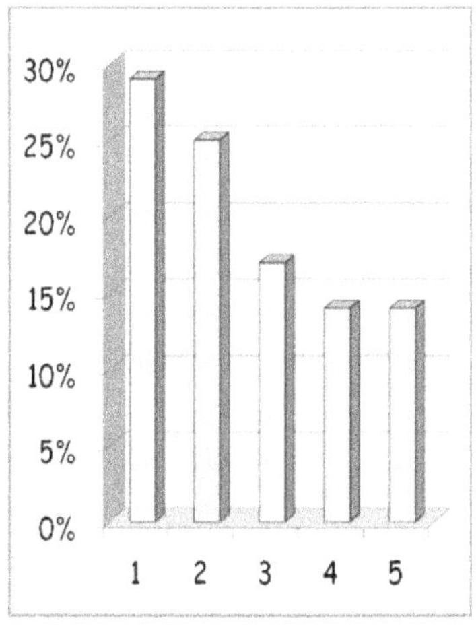

1. Chief Operating Officer (29%)

2. Chief Finance Officer (25%)

3. CEO (17%)

4. VP Supply Chain (14%)

5. Other (14%)

(Source: Aberdeen Group, "Spend Optimisation" report number 7995 dated June 2012, using data from August 2011).

Strategic sourcing will require the application and interpretation of sophisticated strategic sourcing tools and techniques, such as supplier relationship management (SRM).

2. "As is" Analysis

The second and very resource consuming stage in strategic sourcing involves the "As is" analysis stage, which includes:

Customer and Business requirements

What do our customers need and what does the business need?

- Spend Analysis
- Historical usage analysis of goods or services
- Supplier positioning
- Supplier historical analysis
- Transaction cost analysis
- Critical nature of products

Future Spend Analysis

- Forward/expected usage of goods and services
- Trends in the market

Market Analysis

- Assessment of the market capability
- Analysis of power dependency in supply chains
- Analysis of individual marketplaces
- Supplier preferencing
- Relative positioning of your organisation
- Supply chain cost analysis
- The nature of the market and the appropriate type sourcing strategy – global, regional or local
- Potential size (and actual size) of the supply base

Several analytical tools are appropriate for this stage including the earlier Porter's Five Forces, PEST (Political, Economic, Social, and Technological), now widened into STEEPLE (Social, Technological, Economic, Environmental, Political, Legislative and Ethical) and SWOT (Strengths, Weaknesses, Opportunities and Threats), and finally the Kraljic Supply Positioning Tool (classifying routine, leverage, bottleneck and critical items).

3. Consolidate Data and Generate Options

Once the analysis has been undertaken and supply chains have been mapped, the next stage is to consolidate the data and to generate options. When resources are tight in terms of time and skills availability, although not ideal, it is possible to omit some of the analysis stages and go direct to the brainstorming of options.

It is however, good practice to undertake all stages in strategic sourcing but where this is not possible, it is better to attempt some aspects of it than not undertake it at all. Options can be seen as "baskets of opportunities".

In summary, this stage involves brainstorming options to fulfil the requirements, such as identifying the offering of suppliers and identifying whether there are other ways to fulfil the requirement, for example, instead of purchasing PCs, it is possible to purchase a desktop service by outsourcing the PC desktop provision?

Sourcing plans

Once the preferred strategic sourcing options are agreed, these are developed into "sourcing plans" which should be innovative and bring creative solutions to the organisation's requirements in support of the organisation's mission and objectives. Strategic sourcing plans should generate work streams by providing clear achievable milestones.

Measurement

Strategic procurement, including the design and implementation of sourcing plans, should be measured in terms of the benefits that are actually delivered, compared with was set out in the original business case of what they were expected to deliver. This might take the form of a post order audit perhaps one year after the contract had been started. The findings should be reported and discussed in order to learn from experiences and to build on current commercial arrangements.

Achieving goal alignment: stakeholder engagements

Below is a suggested five-step process to developing procurement strategy in conjunction with the stakeholders.

1. Assess the current situation including the organisations culture, organisational structure, people, organisational maturity together with knowledge of the key stakeholders and the current credibility with them.

2. Develop a draft based on the assessment results, ensuring links to the company strategy and stakeholder needs. In collaboration with the stakeholders, set goals that

address their requirements, uses their language and ensures there is internal ownership within procurement.

3. Build buy-in with senior company leaders through workshops and presentations. Document the plan, circulate for final revisions and gain demonstrable commitment.

4. Execute the plan ensuring some quick wins. Measure your progress.

5. Communicate the strategy and progress widely. Share credit with the business and keep marketing internally.

Case Study: Premier Foods

Manufacturer Premier Foods succeeded in increasing its profits against a backdrop of falling sales, in part down to improved procurement performance.

"Procurement gains from working more strategically, without suppliers adding to the grocery trading profit."

The company reported that although sales had fallen, adjusted profit before tax had grown by 6.4 percent over the same period.

They have aligned the organisational structure behind the strategy of growing their brands.

Premier Foods cut its supplier base to create a more productive relationship with its top suppliers. They have cut numbers by 11 percent in the last quarter, and their top 100 suppliers, which represent 45 percent of their spend; have experienced real growth of 33 percent over three years.

Case Study: Local Authorities

Over several years, auditors have commented that it is crucial to align procurement and corporate strategies in order to improve services.

In order to facilitate this, procurement strategies must have buy-in from the top level. Procurement often writes a procurement strategy without a clear understanding of the corporate strategy.

Procurement is the key link in translating corporate objectives into reality.

Research

A Future Purchasing Alliance report was specifically orientated to connecting purchasing strategy with shareholder value. It outlines how leaders within organisations must be sought to pursue new purchasing strategies, and to incorporate value-creation mapping and best practice. It also very usefully acknowledges the softer skills of persuasion and alignment.

However, another piece of work (Quayle, 2002), a survey of purchasing activities in SMEs (Small to Medium Enterprises) shows some alarming results for strategic purchasing. Although issues such as leadership, waste reduction and team working came out as high priorities in the organisations sampled, purchasing, supplier development, EDI and benchmarking came out near the bottom of the list. Purchasing was ranked 14th out of 19 issues. This is quite astounding given the extensive literature discussed above which identifies not only the benefits of effective purchasing strategy in terms of competitiveness and adding value for the organisation, but also that this is essential to compete, survive and grow in contemporary business environments. It also demonstrates the potential scale of the challenge ahead for purchasing professionals just in convincing their organisations of the importance of strategic purchasing.

Procurement and "Value added"

The challenge Procurement has, is to identify which activities will have the most beneficial impact, taking in to consideration the specific strategy of the organisation, its size and sector. These priorities must be built into the strategic plan, ensuring that Procurement has a significant influence, as well as alignment with the overall business strategy.

The areas that Procurement can develop on additional value to the supply chain are as follows:

- Improvement in the product quality from suppliers, for example, this could then mean there are no product recalls.
- Improvement in the levels of customer services provided, for example, the outsourcing and ongoing management of call centres to ensure that the high standards to the customers are met by a specialised team/company
- Reduction in time to market and cycle time, for example, managing a just in time process with key suppliers
- Assurance of supply so that there are no supply lead time delays
- Management and audit of suppliers Corporate Social Responsibility (CSR)
- Management of sustainability and "green" issues; this is a growing area
- Increased New Product Development (NPD), allowing suppliers and procurement to work together

Procurement value added: the evidence

In a survey on procurement practices at 156 large organisations, Bain and Company

(Business Strategy Review, Spring 2007) found that 22 percent of organisations stood out significantly from the rest. They had growth rates of over 20 percent per year and their supply management functions seem to be in "hyper-drive". The Procurement teams at these organisations were delivering significantly more incremental revenue than those of the lower performing organisations. They were achieving greater reductions in cycle lead times and they were much more likely to bring innovation to the company, either through processes or products, through their own efforts or by working with their suppliers.

The Bain and Company study found that high performing organisations had "reinvented" supply management along the following lines:

- The leaders of Procurement and Supply Management looked and acted differently from their more conventional counterparts. They did this by offering higher volume, lower priced contracts to a select group of suppliers. They fostered new competition for existing suppliers by continually searching for new suppliers and developing alternatives.
- They performed independent analysis of the market and of suppliers' cost structures and returns, simulating the impact that greater purchasing volumes can have on per unit costs. This helped establish sound target prices in advance of any negotiations.
- They forecast and demanded continuing cost reductions year after year
- They also put a premium on speed, quality and flexibility and assured supply
- They had much more cross-functional teamwork within their organisation.

Such excellent procurement and supply management organisations made a point of viewing their procurement teams as a source of innovation. The study found that there was a variety of different approaches to this:

- Designing of products to cost; getting involved at the very start of a new concept (because as much as 80 percent of the total cost of a product is determined during the design phase).
- Tapping into supplier knowledge for new and improved products
- Expanding the supplier search for innovation by inviting suppliers to meetings and asking them for innovative ideas on products and how to reduce costs in the supply chain.

The study concluded that today's supply management at many organisations is a complex function that is critical to business success, with responsibility for total costs, quality, delivery and innovation throughout a company's entire supply chain. The strategic contribution of supply management was measured in terms of not only cost savings (the traditional metric), but also increased shareholder value by delivering added value.

Research

A McKinsey global survey of purchasing executives at over 200 organisations (The McKinsey Quarterly 2007) found that those setting the pace in purchasing best practice differ from ordinary organisations along three different "talent" dimensions.

- Hire better people in Procurement and Supply Management
- Set clearer performance targets for them
- Create a strong sourcing culture that allows the Procurement and Supply Management function to align their purchasing activity with the company's overall corporate strategy.

The pay off for those organisations was that they enjoyed annual cost savings from their overall sourcing efforts that were nearly six times greater than the annual savings of competitors.

The study assessed the performance of the respondents' organisations against recognised good practice in Procurement and Supply Management by analysing responses along four dimensions:

- The capabilities and cultures of purchasing professionals and their organisations
- The corporate structure and systems that support purchasing
- The management techniques and business processes supporting it
- The contribution of purchasers to their organisations and the extent of the alignment between purchasing and corporate strategy

Critical Success Factors for Procurement Added Value

A number of enablers need to be in place, so that a procurement and supply management function can implement a value generating strategy; these are as follows:

- Examine the existing procurement and supply management skill sets. It would be useful to conduct a skills analysis to establish what expertise and knowledge the existing procurement and supply management team may have;
- Experience of delivering added value ideas, whether this is gained from working in another organisation or in a different function of the organisation where generating added value was actively encouraged.

- Definition and agreed measures of value, and ensure that everyone buys in these (from the top down) and progress is measured against them and communicated on a regular basis, for example, quarterly.
- Market and category knowledgein the procurement and supply management team. The McKinsey study found that one of the attributes of the high procurement and supply management performers was from their deep knowledge of a particular category.
- Excellent supplier relationships, having clear and personable communication with the supplier base, especially when looking at the area of New Product Development
- The ability to manage markets, using the skills and the knowledge of an experienced procurement and supply management professional. It is imperative they know their categories and the markets that they trade in.
- Thinking and utilising creative skills when looking at traditional procurement processes and ways of working. Think outside the box, do not worry that the procurement and supply management are getting creative. Encourage a relaxed environment for procurement and supply management teams to work in.
- Ability to manage change and transition with suppliers and within the organisation. This may be having project management skills, or the ability to manage change on a regular basis.
- Being able to be objective when thinking about value generation, as opposed to subjective and "that won't work here". Thinking about value generation brings a completely new perspective to the world of procurement and supply management.
- Understanding risk management by closely working with the supply chain, the procurement and supply management function is able to identify potential risks and implement strategies to mitigate vulnerabilities in the supply chain.
- Talent development of the procurement and supply management team. Ensure the development of the team is bespoke and "made to measure", for example, functional rotations through the organisation ensure that the procurement and supply management team get broad business experience. Encourage, promote and provide regular appraisals and feedback to the team.
- Analytical and problem solving environment by providing the tools and the support to allow the procurement and supply management to work on and develop value generating ideas.
- Continuous development of procurement and supply management practice by

staying abreast of best practices in the marketplace.

- Utilisation and possible flexibility of any e-sourcing systems used. Be aware of technological changes and any new systems launched that could help the procurement and supply management in delivering added value.
- Strong internal client relationship, to ensure that they buy into any proposed changes in ways of working. This is key and should be amongst the top five actions to rolling out value generation
- Procurement and supply management managers must participate and often lead the cross-functional teams needed to deliver added value. Supplier's representatives may even be included in these teams, as well as the R & D, Finance, Marketing and other departments.
- Development and in-depth knowledge of the supply chain, by working closely with the internal clients, for example, to understand the processes of manufacture, the delivery of the goods and services etc.

Research: Roles and Responsibilities of Procurement; CIPS

CIPS has considered the key roles, characteristics and objectives of the procurement management function with respect to the implementation and development of a corporate strategy, whether it is in industry, commerce, public service or in a not for profit.

To ensure that as far as possible procurement strategies are in harmony with the time scales and objectives of the corporate plan, the procurement management department should be quick to capitalise on those occasions when, due to external PESTLE forces, directors are particularly aware of the impact, which sound purchasing techniques can have on the bottom line.

An effective procurement management department, staffed by fully qualified professionals, is in a strong position to influence corporate behaviour.

To maximise its contribution to corporate well being, it is essential for all members of the purchasing department to have an in depth appreciation of the strategic objectives of the organisation and how procurement management can contribute to the achievement of corporate goals.

Procurement management professionals should have the ability to analyse the corporate plan in such a way that they are able to generate objectives and opportunities for the purchasing department.

Procurement management professionals should possess sound commercial skills, which can be of benefit to the organisation as a whole, in the development of joint ventures.

Procurement management professionals should in general be supportive of change where it can be seen to be of benefit to the organisation.

Effective communication is critical to the success of any strategy.

One of the key responsibilities of procurement is to be aware of cases where procurement strategies are at variance with the timescales of the corporate plan as a whole. Let us now remind ourselves of some of these that were mentioned, with examples of corporate strategy goals:

For profit driven organisations:

- Increasing profitability
- Developing the business
- Staying independent
- Safeguarding the organisation's future

For public bodies or non-profit making organisations:

- Achieving improvement and value for money in public services
- Promoting democracy and/or political objectives (central and local government)
- Promoting certain values or causes (e.g. commission for Racial Equality, Countryside Commission, Charities)
- Protecting people (health, social care, armed forces and emergency services)

For a company whose goal is to maximise profitability, strategies might include:

- Cutting manufacturing and distribution costs
- Removing unprofitable lines
- Being lean and mean
- Developing new, more profitable products
- Transforming unprofitable customers
- Selling the existing profitable products into new markets

An organisation with the primary goal of expanding the business might:

- Grow through merger and acquisition
- Sell existing products into new markets/sell more of existing products in new markets/sell new products into existing markets / sell new products into new markets
- Reduce prices so as to sell more

A public body whose goal is to achieve improvement in public services might:

- Seek to optimise the use of resources to maximise the benefit

- Improve efficiency and eliminate waste
- Invest in infrastructure and new technology
- Recruit, train and develop its people.

As an example, if a typical goal of an organisation were to cutting manufacturing and distribution costs, the procurement strategies appropriate for achieving those goals would be to reduce supply chain costs by:

- Cutting out unprofitable lines
- Negotiate the organisation out of existing supply contracts for materials or services that support those lines.
- Improving efficiency and eliminate waste
- Rationalise support roles so that core activities focus only on clear prime objectives.

Integrating Procurement with other Corporate Functions

All of an organisation's individual functions such as procurement, finance, marketing, human resources and operations (such as production and logistics) must generate their own objectives that support and align with the organisation's corporate objectives and strategies.

Allied to this is that as a guiding principle, procurement professionals should accept and encourage change where it is beneficial to the organisation.

However, it is difficult to keep procurement strategy on track when organisations frequently and rapidly change direction. An added practical problem is that it takes time to change objectives and so it is not unusual for functional strategies to be out of tune with corporate strategies.

The management of such emergent strategies will however be eased by procurement management networking with colleagues and by remaining close to the business.

Strategy must therefore be capable of being easily and swiftly communicated, and procurement strategies be made flexible. In such circumstances, procurement management should develop a way to document the strategy that is not too onerous to change. For example, if the organisation determines that it is in the business of bringing new products to market ahead of the competition, then procurement may have to sacrifice cost savings at the expense of focussing on innovation in collaboration with the supply base.

This concurs with the CIPS view that procurement never was, and never could be, about cost savings alone. Furthermore, as strategies are sometimes emergent, for example, a supplier generates innovation that the buying organisation had not predicted; then procurement has to respond in a strategic and opportunistic fashion.

Projects are often considered part of programme management that, as a function, is sometimes external to procurement. In such scenarios, procurement should ensure they could contribute to bringing projects to an effective conclusion of on time and within budget.

Strategy development also varies with factors such as the size of the organisation, the sector it is in, the maturity of the organisation and the maturity of the markets in which it operates.

Purchasing is able to make an effective contribution to corporate strategy but only if procurement professionals ensure their entire team has a detailed understanding of the strategy and those to whom the strategy is communicated are able to understand and support it.

Procurement professionals should be able to take the corporate plan and dissect it to generate objectives for the procurement function. By being aware of the macro environment purchasing and supply, management can remain ahead of the game by being proactive rather than reactive to change.

Checklist: 20 Questions for Senior Purchasing Managers
(Source: www.neilfuller.com)
- Do you know exactly how much your organisation is spending externally each year?
- Do you know how much is spent on each category of spend and with which supplier? (a category is a range of purchases – e.g. energy, raw materials, IT)
- Do you know the total cost of the purchases you make, rather than just their price? i.e. the total acquisition cost (TAC) and the life cycle cost of capital purchases?
- Do you know how much value your suppliers provide and create for your organisation's success and reputation?
- Do you know who your key suppliers are?
- Do you have pro-active, close relationships with your key suppliers?
- Do you understand the risks inherent in the purchases you make and are you managing risk effectively?
- Do you know what you should outsource and what you should not outsource?
- Are you outsourcing services successfully?
- Are you managing suppliers of outsourced services successfully?
- Do you know what your purchasing strategies are and are they aligned to your business strategies?

- Do you have appropriately skilled people developing and managing your purchasing strategies?
- What proportion of your external spend is managed by your purchasing professionals?
- If the answer to the last question is not 100 percent, why not? What are you doing about it?
- How do you support your purchasing people to ensure they achieve appropriate business benefits?
- Do you direct your purchasing people to limit their focus to reducing prices by x percent each year or do you direct them to achieve cost-effective, risk-controlled added value?
- Do you maximise the use of IT and ensure that you receive the maximum benefits from its application?
- Do you plan effectively for major negotiations?
- Do you assess the outcome of your negotiations?
- Do you ensure that all your people receive adequate training in negotiation skills?
- Do you encourage team negotiation where appropriate?

Strategy often fails on implementation

Implementing strategy is so often the most difficult aspect. This is also a reflection of the unfortunate reality of decisions being made without any regard to the impacts and how it will be implemented.

The point here that it is the implementation and application that is critical; the design is the easiest part. Merely trying to implement by the planners and strategists "waving the wand" is damaging, wrong and can be fatal. It is a pity that more strategists in organisations (and in politics) do not recognise this simple eternal truth.

Separation between the planners and the doers cannot only give a poor implementation, but it may also reveal a divisive aspect and separation in organisations. Indeed one of the factors in a successful total quality management (TQM) implementation is the involvement of all in decision-making; which then leads onto making continuous improvements at all levels in an organisation.

There are other barriers to Strategic Development, for example:

- Vision/Mission and Strategy are not actionable

- Strategy is not linked to Tactics or to Team Goals
- Strategy is not linked to Resource Allocation
- Feedback is Tactical, not Strategic

The following factors have been identified on why strategy implementation fails:
- Preoccupation with following fashionable ideas, without checking on the appropriateness; e.g. the rush to use ICT that turns out to be not fit for purpose, this being after a wasted spend of millions
- No proper understanding of exactly what needs to changed
- Unclear or unrealistic expectations
- No persistence and considerable effort over many years, it is often not a "quick fix"
- Inconsistencies between declared objectives and the actual behaviour and actions
- Assuming that training employees is all that needs to be done (as trainers, the authors encounter this too often).
- Not changing the organisational (a common problem where many so-called leaders just have no real perception of exactly what the current culture actually is).
- Not recognising that changing things will likely not involve dealing with routine and well-organised situations, consequently, the style "rule book" is unlikely to work anymore.

The following checklist takes forward the above issues with strategy implementations:

Checklist: Strategy Implementation
- It is the people on the ground who make the strategy alive, so work with them
- Have a good business case that has a sense of urgency for implementing
- Communicate not just the strategy, but also what is/is not working,
- Update the measurements; do not measure the old strategy
- Culture drives the implementation, but does it fit the new strategy?
- Ensure the processes support the new strategy
- Reward and reinforce behaviour and actions towards the new strategy
- Break the strategy into small components.
- Review what was said would happen as you are doing it
- Do the review:
    - every 2 weeks for the small components
    - every 12 weeks for the whole strategy

Strategy will always evolve

In most organisations, there is an ongoing need to react to:

- Shifting market conditions
- Fresh moves of competitors
- New technologies
- Evolving customer preferences
- Political and regulatory changes
- New windows of opportunity
- The crisis of the moment

Therefore, there must be ways to develop those capabilities that will help to deliver the business strategies. This will involve a complex, harmonious mix of individual and technology skills. After all, an organisation's capacity to improve existing skills and learn new ones is the most defensible competitive advantage an organisation can have. Learning to do this will involve the following:

1) Clarity of the core competence

A clear core competence should provide the potential access to a wide range of markets and this should make a significant contribution to the perceived customer benefits for the organisations end product/service. It should also make it difficult for competitors to emulate.

2) A considered view of the operational excellence

Operational excellence and strategy are both essential to obtain superior performance, but an organisation can only outperform competitors, if it can establish a difference and then continue to maintain it.

Managers must not here become too preoccupied with improving operational effectiveness. Whilst this could give, in the short term, lower costs and higher prices with increased profitability; if managers let operational excellence supplant strategy, the results in the medium term may then be zero-sum competition, static or declining prices and pressures on cost, resulting in compromising the organisations ability to invest in the business for the long-term.

> **Checklist: A Winning Strategy**
> 1) Goodness of fit test; how well is strategy matched to the situation?
> 2) Competitive advantage test; does strategy lead to sustainable competitive advantage?

3) Performance test; does strategy boost performance? (This assumes it has been effectively implemented)
4) What have we done to:
- Improve customer service?
- Improve customer satisfaction?
- Reduce costs?
- Improve productivity?
- Increase revenues from new products/services?
- Be better than the competition?
(These questions can be asked at all levels in the organisation).

2: The Demand Side: a Driver for Procurement

In this part of the book, we examine that demand drives everything that procurement and the supply chain does, for if there is no demand, then procurement and the supply chain are not needed. Therefore, we will consider the following:

- The Intelligent customer
- Customer requirements and specifications
- Providing customers with value
- The link to customer service and value

The Intelligent Customer

Many writers suggest the core competencies of Procurement should be shared across the whole of an organisation. The argument here is that this would introduce a greater understanding of procurement processes, allowing other departments to act more efficiently. The aim of this approach is that the organisation will become an "intelligent customer" and whilst the characteristics of an intelligent customer will vary, they will always involve an understanding of the nature of the marketplace and the organisation, as well as those specific procurement competencies such as:

- Sourcing skills and knowledge
- Specification development skills
- An understanding of the tendering process
- Supplier assessment and selection skills
- Negotiation techniques
- Contract drafting and management skills

Creating an intelligent customer standard can be incredibly useful to procurement as it offers the advantages of improving transparency in the procurement process and the sharing of vital knowledge, thereby removing pressure from purchasing and supply departments.

There are ways of developing such an integrated, co-ordinated commitment to having cross-functional working:

- The customer's needs and requirements are clearly understood in every corner of the organisation
- Business processes are clearly linked to customer critical outcomes
- Work groups with employees from several functional areas take responsibility for making sure all business processes are co-ordinated and service the customer
- Information is shared between work teams and the functional departments

- Technology supports information sharing
- Policy and procedures changes are made only after consulting other functional groups to assess unexpected impacts on customers
- Problems that arise are viewed as opportunities to improve the process of serving customer; a culture of blame is replaced by collaborative working

Checklist: Evaluating internal relationships

The criteria to evaluate internal relationships will always contain factors specific to the issue at hand, such as:

- What is our primary objective?
- What is the key interest that we are trying to satisfy most?
- What is the absolute minimum that must be achieved?
- What are the desirably, but not essential aspects, that we want to satisfy?
- What are the key things to avoid?
- What are the consequences of continuing with the status quo, or simply doing nothing?

Case Study

A large European Manufacturer achieved 100 million euros in savings in nine months by creating more than 50 cross-functional purchasing teams, that were organised around spending categories led by Procurement and included key personnel from Engineering, Manufacturing, Marketing and Suppliers/ Contractors. They all worked on holistic development of products and optimising processes and they managed to:

- Leverage buying power by renegotiating contracts and changing suppliers.
- Leverage products changes by:
  - Standardising
  - Changing product specifications
  - Designing to cost
  - Locating substitutes
  - Optimising processes by:
    - Reducing joint costs with suppliers
    - Reducing inventory

In all, 45% of 100 million euros savings were attributed to the internal and external cross-functional teams (CFTs) close co-operation and collaboration.

Meanwhile on a more general but highly relevant basis, some strategic considerations on demand are important – the following checklist highlighting once again the importance of cross-functionalism:

Demand planning
- Use a repeatable cross-functional process to obtain a consensus forecast
- Apply various forecasting techniques to obtain baseline forecasts for different demand patterns
- Evaluate the impact of demand management techniques for creating and shifting demand
- Monitor forecast performance, taking corrective action as appropriate

Customer planning
- Evaluate customer requirements and segment customers into different supply chain combinations
- Evaluate supply chain strategic requirements to determine cost to serve objectives
- Configure supply chains to obtain a strategic fit between supply chain and customer requirements
- Identify opportunities to compress time within a supply chain

Inventory planning
- Determine appropriate points to position inventory within the supply chain
- Specify target stock levels based on uncertainties in supply and demand
- Use different inventory systems for managing inventory levels

Supply chain planning
- Use a repeatable cross-functional process to balance supply and demand
- Aggregate demand and produce an aggregate plan to identify supply requirements by location
- Perform "what if" analyses to develop planning sensitivities

Collaboration
- Identify potential supplier and internal and external supply chain partners to collaborate with
- Quantify the benefits from pursuing collaborative relationships
- Establish and implement a cross-functional process for utilising collaborative relationships

Interface with Customers

Perhaps no one would dispute that the objective of the procurement and supply management function is to procure materials, equipment and services of the right quality, in the right quantity at the right time and right price and to provide service that satisfies the client, thereby emphasising a customer-centred approach to the need satisfaction.

To satisfy a customer's needs, procurement and supply management has to make continuous performance improvements. It is therefore appropriate to provide a general outline of a service framework that includes four essential elements necessary to produce efficient and effective service. These four essential elements are:

- Customers (clients)
- Procurement
- Strategy
- Systems/processes

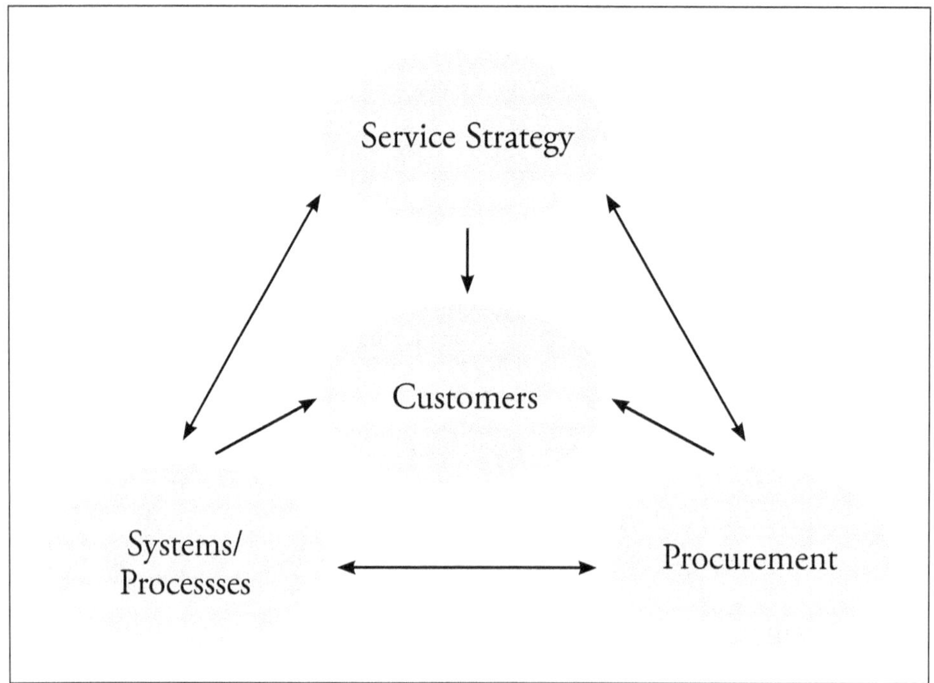

Customers are at the centre of the triangle because services produced from procurement and supply management should always be customer centred.

The inside line from the Customers to the Strategy, indicates that the strategy should put the customers first, by meeting their true, identified needs. Procurement and supply management should correctly identify what the customers want and should ask what goes on in the customer's minds, so that they can fulfil their needs satisfactorily.

The inside line from the Customers to the System indicates that the systems (i.e. procedures, controls, decision-making, equipment etc.) should be designed with the customers in mind for efficient service delivery.

The inside line from the Customers to Procurement indicates that everyone in the procurement and supply management department should be customer driven. This is not only the operational front line staff, but also the other staff in the department, such as computer operators and budgeting control staff who, whilst they do not service customers directly, do need to build up an internal servicing network to service Internal Customers.

The outside line from the Procurement department to the Systems/Processes indicates that people depend on the system to deliver an efficient level of service; therefore, service procedures and systems should be designed to be simple, fast and practical for operation.

The outside line from Strategy to Systems/Processes indicates that the systems should follow logically from the strategy and must be well integrated with the strategy.

The outside line from Strategy to Procurement indicates that everyone in the Procurement and supply management departments should be aware of the strategy, e.g. to provide fast and reliable service on time to customers with good quality goods at competitive prices.

Procurement and Internal Customers

Case Study: Study Babcock

Procurement at Babcock is working ever more closely with operations to satisfy customers' growing demand to share risk with its suppliers.

In a complex and multi-level supply chain, this change of approach needs to be reflected in the contracting model below the top tier.

To achieve this, Babcock found it essential that operations and procurement were closely aligned in presenting the need for change to a supply base well established in its current way of working. If the project managers, who own the day-to-day relationships with the suppliers, did not present the same case for change as the category manager responsible for reflecting this change in the new contracting model, they would quickly fail.

Where Babcock achieved success was working jointly with procurement to communicate the benefits of the new approach and making it visible internally, and to the supply base, that they were aligned in their thinking.

The internal case for change was important because to make the new contracting approach work they would have to move away from a tradition of micro-managing suppliers to give them space to make their decisions balancing risk and reward within the scope of work.

Results on the first ship where they employed this new approach were impressive and the reduced overall cost of the work justified the change. They saw improvements in the health and safety record that suggested with more responsibility came a more responsible approach.

That a significant change, affecting both Babcock internal cross-functional teams and supplier teams, was achieved in a short time is testament to the close relationships and joint approach, which was fostered between operations and procurement.

Providing value to customers

Case Study – Novartis Pharmaceuticals "Value-Added"

One of the things they are working on is how they measure value propositions not just price savings, such as: cost avoidance, supply chain security, risk management and quality. They are building our balanced scorecard and raising awareness with their senior management that they cannot deliver nearly double digit cost reduction year on year. They realise that it is not possible unless you re-engineer what you buy. So, that's what they are doing.

This shift requires them to have breakthrough conversations with internal customers/stakeholders that can unlock significant additional value.

What other opportunities/projects are there? Who do they need to talk to in the business to build support for the ideas? The concept is that procurement start to become facilitators and leaders of change, as opposed to predictable.

They have adopted the use of focused customer surveys. They sit opposite key stakeholders and ask a very structured set of questions and they score us 0 – 10, as well as giving critical and honest qualitative comments.

The survey explores the type of value, quality, communication, responsiveness and creativity they get from the procurement team and what is important to them. Procurement analyse the results and come up with ideas for improvement.

Customer Requirements and Specifications

As we have explained in *Excellence in Procurement* (2008), an initial requisition from users or the customers is commonly used to identify their requirements. The format of the requisition may range from a simple requisition covering a standard requirement, right through to a complex project where a more thorough analysis precedes the final requests.

The need is what has to satisfied, it also importantly represents the demand that "kick starts" the whole process. At the root here, from the procurement perspective is the specification.

Specifications are a description of what a customer/user wants and therefore communicate what is required, to meet the needs. They are a statement of need from internal sources that is to be satisfied by the procurement of external resources. They can rightly be seen as the cornerstone of the whole procurement process as everything that happens after the specification will be dependant and results from the specification, including, as we will see, legal aspects in contracts.

Specifications therefore do need to be clear and to communicate; they may therefore take the form of industry used standards, as every standard is a specification.

Standards have often been originated by organisations such as The British Standards Institution (BSI) and The International Standards Organisation (ISO) and where such standards are found, it will usually imply that there are many supply sources. It can however also mean that the use of such a standard may actually preclude other suppliers, which in turn, may be against legislation on preventing competition.

Where standards are a part of specifications, it is useful to check that the current version is being used as standards are often regularly updated.

It should also be noted here that the use of the BSI 5750/ISO 9000 standards for services does not necessarily guarantee that it is a "good" service. For example, IS 9002 and its forerunner BS 5750 part 2, cover the procedures that have to be followed to give the service standard required. They make no comment what so ever about the service that is required, as it is for the organisation holding the standard, to determine what these service levels are.

Accordingly for service supply, whilst IS 9002 tells you that the organisation has procedures to ensure the compliance with a standard, it tells you nothing about "goodness" of the standard. IS 9002 therefore accredits the means, not the end.

Determine the specification types

Specifications should comply with the following criteria:

- Are the requirements stated clearly, unambiguously and with only the essential characteristics stated?

- Will it enable suppliers to decide and cost their offer?
- Will the suppliers offer be able to be evaluated against the specification?
- Does the specification enable opportunity for all suppliers to make an offer?
- Does it include any legal requirements?

The development of specifications will usually require liaison between users, procurement and maybe potential suppliers. Trade associations and other users can also help, as can independent people who can check and verify the final draft specifications.

Specifications may take various forms as follows. It will be seen that many of these, find a better fit with only products:

- **Technical specifications:** such as a highly detailed description; e.g. especially with engineering products.
- **Sample specifications:** such as to assess the suitability of chemicals or fabric on products.
- **Brand specifications:** such as a specific brand that may denote the customer's preference; it is also actually identifying a standard. As the acceptance of a brand will limit the supplier options, then any such use will need to be specially justified.
- **Design specifications:** such as to identify dimensions and outlines.
- **Form specifications:** such as the shape and appearance.
- **Functional specifications:** such as to ensure the product or service performs 'fit for purpose' or what it has to achieve
- **Performance specifications:** Such as the output range within which the item must function, these as will be seen next, are very useful for services.

Performance specifications/contracts

As performance is the output(s) required from the product or service, the aim with specifications is to provide a clear and objective view of the expected output. Therefore, the nature of the product/service may determine that a performance related specification is required, and perhaps becomes part of the formal final contract.

The following questions can be asked and the answers will assist in determining objective performance outcomes:

- Clarity; what has to be done? This must be very clear, along with who is accountable with clear levels of responsibility and authority.
- Competence; do the knowledge and skills exist.
- Consequences; why is it being done? These must be clear.
- Competition; what other tasks are there to do? Prioritising may be needed.

- Co-operation; who else is to be involved?
- Control; how is it known that a desired and satisfactory end has been reached?
- Commitment; do the suppliers have the confidence to do it willingly and well?
- Context; are the right surroundings and support available?

The UK public sector for example, has used performance contracts widely in recent years, such as in the provision of services such as ambulance, police, hospitals and fire rescue. The aim here is also to ensure that government objectives can be maximised by the setting of targets to be achieved, that will also, bring improved performance.

These expected conditions can however fail to materialise when for example, managers with information and bargaining power and with no strong incentive to "comply", can manipulate targets to ensure performance is judged satisfactorily.

For performance specifications, to work correctly the objectives must be explicitly stated with assigned weighting and priorities translated into clear and agreed performance improvement targets, perhaps with clear incentives and disincentives about compliance.

Differences between Technical and Performance Specification

The following shows the important differences between the two types of specifications:

	Technical specifications	Performance specifications
Supplier	Receives an exact and clear specification	Responds to the outcomes required in the customers required operating conditions and environment
Buyer	Has certainty of what is being bought. However these may not the "best", as other options that may satisfy the need are excluded	Must very clearly specify the requirements and outcomes needed
Technical risk	With the buyer	With the supplier
Supplier Innovation	Low/little	Highly likely
Examples	Simple and branded products	Services and complex projects

It should be noted that the above technical specifications and the subsequent, so-called technical assessment in the evaluation process, are not the same.

The technical assessment looks at things such as compliance with the specification; (and this is either the technical or the performance specification).

Performance contracts

It is important to appreciate the link between specification and contracts. Performance contracts are an enforceable agreement between suppliers and buyers as they link incentives and disincentives to the contractual performance outputs. The supplier is required to provide guarantees, for example:

- with a timely completion
- the achievement of performance specifications,
- on quality and cost parameters

Liquated damages may be a part of such contracts; this being a pre-determined estimate of loss by the buyer and payable by the supplier in the event of failure to meet agreements. Liquated damages for delays are determined by a time scale (e.g. daily) and normally will equate to the buyers financial loss. Liquated damages for failure to meet performance are normally based on an amount for each percentage point the failure falls below the guaranteed performance level. We will be looking at contracts later on.

Role of procurement with specifications

The users' specification means procurement is able to have:

1. Information on available supply
2. A basis for a supplier appraisal
3. Indications of risks on suppliers and products
4. Indications where the business able to standardise

Ultimately, procurement aims to procure services that are fit for purpose and the characteristics that give this may be determined by the specification.

Once then, the service requirements have been established/specified, it is important to summarise the details with the user or customer to ensure that what is being sourced is to the specification they require. Additionally, lines of communication will need to be established to ensure there are minimum delays should problems occur, and areas of responsibility should be highlighted and agreed.

Providing Customers with Value

Value can be a strange word as it has many different meanings, for example, value for a supplier may not be value to a customer. Value therefore has some degree of subjectivity.

Here we will use 'value' in the sense that the customer that defines what value is, therefore some will be more interested in quality, some in availability/time, and others with the cost/price of the product/service being purchased.

Price and value are however not the same – there is a saying that goes 'we can know the price of anything, but the value of nothing.'

The strategic success here is to satisfy exactly the customers' wants and values, and at the same time to satisfy what is best overall for the organisation. This is not always easy to achieve, but it is helpful to examine what it is that actually creates value.

We need firstly to see here that value and the process of procurement are only parts of the overall whole Supply Chain process, that will cover the following:

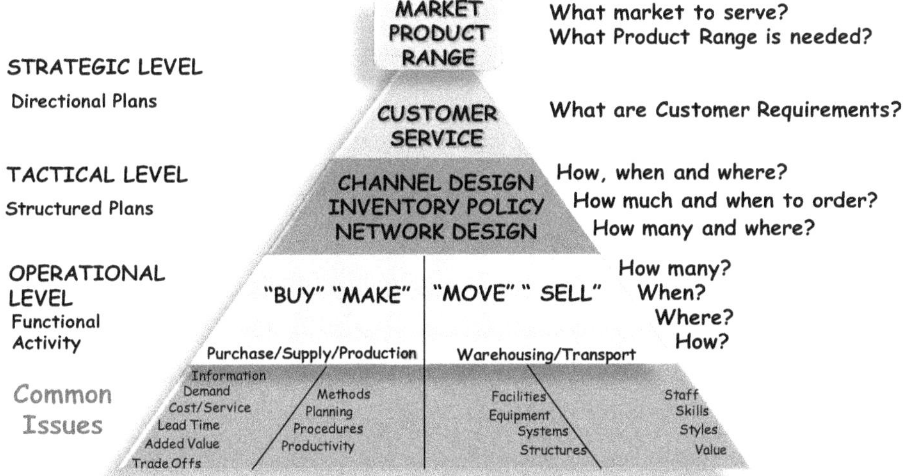

Whilst the concept of the supply chain is simple, its outworking varies enormously, as shown below, which highlights four major types of supply chains:

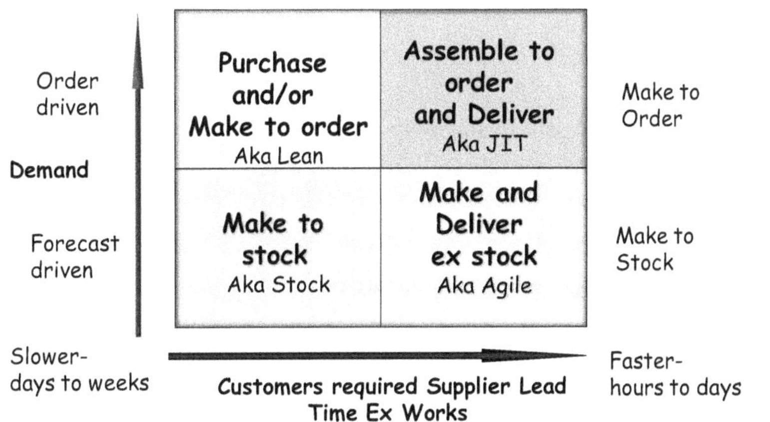

The Supply Chain is therefore a dynamic system with the following parts:

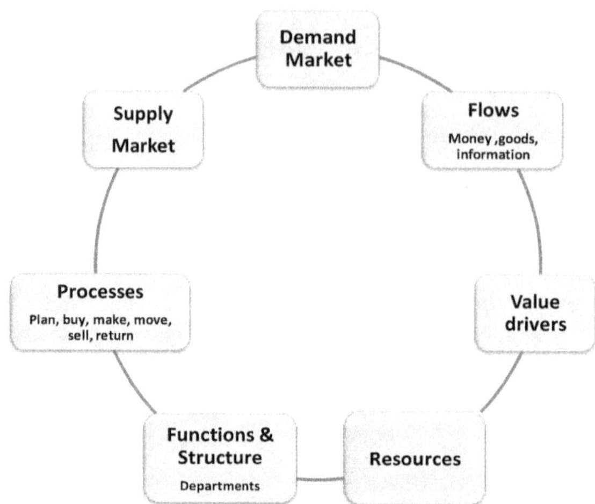

It is important therefore to identify what are the specific value drivers. One view that helps is to consider the Supply Chain 7xVs; these being where:

Volume + Variety = Variability + Velocity + Volatility =
Visibility (low) and Vulnerability

Whilst we expand on these shortly, these Vs are commonly in the supply side of the supply chain and are considered as "problems". In solution, there are also the following Supply Chain '6Rs' solutions to these problems:

- Rationalisation
- Reliability
- Responsiveness
- Resilience
- Relationships
- Risk management

Let us examine further this relationship between the Vs and the Rs. As we will show, these will ultimately provide value solutions for Customers.

The 7xV Problems

We will start by looking at why the Vs create problems:

Volume and Variety

The relatively recent growth in product variety has followed on from alleged changes in consumer demands, which in turn, have sponsored the response of providing choice and therefore creating high product variety.

Whilst increases in variety has happened, it is also common to find that over time the position is where 80% of volume (demand) comes from only 20% of product variety (lines).

This is often because – whilst increased variety gives some initial increases in volume – over time, the volume per line item reduces, as it now competes with more variety; a vicious "competition of variety" circle.

Additionally, another problem is now that the predictability of demand is then spread across an increasing variety of product ranges.

Variability

Variability brings uncertainty, resulting in both poor reliability and reduced confidence in whom or where, the variability is seen to emanate from. In supply chains, variability is common in both the demand volumes and in the supply lead times; hence the expression, "uncertainty is the mother of inventory".

As organisations will often over or under compensate for the variability; this affects the up and down streams of the supply chain (as in the well-known Forester or bullwhip effect).

Velocity

Velocity is about movement and speed, and in the supply chain this is the rate of the flows of goods, information, and cash, and the speed of change generally. Additionally, whenever the movement slows down or stops, then we will automatically add cost, such as with storage, demurrage and delay costs.

Volatility

Volatility is violent changes over quite short time scales e.g. "lumpy" demand that is fast today/slow tomorrow, with no historical pattern, e.g. stop/start flows of product and information. Volatility therefore represents unexpectedly high levels of turbulence, and/or extreme degrees of fluctuations. In supply chains, this will create more variability, and if it occurs relatively frequently over time, a reduction in confidence of the "repeating" source.

Visibility

Visibility is all about having transparency and seeing "what's going on". In supply chains, this is the visibility of both demand and supply; here the common causes of having poor/low visibility are:

- no real-time demand sharing with, or access by, customers to the suppliers
- no track and trace on product delivery
- lack of intelligence

Vulnerability

This represents an exposure to risk where:

"Risk is the probability that a particular adverse event occurs during a stated period of time, or results from a particular challenge …

Risk is the numerical measure of harm or loss associated with an adverse event."

Risk is effectively the accumulation from all the previous aspects described above and creates a lack of confidence in the following:

- Order cycle time
- Order current status
- Demand forecasts received
- Suppliers' capability to deliver
- Manufacturing capacity
- Quality of the products
- Transportation reliability
- Services delivered

Another example of the lack of confidence is shown from the customer-facing end of a business where a sales team believes that order cycle and order fulfilment times are not reliable, so they then devise their own means of addressing this and order stock so they can have supplies to support their key customers.

Effectively this is placing a phantom order (i.e. for their own private buffer stock) which clearly causes inefficiencies. Sales now start over-ordering since they do not have timely visibility of the correct demand signals, or they know from experience that supplies may be late or insufficient to fill the complete orders.

Meanwhile suppliers Production plans may also be based on inflated production lead times due to their own similar lack of visibility and control. Safety lead times are often used in standard Materials/Manufacturing Requirement/Resource Planning (MRP/ MRPII), since production planners do not want to be blamed for production delays.

This, coupled with a lack of means to expedite, or flexibility in manufacturing also means that any yield shortfalls or production downtimes have to be made up by investing in additional production.

Such impacts from a loss of confidence show that:
- Without visibility and control, it is common that the supply chain is plagued with buffer inventories
- Buffering is employed to hedge against the uncertainties and risks in the supply chain
- Excessive inventory leads to higher financial risks
- Investing in excessive capacity to hedge against uncertainties and risks

We can also readily identify impacts of loss of confidence with logistics providers, who also have to build slack into their operations; meaning quoted transport lead times will often have built-in safety times, and therefore extra shipping capacities may need to be purchased. The lack of visibility of shipment and requirement schedules means unnecessary expediting of shipments, or the wrong mode of transportation is used.

All the above means it is going to be increasingly difficult to be responsive to customers, to react to changes in market conditions, and to be competitive in providing customer service.

Lead times quoted to customers will also tend to be longer, since added protection is needed when people have little confidence in the supply chain. Contracts may now be constructed in ways that do not give much flexibility to customers, and special requests by customers are now turned down. The supply chain is no longer competitive and is susceptible to market risks.

Vulnerability in supply chains also unfortunately collaborates with some of other Vs, as the consequences of risk are for example some of the following:
- "Lumpy" and slow flows of product/information, i.e. volatility and poor velocity
- Lead times variability
- Poor ICT and visibility
- Poor service with no customer value
- High costs with poor metrics
- Inadequate understanding of SCM and customer service
- Stock outs, yet have high overall inventory levels
- Slow responses to change
- Company failures
- Poor customer service/lost customers
- Higher costs
- Disillusioned people

This reveals not only poor operational effectiveness, but clearly at the core, a very poor strategic direction. Therefore, what are the available strategic and operation solutions?

The 6R Solutions

We have already identified these earlier as being Rationalisation, Reliability, Responsiveness, Resilience, Relationships and Risk management. We will look briefly at each in turn.

Rationalisation

The aim here is to reduce product or service complexity/variety and increase customisation, whilst still being able to maintain or increase service sales and profits. The way forward therefore is to rationalise/change the products, and redesign the supporting supply chain.

Reliability

This is consistency in what is done, and, in what is said/promised. Reliability is therefore the enabler of certainty and confidence and the "destroyer" of variability and lack of confidence.

Interestingly, reliability always features in the top 3 characteristics that buyers look for from service suppliers (along with cost and service performance e.g. on time, in full (OTIF)). For example, *The number one thing suppliers must get right is reliable fixed lead times; otherwise, simply, we will change suppliers.*

Doing what you say you will do is important here. It will in turn lead to trust and good relationships.

Responsiveness

Flexible responsiveness refers to varying and changed demands and service requirements, and is regularly achieved by having shared information among supply chain members. Here, whilst the traditional view is that "information is power" and is associated with the belief that power is diminished when information is shared, in supply chains the reverse is true.

If information between supply chain members is shared, its power increases significantly. This is because shared information reduces uncertainty; e.g. it reduces the need for safety stock.

As a result, the supply chain becomes more responsive and, ultimately, could become demand driven, rather than forecast driven.

Resilience

Resilience means not being vulnerable to risk or unexpected disturbances.

It is often achieved by using normal best practices; it also however does require a proactive strategic design. An example of such a design is one that will follow the six steps:

1. "Win the home games first" by having internal cooperation and strong relationships in a cross-functional approach that has customer service/demand as the main driver

2. Cooperate externally on joint problems

3. Know the weakest links (e.g. as revealed by the Theory of Constraints) and know where the associated risks are

4. Strengthen the weak links or reduce/avoid the risks

5. Create lean and/or agile supply chains e.g. spare capacity, backup systems, standard materials, standard operations, postponement, short lead times, make to order (not to stock) etc.

6. When all else fails, have emergency procedures and contingency plans

The benefits here are much more than cost reduction, and include the reduction of market risk, for example:

- increases in sales and market share
- penetration to new markets
- speedy new product introduction

The contention is that by making improvements, this creates a virtuous circle of confidence; in turn, this gives resilience and a significant effect on mitigating supply chain risk. This requires that "working with others" must work, a topic discussed next.

Relationships

How we choose to work with others (e.g. as in "win the home games first") and external customers and suppliers, will directly affect the supply chain and its performance.

Supplier Relationship Management (SRM) can also mitigate supply chain risk as it involves changing from "Managing Supplies, to Managing Suppliers". As such, SRM recognises as a core principle that "you are only as good as your suppliers" and asks 'fundamentally, what is the point of setting a supplier up to fail?'

SRM can be defined as follows:

"SRM is an holistic discipline, to work collaboratively,, with those suppliers, who are vital to our success, by maximising the value of our relationship."

It will also mean that, "vision for me must be viability for you."

Before the SRM approach, it was common to find that supplier meetings focussed on "yesterday's" contract/service issues, and were undertaken in an often adversarial and competitive manner. Adopting SRM will therefore mean working out how best to work and collaborate, which extends to continually solving problems that will drive organisational learning and challenge people to grow. For suppliers, by working towards becoming a customer's supplier of choice, they develop a longer-term view of adding value. Essentially, therefore, SRM brings in a changed view in managing suppliers and when there is no such longer-term relationship management, this tends to lead to:

- Short-term savings, but these are eroded over time
- Cost emphasis, but with the exclusion of extra value
- Decreasing supplier service
- Animosity in customer/supplier relationship
- Suppliers who "drop" customers

Case Study: Changed view in Managing Suppliers – Toyota's view is:
- Suppliers are seen as "extensions"
- Select suppliers with care (as is done with our own staff/personnel selection)
- Develop suppliers (as done with our own staff)
- Use a long term partnership approach
- Tier structure with levels of responsibility
- Set up strict cost targets and timing e.g. expect 3-4% price reduction per year
- Integrate methods/systems (e.g. on JIT, New Product Development)

SRM will focus on all of the "usual suspects", for example:
- Demand forecast sharing (e.g. Volume/Variety)
- Order lead times (e.g. Visibility)
- Inventory status sharing and reductions (e.g. Visibility)
- Packaging
- Shipment size/frequency (e.g. Volatility)
- Supplier lead times (e.g. Variability/Visibility)
- On time delivery (e.g. Variability/Velocity)
    plus
- Improved relationships
- Joint KPIs
- Innovation
- Joint problem solving

We will be examining SRM in more detail in Part 3 of this book, additionally it is fully covered in *Quick Guide to Supplier Relationship Management in the Supply Chain* (Emmett, 2011).

Risk Management

The principles of risk management involve being proactive to avoid damage/harm by applying the rule that "prevention is better than the cure". Done effectively, it can give benefits of smoother operations with fewer disruptions, lower costs and more value.

However, it firstly needs a recognition of risk that must also be taken on by others in the supply chain (back once more to relationship approaches) and whilst legislation does makes risk management mandatory in some areas (e.g. health and safety, fire) it really must be something that is actively strategized for in supply chains. Risk Management is not an organisationally widely accepted process, yet done well, it will systemically better identify, analyse and respond to risks.

Taking on Supply Chain Risk Management (SCRM) therefore, could aim:

"To ensure the supply chain continues to operate as planned with smooth and uninterrupted flows of materials, information and money from suppliers to customers" (Source: After Waters, 2007)

Just like in supply chains, SCRM will need to cover all internal departments, like marketing/sales, distribution/logistics, production/manufacturing, procurement/purchasing, finance, HR etc., as well as the external customers and suppliers.

The link to customer service and value

After delivery of a product or service, customers have both perceptions and measurements of what has been delivered to them. Effectively these perceptions and measurements have come from the outcomes of the 7Vs and the 6Rs. The measurements of customer service are the "normal" Five Rights of Quality, Quantity, Time, Place and Cost. There are also many other common customer expectations covering things like, support, commitment, safety, morale, ethics along with other factors like value.

Quality

Or *"Is it what I want"*, with the questions here including 'does what we have received meet our:

- Functional or Technical specification?
- Performance specification?'

If these have been met, then additionally does it do what we want it to, and is it "fit for purpose" and "right first time, every time"?

Quantity and Time

Or *"How many I want"* and *"When I want it"* – the questions asked here are:

- Is it On Time (OT), and
- In Full (IF)

Therefore besides being, on time, in full (OTIF), it is also received undamaged and with full and complete paperwork.

We commonly find with the IF measurement, that if the order is short or is received damaged (therefore, it is not "in full"), then these are reported (as indeed are any price differences) to the supplier.

However, it is very common to find that any time variations (OT) are frequently not reported back to suppliers, and therefore they are never acted upon. This is a mystery for anyone who is concerned with inventory management, as lead time is a critical competency in determining inventory levels – as already noted above, 'uncertainty is the mother of inventory'. For those who require more on this critical topic, it has full coverage in *Excellence in Inventory Management* (Emmett and Granville, 2007).

Place

Or *"Where I need it"*

Of specific interest here for buyers/imports is changing to Incoterms Ex Works (EXW), as this buyers option offers better freight control and price reductions, but importantly, better lead time visibility and control; this is well covered in *Excellence in Global Supply Chain Management* (Emmett and Crocker, 2010)

Price

Or *"How much is it"*

Price is cost, and profit, and a question to ask here is, 'what is the visibility and awareness of the costs and profit?' Often such an examination can be undertaken, and is enabled with both good relationships and in the specific types of contract (like "open book" contracts) with suppliers. There should also always be an examination of the Total Acquisition Costs (TAC), and additionally, for items that we will own, the Total Costs of Ownership (TCO) figures.

Others

After delivery, we may need the following from suppliers:

- Support; e.g. after sales service
- Commitment; e.g. ongoing assistance

We need to ensure these have already been noted in the original specification and that the appropriate costs/service levels have been part of our evaluation and ultimate award. However, this may not always have been possible. We also will often have expectations on the:

- Safety of the product/service
- Morale; the "well being" of people, for example, our own motivation levels and those of others in the supply chain, e.g. Suppliers
- Ethics; covering the growing interest and legislative measures on sustainability, environment and green issues along with fairness and anti corruption/bribery matters.

Value

It is our contention that value is defined by the customer and is effectively what the customer expects. As shown above, these expectations can be ascertained from objective measures (e.g. on the quality, quantity etc. KPIs). However, many expectations are subjective perceptions (e.g. some of the 7 Vs/6Rs and also those "others" above).

The customer's ultimate value can only follow delivery and the acceptance of a product for use, e.g. availability in stock, or the use of a service.

Value is therefore found in the customer measurements and perception of benefits and these are judged, either objectively or subjectively.

Therefore value is the customer's measurement and perception of benefits, less the TCO (= TAC + Whole Life costs/Life Cycle Costs + Disposal costs).

3: The Supply Side and the Procurement Organisation

Having earlier considered strategy and customer demand, the next aspect of strategy is to consider how we work with suppliers and what the appropriate procurement structure and processes should cover. In this long section of the book, we will therefore consider the following:

- Reviewing: who are the customers?
- Introducing relationship management
- Introducing supplier service
- Reviewing the 3 supply chain roles
- Cross-functional management
- ICT and E-Procurement
- People development and learning
- Measuring supply lead time
- Outsourcing of non-core activity
- Continuous improvement
- Suppliers have needs
- Supplier development
- Maximising supplier performance
- Post-contract award contract management
- Corporate social responsibility
- Anti corruption practices

Who are the customers?

Determining who the customers are is not always as straightforward as one might think. In addition to the people external to the organisation, such as the consumers (who are often called customers), there is also the internal customer, who is working within the organisation. There is additionally, we suggest, the role played by the suppliers.

Suppliers as customers

If a true Total Quality environment is to be created, then consistency of high quality inputs, service or products, depends totally on the consistency of high quality inputs in the form of components or materials. As such, it is vital to integrate the suppliers of the organisation in order to create a mutually beneficial relationship. (Indeed, we will look soon at seeing suppliers like we see customers, in our section called 'supplier service'). In the first instance, it is important to ensure that both parties clearly articulate their needs and expectations in order that quality specifications can be met.

External customers

Customers come from a variety of sources and their needs and wants will relate directly to their purpose for buying. In considering customers, our first thoughts tend to go to the direct customers, those who purchase the service or goods directly; but there are a number of other customer groups who also need consideration, as follows.

Intermediary customers

These customers purchase the service or product on behalf of somebody else. In order to make that transaction as smoothly as possible the intermediary customers themselves are likely to have their own requirements of the product or service and its accessibility. Within the context of the customer, one has to consider organisational customers – people who buy on behalf of an organisation. This decision to buy is seldom taken in isolation and customer roles here can be aligned to what in marketing terms are called buying roles:

(1) The initiator is the person or people who initially propose that there is a need to be met.

(2) The influencer is the person or people who reinforce the perception of that need.

(3) The decider is those who decide how appropriate it is that the need be met.

(4) The buyer is the person or people responsible for the purchasing process.

(5) The user is the person or people for whom the purchase has ultimately been made.

A satisfied customer is likely to buy the product or service again, and to talk positively about both the product/service and about the organisation. It is also significantly more beneficial to keep customers than it is to win new ones.

Internal customers

Within every organisation there are a number of sub-systems, departments or functional units with different roles and remits, which all contribute to the eventual output of the organisation. It is interesting to consider the nature of communications which take place between these different units, bearing in mind their organisational interdependency. Communication between departments tends to be minimal. When there is dialogue it is often either a functional exchange of information or relating to a problem. The emphasis is on relationships that are reactive by nature, rather than the development of constructive and proactive relationships.

The notion of considering the people within the organisation as customers highlights the difference in the ways external and internal customers are treated, despite the fact that the organisation is equally dependent on both. In order to redress this imbalance a number of key issues relating to the internal customers need to be clarified, namely:

(1) Who are the internal customers?

(2) What does this organisation expect of them?

(3) Are these expectations realistic?

(4) What are the internal customers' expectations of this organisation?

(5) Are these expectations realistic?

(6) What can we do together to make the systems work better for everybody?

The answers to these questions may be sought by the use of formal customer satisfaction methods; although it is often better to try to use personal contact between managers and staff in the form of informal discussion or conversations. By seeking the information in this face-to-face way, an organisation is demonstrating its commitment to listening to the people it values.

Introducing Relationship Management

Any organisation working anywhere in the supply chain is fundamentally working with others; so fundamentally, the issue of people relationships and their effective management is critical as the supply chain is the ultimate team game.
Two definitions reveal this importance:

1. The Office of Government Commerce defines supply chain management as the: *"Coordination of all parties involved in delivering the combination of inputs, outputs or outcomes that will meet a specified requirement".* (Supply Chain Management in Public Sector Procurement-a Guide in *OGC,* June 2006)

2. *"A network of organisations that are involved, through upstream and downstream relationships, in the different processes and activities that produce value in the form of products and services in the hands of the ultimate consumer". (Christopher, 1998)*

"Coordination of all parties" and a "network of organisations" are the prime words used in these definitions, therefore we can see that a simple aim of supply chain management must be one that will integrate, coordinate and control the whole supply chain.

These concepts are well-known and largely accepted, but what is commonly not so accepted is that this integration and coordination must also be done "in the hearts and minds of people". Whilst the use of technical tools, systems and techniques does also enable supply chain management, these should not be used in isolation, for as noted by

Peter Drucker, *"because the object of management is a human community held together by the work bond for a common purpose, management always deals with the nature of man."*

Therefore to manage procurement and the supply chain effectively, we must have a strategy that emphasises collaborative relationships both internally (between the people processes and structures), and externally (between suppliers, customers and other relevant organisations).

Collaboration is the supply chain and is a prerequisite for effectiveness. Otherwise, a one-sided power play is likely to exist, perhaps accompanied by short-term gains for one party. However, this is short-term gain is more than likely destined for longer-term failure, due to a lack of engagement to release the total value from the all of the other parties in the supply chain.

Traditionally, organisational behaviour mirrors their existing culture and structure; therefore, we will often find blame and adversarial communications in functional silos. These silos are also independently managed with accompanied internal politics and power plays.

Whilst it is irrefutable that the reality is interdependence, we still find inconsistent access to information, with isolated functional-only reporting that has built-in conflict, with overall minimal levels of internal and external collaboration.

To change this – a topic we look at soon – organisations must therefore develop end-to-end approaches to their:

- Culture (by a share to gain collaborative approach)
- Processes and structure (by having cross-functional elements)

As has been noted elsewhere, we need to replace competition by cooperation, as "we have been taught to compete, not to cooperate" (after Professor Allan Waller). In many ways, this is analogous with effective team playing where people with different skills work together to achieve a clear and commonly accepted goal.

Collaboration in Supply Chain Strategy and Tactics

Collaborative relationships in Supply Chain Management (SCM) will therefore need to involve a strategic view that sees that the supply chain networks extend both upstream and downstream and that these networks are varied and complex, with many supplier/customer interactions and with much trade off opportunity. Additionally, this strategic view must recognise that competitive advantage and the optimum cost/service balance are only found, by, managing collaboratively, all of these network relationships.

This is the strategic future for supply chain management, which is also seen as a philosophy and approach to use that will guide what needs to be done.

Meanwhile, the tactical management of the supply chain will concentrate on the functional processes that will deliver the required levels of cost/service to meet the strategic plans. As such, there is the need to integrate/coordinate and control both the internal organisation and the external Suppliers/Customers. This is the tactical "implementation and doing" aspect of SCM.

Links to the Supply Chain Rules

In an earlier work, we identified the following 8 Supply Chain Rules *(Emmett, 2005)* and we reproduce a summary of the rules here, with the collaborative and relationship aspects highlighted.

Supply Chain Rule number 1: "Win the home games first". This is all about changing the internal workings to be collaborative by removing silo functions and staffing the functions with "T"-shaped people, who still have the functional depth, but have gained cross-functionalism.

Supply Chain Rule number 2: The format of inventory and where it is held is of common interest to all supply chain players and must be jointly investigated and examined.

Supply Chain Rule number 3: The optimum cost/service balance will only ever be found by working and collaborating fully with all players in the Supply Chain, starting internally (see rule number 1), and extending externally with suppliers and customers.

Supply Chain Rule number 4: Time is cash, cash flow is critical and so are the goods and information flows; fixed reliable lead times being more important than the length of the lead-time.

Supply Chain Rule number 5: The Customer is the business; it is their demand that drives the whole supply chain; therefore finding out what customers value and then delivering it, is critical.

Supply Chain Rule number 6: It is only the movement to the customer that adds the ultimate value; smooth continuous flow movements are preferable. The movement to the customer, undertaken as quickly as possible whilst accounting for the associated cost levels, is really all that counts in adding value. The ultimate value is only found from the customer.

Supply Chain Rule number 7: Trade off by looking, holistically, at all the supply chain players; stop incrementalism and get the whole supply chain working together.

Supply Chain Rule number 8: Information flows lubricate the supply chain; therefore using the appropriate ICT is critical.

Five of these rules have collaborative and relationship aspects directly mentioned, in the other three, this will also be needed, for example; lead times improvements involve working better with external suppliers; movement flows to the customer involve many players as do also, the information flows. Indeed as mentioned earlier, whilst the Supply Chain is driven by flows of materials and information and money, it also needs people working together in flow, that special state when people are connected and think together; when there is a positive relationship with no separation; when people (and organisations) are connected by "hearts and minds". Only then, can supply chain success be realised.

Supplier Relationship Management

Supplier Relationship Management (SRM) is essentially changing from a basic buying process of managing supplies, to one that extends to managing suppliers. Subtle word changes, but this requires a profound difference in application and in thinking.

This will therefore involve a change from having supplier meetings dominated by "yesterday's" contract/service issues and conducted in an adversarial and competitive manner, towards one of working with suppliers by concentrating on how best to work together collaboratively. This involves continually solving problems and driving towards organisational learning that challenges people to grow.

Along with a longer term view of adding value, effective SRM will move away from a cost emphasis (as this can effectively exclude obtaining any extra value) and also moves away from those short-term saving approaches that become eroded over time.

SRM therefore aims for increasing service from suppliers by removing any animosity in customer/supplier relationships.

SRM Practice

There is much evidence that SRM is practiced and has been for many years, as the following examples clearly show:

> **Case Study: Toyota supplier partnering involves:**
> - Mutual understanding
> - Trust
> - Commitment to co-prosperity
> - Respect for each other's capability
> - "GOYA" (Get off your ass") and "Go and see and talk and listen"
> - Interlocking structures
> - Alliance structure
> - Parallel sourcing

- Interdependent processes
- Control systems with
- Measurements
- Feedback
- Target pricing
- Compatible capabilities
- Engineering excellence
- Operational excellence
- Problem solving skills
- Information sharing
- Accurate data collection and dissemination
- Common language
- Timely communications
- Joint improvement activities
- Value added and value engineering
- Supplier development
- Study groups

Case Study: Dutton Engineering UK in the 1990s

"Suppliers as Partners" initiative
- Apply TQM principles
- Philosophy of trust and empowerment
- Teamwork widely used, including with suppliers and customers
- Supply base of key partnerships (had 80% of materials from 12 suppliers)
- Aim: to minimum total acquisition cost (TAC) with, maximum service

Methods used
- Held a supplier day with an agenda of:
- Explained TQM, e.g. involve all employees, proactive to continuous improvement, cooperation and teamwork
- Suppliers invited were told were to be single sources
- Future to be based on:
  - ✔ Openness/trust
  - ✔ Clear joint objectives

✔ Long term view with no year-end renegotiations

Basis of supplier selection was:
✔ Culture of TQM 30%
✔ Quality 25%
✔ On time delivery 25%
✔ Price 20% (TAC is used as this "is more than the price on the invoice")

Approach of "Partners as suppliers":
✔ Trust implicitly e.g. no inspection
✔ Kanban supply e.g. two bin, suppliers call in once/twice a week, no orders are placed
✔ Some non Kanban by team leaders with a single PO
✔ Reduce non value added e.g. no delivery notes, invoice once per month e.g. goods as listed on computer disk, e.g. POs down by 80%
✔ Reduce TAC e.g. suppliers offload delivery vehicles, joint design of packaging

Benefits
- For Dutton
  - ✔ Secure supply
  - ✔ Reliability in delivery
  - ✔ Improved quality
  - ✔ Purchase administration was reduced to 20% of what was done before
  - ✔ Reducing TAC
  - ✔ Growing sales
  - ✔ Lead onto outsourcing of transport, cleaning, gardening and some "standard" manufacturing with own plant kept for prototypes and small runs

- For Suppliers
✔ Long term, so can plan forward
✔ Freedom to perform
✔ Paid on time
✔ Financial stability

Source: "Focus" (CILT magazine) February 1996

Case Study: a contrast in UK experience in the 2000s

National Stadium at Wembley, London
- Design-and-build contract
- Fixed-price, lump-sum.
- All risk is passed to the contractor as "we protect against failure"
- Labour and people problems
- Opened in March 2007, almost a year late
- Over budget
- Litigation

UK Heathrow's Terminal 5, London
- Work in partnership with contractors. Contract required totally integrated teams, including the principal subcontractors, through main contractors and designers to the operator (BAA) and the end user (BA)
- Contractors are paid on a cost-reimbursable basis, with performance bonuses
- Risk is accepted by BAA as "we have a shared interest in successful outcomes"
- Opened on time in March 2008
- On budget

"T5 people always talk about the contract; it's what everything we do here is based on. Usually in this business, the contract tells you what to do when things go wrong, but our contract tells you what to do to make things go right."

"We took in our suppliers as partners and got them involved at a much earlier stage than is normally the case. Usually in this business there is a complete break between the consultants who design the things and the contractors who build them-there is no meeting of minds."

*(More SRM case studies are in the **Quick Guide to Supplier Relationship Management**, 2012, by Stuart Emmett)*

Such good examples of collaborative relationships however remain the exception rather than the rule. This could indicate a lack of knowledge, but it also reveals a failure to learn and to change, and of sticking to "rowing the boat we know", a topic we will also explore later. It can also be because of lack of clarity and meaning in the words supplier relationship management as this is all too commonly, and confusingly, seen as a software program. For example, the main ERP supplier SAP advertises its supplier relationship management software as covering the integrated source-to-pay process, and that its SAP SRM application automates, simplifies and accelerates procure-to-pay processes for goods and services. Whilst there is no doubt at all that this is a valuable offering, SRM is very much more than any standard source/procure to pay procurement process.

Additionally with procurement software programs and systems, "Most systems focus either on contract management or supplier performance management, while a number of organisations reported confusion among internal stakeholders as a result of transactional procurement modules in their ERP systems being badged as SRM. (*Source: Alan Day*)

SRM definitions

"SRM is an holistic discipline to work collaboratively, with those suppliers who are vital to our success, by maximising the value of our relationship where such a vision for me, must also be viability for you".

Whilst SRM definitions do vary, many are one-sided and see SRM as being the monitoring/improving of the suppliers performance (win/lose?).
The definition should however be a two-way; otherwise, why should the supplier choose to engage? The UK Chartered Institute of Purchasing and Supply (CIPS) meanwhile encapsulates these points in its definition of SRM as being the *"process for managing the interaction between two entities, one of which is supplying things to the other entity. SRM is a two-way process in that it should improve the performance of both the buying organisation as well as the supplying organisation and hence be mutually beneficial. It involves proactively developing relationships with particular suppliers"*.

To indicate what is important in SRM, research on SRM introductions indicates the behavioural aspects take up around 70/80% of the implementation of a full SRM program, whereas the technical aspects, such as software, are only some 20/30%.

Knowledge of such a correct reality is critical to counter the many who actually believe the main way to make the change is to use only technological tools and techniques (such as software programs). As we have already noted, the use of technical tools, systems and techniques do also enable supply chain management; however, these should not be used in isolation. Clearly, the behavioural aspects must dominate.

SRM's Reported Benefits

If we look at having bad relationships, then the following have been identified:

- High administration costs
- Time spend price wrangling
- Time spent resolving problems
- Too many meetings with too many people
- Unwilling to consider simple solutions to problems
- An atmosphere that discourages innovation

(Source: Toyota in Institute of Business Ethics, Supplier Relationships Report 2006)

Accordingly, it could be argued that the benefits of an SRM program are:

- Lower administration costs
- Little time spent on price wrangling
- Less time spent resolving problems
- Fewer meetings
- A willingness to consider simple solutions to problems
- An atmosphere that encourages innovation

As noted earlier, improvements using SRM will usually focus on the following:

- Demand forecast sharing
- Order lead times
- Inventory status sharing
- Inventory reductions
- Shipment sizes
- Shipment frequency
- Supplier lead times
- On time delivery
- Packaging

However, with an SRM program, the following will also be evident:

- Improved relationships
- Joint KPIs
- Innovation
- Joint problem solving
- Reduced cost/risk
- Increased efficiency/quality/innovation/service, by:
  - ✔ Working together to make it easier to do business together
  - ✔ Developing trust

Introducing Supplier Service

Organisations are now well-versed in customer service, indeed the customer *is* the business for many. This was not always true, but now the growth and acceptance of the importance of customer service is well recognised (if not always well practiced).

At the other extreme, conceptually, from customers, we have suppliers. And as suppliers, service is a concept very similar to that of customer service. It presents some interesting and possibly controversial views on supplier relationship management, which one day, hopefully, will become as well recognised and important as the customer side (suppliers are critical in delivering customer service, as if there is no supplier, then there is no service for customers).

Meanwhile let us amplify further the importance of supplier service/relationship management.

The supply chain is also the supply-demand chain and is the supplier-customer chain. The supply chain can also be visualised as a series of connected links of suppliers and customers:

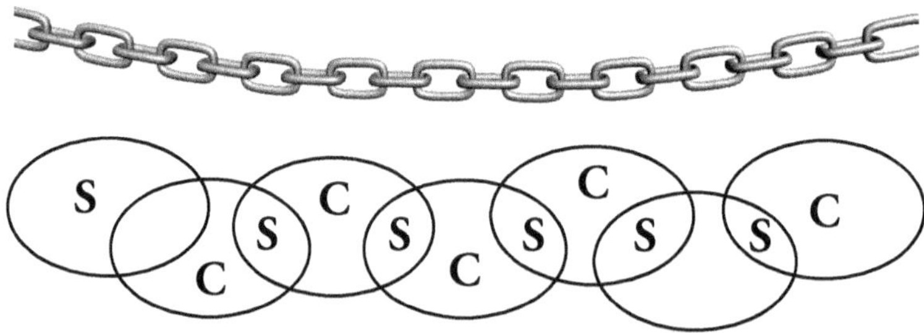

S = suppliers
C = customers

There are many and multiple supplier/customer connections in any supply chain. Such connections can be internal or external ones, involving internal departments in an organisation, or, external suppliers or customers. For example;

- the passing on of paperwork to the next person,
- the passing on of a sub assembly on an assembly line or
- the supply of component part from an external supplier

Of course, and to state the obvious, suppliers have customers and customers have suppliers – additionally, one may be a customer in one transaction, but then a supplier in another transaction.

Suppliers will, naturally and normally, view the next connection link as a customer. However, rarely will customers view their suppliers in the same way as they do their customers. Yet in the supply chain process, they are both connected dependently.

If buyers would see suppliers, the same as they see customers, then supply chain relationships should change and then, overall, the end service to the ultimate end customer should be "perfect."

This is therefore what we have called here, supplier service. Whilst we do not really want to add to the multitude of jargon that already exists in our profession, it is our belief that seeing suppliers in a similar way to how we already see customers will bring a paradigm shift in our thinking. Seeing suppliers this way therefore, will mean that the following rules and actions have to apply with suppliers:

Supplier Service Rules

- Believe that suppliers possess good ideas.
- Gather supplier feedback at every opportunity.
- Focus on continual improvement.
- Actively solicit good and bad feedback.
- Do not spend vast sums of money doing it.
- Seek real-time feedback.
- Make it easy for suppliers to provide feedback.
- Leverage technology to aid your efforts.
- Share supplier's feedback throughout the organisation.
- Use feedback to make changes quickly.

Definitions of Supplier Service

Supplier service can be variably seen and the following five views represent some different definitions:

1. Supplier service is seen as a need satisfier

"Supplier Service is a function of how well an organisation meets the needs of its suppliers."

2. Supplier service is seen as taking care

"Supplier Service is a phrase that is used to describe the process of taking care of our suppliers in a positive manner."

3. Supplier service is seen as keeping promises

"Supplier service is the ability to provide them with feedback in the way that it has been promised."

4. Supplier service is seen as adding value

"Supplier service is a process for providing competitive advantage and adding benefits in order to maximize the total value."

"Supplier service is the commitment to providing value added services to external and internal suppliers, including attitude knowledge, technical support and quality of service in a timely manner."

5. Supplier service is seen as all of the supplier contact

"Supplier service is any contact between a supplier and a company, which causes a negative or positive perception by a supplier."

Total supplier service

Top leadership must therefore have the commitment to suppliers and supplier-focussed procedures will need to be in place. What is important to accept is that the supplier is:

- a part of the business
- an important person to have contact with
- one we depend on
- a human being with feelings and emotions
- not one to win arguments with, but, is someone who can help us to build our business and give us a competitive advantage

Supplier Satisfiers

All suppliers will expect as a minimum, the following:

- Reliability
- Responsiveness
- Accessibility
- Accuracy

Providing suppliers with the above will prevent them from being dissatisfied. However, these will not, by themselves, provide satisfaction. To provide supplier satisfaction, then the following are required:

- Fully met their expectations (and therefore prevented dissatisfaction)
- Responsiveness
- Courtesy
- Empathy
- Provide exceptional quality
- Good people relationships

- Delivery of value
- Handle well any complaints
- Give them repeat business

Supplier Perception

One of the obvious difficulties in meeting supplier's expectations is that "Perception is Reality." Therefore, we are entering into a space of human variability and subjectivity.

Everything that is done for suppliers, will be the supplier's perception, and how they perceive it is real to them. A buyer's reality should therefore be the supplier's perception of the buyer's performance.

Many people however are uncomfortable with this "reality check" and see it as an unsolvable conundrum that confuses whatever "normal" buying is supposed to be.

However, one very clear reality (one often not recognised), is that attitudes and feelings will definitely affect the way any service delivery is perceived. Accepting this view will require some flexibility from management, such as giving discretion to staff to deal with suppliers and not only relying on any standard and fixed structural procedural manuals and guidelines. After all, suppliers are individuals and organisational procedures must support this. Service is all about delivering, not only about what it is like doing business with your organisation, but also with you personally. Feelings and attitudes are therefore an important aspect.

The importance of attitudes

Please consider the following diagram:

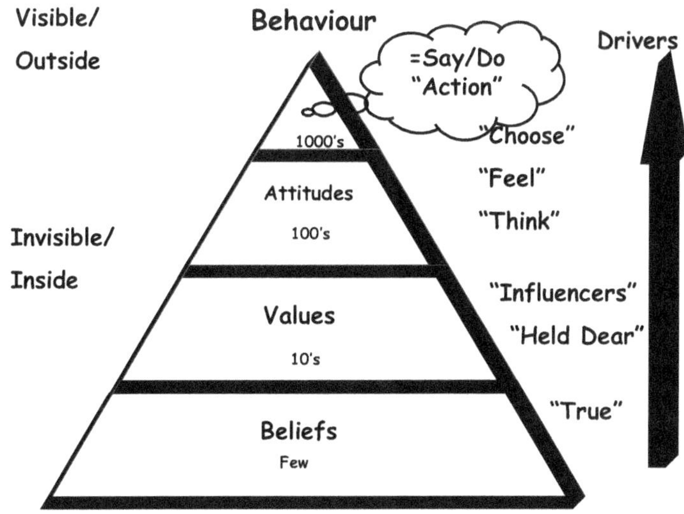

Our attitudes, are underpinned by our beliefs and values, will work through into how we behave (defined here as what we say or do). We will therefore tend to judge from our perspective alone and will not always consider the other parties fully enough.

Good supplier-focussed people will therefore have a deep belief that supplier service is important, they will value this and will then lead by example, so that this belief, will then work through into their attitudes and be shown and reflected by what they say and what they do.

Good supplier-focussed people will therefore:

- pull more than push
- be two-way communicators
- makes concessions, "I think this, but what do you think"
- problem solve and explore interests
- hold views and reasons that "working together works" and is the best approach

Of course, the opposite is also true and often when buyers report problems with suppliers; this can be because they do not have a belief that suppliers are important. As said by Henry Ford; "If you think you can or think you cannot, you are right"

Simple perhaps, but profound in its application and to changing what is done with suppliers. When beliefs are impacted and changed then many other changes will automatically result.

Supplier complaints

Common complaints from suppliers are for example, when:

- Their expectations are not met; e.g. a delayed payment
- Inflexible responses has been received; e.g. when a procurement department (the only department the supplier has had contact with), makes a response to a delayed payment enquiry by saying, it is "nothing to do with me, check with the accounts department"
- Mistakes have been made; e.g. forgetting to say something has changed.
- Communications are poor; e.g. telling one way with no listening and checking understanding
- Delays have been made in payment; e.g. cash flow is critical in all business, cash flow problems are a major source of company failure/bankruptcy, therefore unplanned delays mean supplier cash flow problems. Where however, these delays are known in advance, then suppliers may "compensate" by charging higher prices, reducing service levels, look for alternative customers or even withdraw from the business.

- Dealing with unprofessional people; e.g. "we have just given the supplier a bloody nose" (a comment from a senior buyer in a major UK utility company)

The Supplier Service-focussed organisation

To move towards being be a supplier service focussed organisation, then it is necessary to know:

- Who your suppliers are
- What they expect and need from you
- How well you are meeting their expectations
- How to provide supplier care and follow up
- What needs to be done to make improvements
- What are the barriers to making these improvements
- How you can remove these barriers

The following view of a supplier service-focussed and non-supplier-focussed organisations shows the differences and what is important:

Supplier service focus	Non-supplier focus
Profit comes from supplier and customer satisfaction	Profit comes first, then supplier and customer satisfaction
Preventing problems	Detecting problems
Explicit standards	Vague standards
Complaints are seen as a chance to learn	Complaints are a nuisance
Run by people working with other people using systems, if appropriate	Runs by systems and procedures and then people

The supplier service-focussed organisation will therefore have the following five key attributes:

Reliability: Dependable, accurate performance consistently and in all of the details.

Ownership: Front line ownership, so that those who receive complaints are also able to sort them out.

Responsiveness: Clear evidence of a willingness to help.

Attitudes: Courtesy, friendly, empathy and caring by employees for the suppliers "unique" requirements.

Appearance: Clean and tidy facilities, equipment, people etc.

Benefits of good supplier service

As has been seen, the road to improving supplier service may not be easy; however, the benefits can be huge and long-lasting. The following benefits will all contribute to the survival, wellbeing and profitability of any organisation:

- Reliable service with a marketable product with a price difference
- Market changes, can be better handled and managed
- Continuous improvement becomes a part of the culture, with innovative and responsive staff
- A positive view of your organisation from shareholders, the community and potential employees, with competitors who "fear" your organisation
- Suppliers who now see the organisation as:
  - ✔ responsive and listening
  - ✔ collaborative and sharing
  - ✔ understanding what is critical to their own success
  - ✔ "good people to deal with"

The way suppliers are handled is therefore fundamental to SRM. The following checklist gives more ideas on dealing with suppliers from the view that buyers are the supplier's customers:

Checklist: Ten golden rules for becoming an attractive customer

1. Be a demanding customer.
Challenge your suppliers, but do not crush them. If hard-hitting negotiation is the only tool in your bag, you have problems. Attraction does pay off, but you need to check opinions with key suppliers: Do they see you as only pushing prices?

2. Determine which suppliers are important.
Attraction is not to be spread around like so much peanut butter. Identify which partnerships will pay off in the long term, and invest in them.

3. Recognize, explicitly, that attraction is double-edged.
You will need to work hard to be seen as your key suppliers' most attractive customer. This also implies joint improvement efforts, not unilateral demands for the supplier to make them.

4. Increase the supplier's comfort level.
Make sure that supplier managers know their ideas are welcomed, acknowledged, and implemented. Make it easy for them to provide them. Be fair and scrupulously honour contractual obligations.

5. Help the supplier properly evaluate its expected payoffs.
A typical negotiation technique is to hide information. In fact, keeping information from key suppliers leads to poor evaluation and diminished attraction, of both customer and supplier.

6. Manage the misalignment.
It is virtually impossible to align the objectives of purchasing, manufacturing, R&D, finance, and other functions. It is even more critical to understand and manage misalignment between the partners.

7. Manage the perceptions.
Understand that it is perceptions that matter, and that these are often totally unrelated to reality. Proactively manage the "stories" and "feelings" about a supplier.

8. Understand and manage how the supplier allocates resources and ideas.
Develop the reputation of being the most open customer to new ideas, by accepting as many ideas as possible and implementing them. Develop metrics that support implementing supplier ideas, and reward those in your company who do so.

9. Help your suppliers leverage the learning.
If you not only allow but also deeply encourage your suppliers to use the learning with their other customers, you will increase attraction and be the place where new learning is focused.

10. Sell the opportunities in your company to the supplier, and understand which other customers and initiatives are in the priority list of the supplier. You want to be at the top of it.

Source: Cordon and Vollman (2008), "The Power of Two"

The Three Supply Chain Roles

Following from the above discussion on supplier service and earlier on value, this leads us to conclude that all organisations have three roles in supply chains; these are as a:

1. Supplier
2. Customer
3. Value creator

With the first two roles, we need to see the connections and the effects that both of these roles have. For example, as we have just explored above, what would change if we were to see suppliers in the same way that we view customers?

As has been shown above, some of the most important principles of offering such supplier service are therefore the same as customer service principles, these being:

- Suppliers (and customers) have needs and expectations.
- Supplier (and customer) service can be a source of competitive advantage.
- Supplier (and customer) service is always delivered by people, so how they do it, is more important, than what the product/service being delivered actually is
- Supplier (and customers) offer different levels of service

The third role in supply chains of being a value creator is where each party in the supply chain is able to create value. This has two aspects:

- Value is found when something; satisfies a need, conformed to expectations and/or, gives "pride of ownership", i.e. it is "valued" over something that is not. Here then the perception of value will differ. We have the view that value is simply what the customer says it is; as customers will have different perceptions of "worth" and "price."
- Value is also the opposite to cost and in most processes, more time is actually spent on adding cost & not on adding value. A business will not find it worthwhile to invest and automate wasteful non-value added activities. Waste is the symptom rather than the root cause of the problem. Attention should therefore be given to those activities that do add "real" value, for example:
  – Make it faster , through, form changes (e.g. redesign a product)
  – Move it faster, through, times changes(e.g. shorten the transit time)
  – Get paid faster, through, place changes (e.g. sell Ex Works)
  – Serving the customer better

A supply chain view of added value would also recognise that it is only the movement to the customer that is adding (the ultimate) value. Stopping or delaying the flow, adds costs. It is only the movement to the customer that adds the ultimate value; smooth continuous flow movements must therefore be preferable.

Value and competitive advantage

As is now well recognised, supply chains compete as well as individual organisations and increasingly it is the supply chain that brings competitive advantage for many organisations. In turn, competitive advantage can be seen as being a cost leader or a service/value leader; as was shown earlier in Part 1 of this book.

Value creation involves suppliers

The challenges to be faced in value creation will involve doing things faster, for example, making products faster, moving them into the marketplace faster and getting paid faster.

Supplier rationalisation based on product quality and reliability in lead-time and delivery performance, will, be required. This means facing up to challenges such as:

- Reducing inventory
- Responsive order processing
- Short and reliable last times; this is not just the supplier lead time, it is the overall supply lead time from all those involved in all processes
- Product received that is the "right quantity, right quality, at the right time and the right cost."
- Using appropriate ICT
- Close working relationships and understanding of all the supply chain "players"

This focuses, for a specific supply chain, onto all of the current material and information lead times, the storage/static times and the payment/credit times; as well as the associated customer service requirements of availability, delivery schedules/frequencies and the requirement to provide customers/users with continuous reliability over the long term. How well all of these aspects are managed will actually affect profit and a business strategy. Suppliers are also connected into this, as shown in the following diagram:

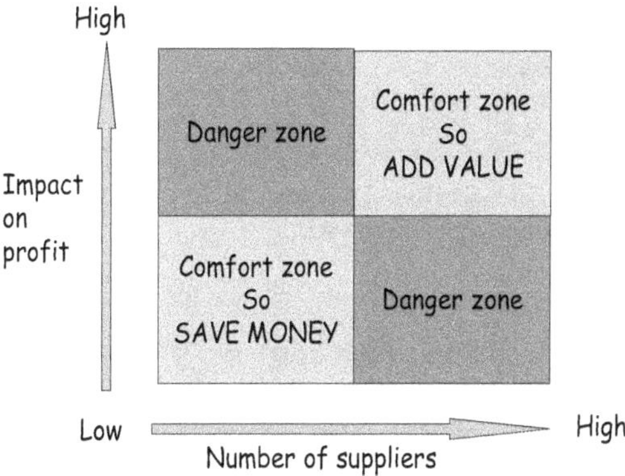

Clearly, suppliers should be consciously better connected to their clients' businesses; we believe this must be more actively considered by many organisations, so that the links between suppliers and customer service will then be better managed.

Value, relationships and exchanges

Adding value and value creation is rarely achieved by single views or by one party alone. As we have shown above, value creation is a two-way street that involves parties making choices in how they can work together by deciding what relationship is required, and what needs to be exchanged between each party.

Exchanges here are anything that is exchanged between suppliers and buyers/users/customers so that value is created for mutual benefit, for example exchanges of:

- People, e.g. on secondments, job swaps etc
- Materials, e.g. designs, joint procurement
- Plant and equipment, e.g. sharing
- Money, e.g. loans, investments
- Information, e.g. patents, real time access to each others systems
- Methods of work e.g. ideas, different ways

Looking at the short and long-term positions of value creation related to relationships and exchanges, such connections can be seen as follows:

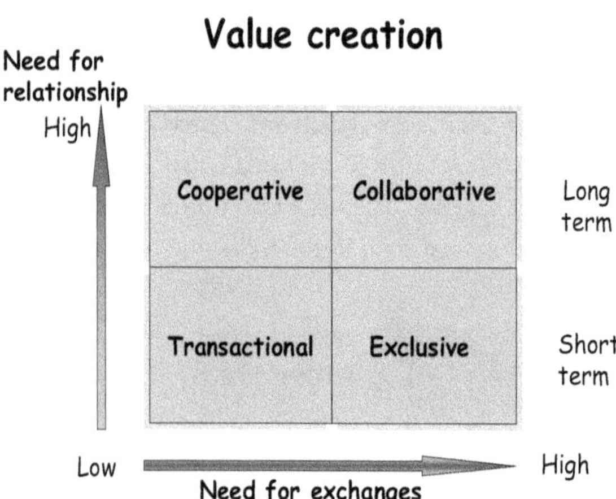

The various positions above are amplified opposite:

Position	Need for relationship	Need for exchanges	Comments	Procurement Portfolio (Kraljic) examples
Transactional	Low	Low	Each party having separate main goals and are only together for a short term deal	Routine and leverage items.
Exclusive	Low	High	Needs some specific exclusive exchange for only a short time	New product launch.
Cooperative	High	Low	Working together is needed to secure supply, but there is little need for exchanges	Bottleneck items.
Collaborative	High	High	Both parties are in it for mutual gain and have open access to each others resources	Critical items.

As already noted, adding value and value creation is rarely going to be achieved by just the one party and requires suppliers to be connected with customers/users/buyers. Where there is any dissatisfaction, then this needs working at, unless of course power plays are in force that prevent this happening. If such power plays do occur, then it's possible that this will prevent full value creation.

Accordingly, making such connections will take the view that suppliers are like "cogs in the machine" and cannot be viewed as being "easily replaceable." Additionally, replacement suppliers may not be available now or "forever", and then losing a supplier may cost sales and customers. Harnessing the supplier's knowledge can therefore add value to both organisations.

Various supplier/customer requirements

If we look at the 5 Rights related to the Kraljic procurement portfolio, then we can see that buyers actually have a hierarchy of requirements. This is shown below:

The Right	Bottleneck/critical items Aim: Secure supply and therefore , lower the risk for non supply	Routine/leverage items Aim: Reduce price by playing the market, possible outsourcing etc.
Quality	Secondary	Secondary
Quantity	Secondary	Secondary
Time	Number one	Secondary
Place	Secondary	Secondary
Cost	Secondary , maybe last	Number one

On a cost/service and supply balance from the buyers'/customers' and demand perspective, the following is indicated:

- Bottleneck/critical items have service requirements/KPIs first, especially the lead time on delivery, with the cost KPIs secondary
- Routine/leverage items have cost price requirement/KPIs first and the service aspects KPIs are secondary.

The matching response related to Kraljic, from the suppliers' and supply perspective, is as follows:

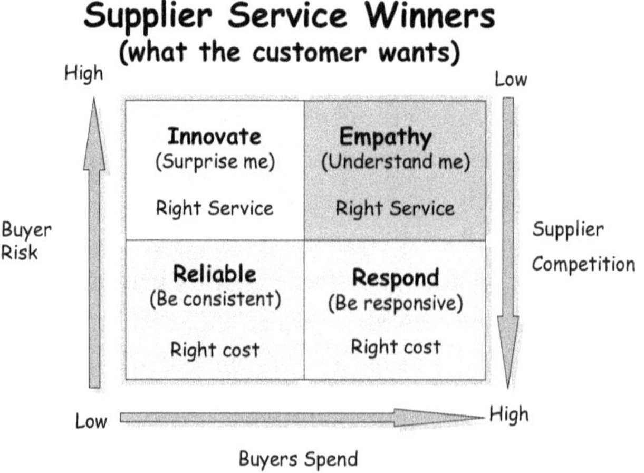

This can be amplified further into an ideal-typical perspective as follows:

Service winner	Buyers Strategy	Matching Supplier Behaviour	Suppliers Market position
Responsive	Leverage items with Supplier Sourcing "Plays the market"	React rationally with price cuts	Certainty of competition in the short and long term
Reliability	Routine items with Supplier Outsourcing "Organises and let's go"	React by exploring options and "fit"	Certainty of competition in the short term, followed by stability in the long term
Innovative	Bottleneck items with Supplier Development "Secures supply and attempts to diversify"	Proactive entrepreneurial behaviour with new product designs, or, Reactive positions when maintaining the monopoly	Uncertainties of being able to innovate, high R&D costs, followed by possible monopolistic position
Empathetic	Critical items with Supplier Collaboration "Work collaboratively with suppliers"	Proactive team work and problem solving	Uncertainty initially (forming/storming) followed by long term performing

The question to be asked here is, will the above-mentioned supplier behaviours line up with the buyer's strategy? If there is congruence, there is agreement, and progress forward will be made as both buyer and supplier will have their needs met.

If there is no congruence, then whilst there are possible negotiation options and positions may then change, the outcome can be an eventual "no deal."

Clearly therefore, the appropriate behaviours by either party are affecting the supplier/buyer relationship. This is easy to accept (the "you get what you give" or, "what you give you get", and the "what you sow, you will reap" scenarios).

Interpersonal behaviour in the supply chain

The above discussion also shows us the common and continuing organisational problem; the underpinning inter-personal behaviour of the people involved. These individual people are the suppliers/sellers/buyers/users and customers, who may actually do some things for their own reasons and not necessarily in line with what the employing organisation expects.

This is briefly explored below and it will be seen that this can cause "interference," as what is actually going on may be different to what was expected or planned to happen.

Leverage buying and responsive supplying takes us to toward the transactional/ adversary-buying behaviours that requires, as a service winner from suppliers, their rational response. The logical and stable thinking patterns revealed here are more of a logical left-brain approach. Providing this happens then there is good fit.

Routine buying and reliability supplying is also more towards the transactional/ adversary buying behaviour and requires as a service winner from suppliers, a response that explores options and of continually sensing for a "fit". The suppliers perhaps use exploratory and innovative thinking patterns; which is a creative right brain approach. This may however conflict with the buyer's view of seeking a rational, logical response. However, it's likely the supplier cannot give this until they have explored more creative options; a possible "no meeting of minds" here.

Bottleneck buying and innovative supplying is more towards exploratory buying approaches that require service supply winners of intuition and exploration and eventual product change. This creativity also requires a more right brain supplier approach, and if buyers do approach suppliers this way, then there is a good fit. However where the sellers wish to maintain any supply monopoly, then they will be displaying more rational and logical left-brain behaviour.

Critical buying and empathetic supplying approaches require collaborative responses involving both logical thinking and emotional feelings; a typical combined right and left-brain approach. This is however difficult for many individuals to use and apply; hence a team approach can be used here to give a more effective balance with both logical and emotional traits introduced, and used as and when appropriate.

Meanwhile, the following summarises these views, taking into account the appropriate brain sides of left (more logical and competitive) and right (more emotional and cooperative).

Buyer's view	Buyer brain side	Seller brain side	Seller's view
Leverage	Left	Left	Responsive
Routine	Left	Right	Reliability
Bottleneck	Right	Right, but possible left	Innovative
Critical	Left and right	Left and right	Empathetic

Clearly again here, whilst this is an ideal-typical model, one should take note of the more appropriate brain sides that are needed for the various views; again, "one size does not fit all." For success, approaches that recognise these varied and applicable options must therefore be considered.

SRM Challenges

There can be many challenges in making changes, for example:

- No trust
- Poor communications
- No "big picture" view
- No risk taking
- Prefer power based adversary transactional approach
- Want quick and short term wins
- No sharing of benefits
- No planning
- No support for any changing "how we do things"
- "Output is king and anyway, we are too busy fire-fighting"
- Fear of change
- Fear of failure from the existing blame culture
- Convincing significant stakeholders
- Overcoming the barriers, where for example: "The most powerful is seen as wielding the big stick"
- To first engage, then listen, and lastly act

This shows that the challenges involve recognising, fully, that the major barriers are going to include trust. Here, built up historical mistrust can remain and also, difficulties in sharing information, where information is seen as power, leading to a reluctance to relinquish power and to share information.

We can refer back here to earlier comments sets from research on SRM implementation that indicates it is the behavioural aspects that are around 70/80%, whereas the technical aspects, such as software, are only some 20/30% of such a change.

It is rarely easy changing "the way we have always done things around here" and therefore careful consideration is needed to ensure that a program is not started without taking all these aspects into account. Additionally, abandoning a program too easily is dangerous as it destroys any creditability and belief. A program should also never begin unless senior management supports it fully and openly, and matches their words with actions. There also needs to be an expectation of eventual success, and along the way, to publicise succes..

It will help to anticipate problems by ensuring that more time is made available in the early days, along with extra management resources. Open communication is needed for a good exchange of information, which involves listening before acting and being able to receive and accept criticism. Above all, commitment and will, with all trying to succeed.

Change as a paradigm shift

If we look at what has changed in recent decades, we can identify the following:

Past normal and status quo	Emerging new status quo
Factory model with cheap and plentiful standard products for a mass market	Craft inventive model with bespoke products for a "fashion" driven economy
Manager as the main technical expert	All are experts, for example everyone has two jobs, one as per the job description, the other, to improve it
Behaviourism with reward/punishment	Empowerment
Central and bureaucratic control	Organic, self and fluid controls
Brain is mainly seen as being logical, for example, IQ testing only	Brain is also seen as being emotional, for example, the "birth" of emotional intelligence and EQ profiling
Narrow local problems with local, perhaps national solutions	Wide global problems requiring holistic solutions
Cost reduction	Service/value for money enhancements with Total Cost analysis
Competitive approaches	Collaborative approaches

To enable such changes requires changing the way we think for as has been noted, *"As a person thinks, so they are" and "if you think you can or think you cannot, you are right"*.

Thinking comes from our mental maps that are like computer programmes and give us predetermined actions. For example, attitudes/beliefs/values inform what we perceive as our "reality."

Whilst with computer programmes we can check and re-calibrate the parameters when needed, for example, with inventory systems where supply lead-time is often not a constant, when it comes to our own mental map parameters, how often do we challenge ourselves or evaluate?

Changing our thinking means acquiring different perspectives. Such change may be uncomfortable and may be rejected, for example, some may say "Trust is the emotional glue that involves commitment to others" whereas others believe "Emotions have no part to play in business".

People working together in flow

The way a person thinks creates their immediate worldview, and determines how they work together with the collective of people in organisations. In turn, such influences will guide and shape the organisation.

We can therefore identify the following types of organisations (after an individual's brain influences):

"The Left Brain Company"	"The Right Brain Company"
Short term results	Long term success
Problems reoccur as only the symptoms are treated; ("Band aid" solutions)	Problems are tackled by looking at the cause/thinking
Rational and Silo thinking using mainly Science and Technology	Emotional and Holistic thinking with Motivating/ Empowering people
"Facts" and "the numbers speak for themselves"	"Solutions" and "it is how we connect that is important"
Follows existing and known ways	Experimentation

The Left Brain organisation type is clearly an obstacle to having effective SRM – as noted earlier, research indicates that behavioural aspects are around 70/80% of making the change needed, whereas, technical aspects are only some 20/30% of change. Such reality is critical and counters those who believe the main way to make the change are to use only technical based tools and techniques. These can assist, but they are not the most important and will not enable effective change and SRM practice. As noted by Jan Carlzon in *Moments of Truth* (1987):

"Running a business is not always a matter of logic and mathematics. It is just as much a question of understanding the psychological impact."

Let us always remember that whilst the Supply Chain is driven by flows of materials and information and money, it also needs people working together in flow – that special state when we are connected and think together; when we have a positive relationship with no separation; when we have connected our "hearts and minds." Only then, can we realise supply chain success.

Cross-Functional Management

We do continually find a lack of joined-up thinking and practices in organisations, where the consequences of having poor internal structures and relationships create follow-on, blame-game disruptions which are not of course, going to be mentioned in any organization's annual report. However, whilst they are so often very visible to connected outsiders (like suppliers and customers), they maybe thinly disguised in annual reports by using words like "structural problems have affected this year's results".

In Procurement and the Supply Chain, we should not be compartmentalising all of the individual parts. Putting things into boxes will likely mean that we lose the overall system meaning. Therefore we must see and think about the whole of the structure and the processes, the total organisational culture, the purpose of the organisation and the associated power and people aspects that will deliver the results.

We must see the interactions, in and between, all of the parts. We must take a more expansive holistic approach. By focussing only on the parts, the whole is not considered and in looking only at the parts, then the purpose and meaning for the whole is lost. Simple really to say, but not at all well understood.

Structure and Processes

An organisation's structure has a major influence on the running of not only the organisation, but also on the people within it and on the external suppliers, customers etc.

The structure provides the stability with fixed and known rules and procedures. Within the structural framework the operational processes of the organisation take place, and here then, we find, as with all processes, variability, dependency and interfaces.

Processes do things in conjunction with structures; these are the fixed settings that include things like rules and procedures, organisational charts and formal culture. Structures therefore have a powerful influence of how people behave and how things work in organisations.

It is the working together of structure and process, which creates an organisational system, so let us therefore remind ourselves what the organisation is fundamentally about. An organisational system has a purpose and for optimum performance, all elements/parts must be present and must be arranged in a specific way. This arranged way will change when we require a different performance.

Additionally, such systems will change in response to feedback. Many systems generally will attempt to maintain stability and control the system performance by making adjustments based on feedback. However the unexpected can happen, as we will soon see.

A system is therefore an entity that maintains its existence and functions through the interaction of its parts. The behaviour of a system depends on how the parts are related, rather than just on the parts themselves. This requires thinking in "wholes" and not just with the "parts." Of course, the more complex for example, the supply chain systems, then the more difficulties are going to be found.

As systems are clearly often going to be complex in the detail and in the dynamics, they also require a change in managerial thinking.

Changing the Thinking

It seems many fundamental change initiatives fail in the UK. Look for example at the quality movement. In the 1980s this had a wide audience. By the 1990s, however it was rarely heard of, apart from those organisations who had succeeded. Why is this? Many reasons for sure, but one strong reason is our preference for using tools that we believe will instantly fix things. When they did not, then the view was that "quality does not work here."

We do often seem to want an instant solution that is a prescriptive, for example, "use these tools, then that will work" and "because it worked for company x, then it will work for us". Nevertheless, it's likely that there will be trouble ahead, as rarely will this tool-fixing be effective without knowing the thinking that goes behind them.

As inferred earlier, the difficulty here is that the way we think is a product of our socialisation and education, in short, of our culture, and "the way we do things around here". We earlier explored some reasons for this – another connected view is that our traditional thinking of breaking things down into parts, ultimately leads us to sub-optimising. This breaking down thinking going back to the days of Adam

Smith and pin production as explained in the *Wealth of Nations* (Smith, 1778). This became the basis for mass production; which clearly at the time gave a large step change in production practices, and went on to create wealth for many Western nations.

To manage such an industrial change, required top down bureaucratic controls that could separately measure each functional process by analysing and breaking them down into parts and looking at each part separately.

Finance is also part of this bureaucracy, with its traditional view of vertical transactions in cost centre silos that look mainly at internal functions with periodic reporting that is static, backward looking and historical.

Effectively then a reductionist approach is taken which can give sub-optimal solutions, e.g. we may fix only the one problem part, but we may still have recurring problems, and these may have been made worse by our attempts to fix something elsewhere.

This takes us back into systems thinking, that reveals what eventually happens from over concentrating on the parts – the parts can eventually become stronger than the whole and the whole can then be ignored.

However, it is actually the whole system and how the parts work and flow together that is important, as the whole is greater than the sum of the parts. (For more on systems thinking, see *Quick Guide to Systems View of the Supply Chain,* Emmett, 2012).

What is needed then is to change the thinking that got us to where we are today. After all, as Albert Einstein said, "The significant problems we face cannot be solved at the same level of thinking we were at, when we created them."

In moving forward, we can have a better foundation that will not only rely on using "one size fits all" tools. We need to analyse by seeing the interactions, in and between, all of the parts.

This expansive, holistic approach to dealing with complex, dynamic problems with perhaps not obvious solutions, is one where performance is being controlled by the system. To move this forward, we also need to consider how to change the organisational structure, which requires a conceptual framework that allows for both objective facts and subjective feelings by concentrating on the interrelationships that drive the overall system's behaviour.

It is only people who can leverage and influence these interrelationships. Therefore, system leverage will often come from changing our mental models that are supporting the system structure.

Peter Senge noted in *The Fifth Discipline* (1993 and 2006):

- Problems are nearly always caused by way we do things

- Changes are usually far away in time and place from where the problem appears
- When it is identified, no one believes it is related to the problem
- If it had been identified, then it is nearly always pushed in wrong direction, thereby intensifying the problem
- One small policy change can solve problems easily

Changing the structure

It is suggested that one policy change needed is to create a cross-functional model (CFM). We have already commented on this earlier, and whilst there is no one easy, way to do this, it will need careful compromise on the following two aspects:

1) Organise around processes and not tasks

Management needs separating from operational supervision and management needs to be generalised at the senior levels. Supervision is then about the people actually doing the work whilst the operations may remain hierarchical and functional, but they now report into (several) cross-functional, process-based managers.

Operational supervisors will also need training in cross-functional appreciations and as has been noted elsewhere, we will need "T"-shaped people who have depth of knowledge and skills, in a function (for example, a finance department), but will also have cross-functionalist knowledge that connects fully with all sides of the function. This process, across these different functions, is then managed by the process-based managers.

2) Keep a team focus

This will encourage self-management when used with clear SMART objectives with the reward mechanism being the overall process team performance. Multiple competencies are needed, for example having knowledge on all of the supply/demand "sides", including knowledge and more contact with suppliers and customers. This should be irrespective of whether these are internal and external suppliers/customers, as any customer is the ultimate "end" link in the individual sub-process.

To emphasise this team approach, the following research is useful:

Checklist: Teams and Purchasing Executives

What should purchasing leaders do to improve team performance? Here are nine recommendations derived from research:

1) Provide E-Sourcing teams with guidance and authority
The impact of autonomy in the research is remarkable. Teams enabled

autonomously to decide upon their strategies and action plans, perform significantly better than teams who have less freedom. This stresses the importance of well-communicated definitions of roles and responsibilities to prevent frequent management intervention. After a clear briefing, sourcing teams need a "license to act".

2) Make sure that all team members are rewarded for their Team contribution

It may be difficult for purchasing managers to influence the reward structure of non-purchasing team members, since this can be done only in consultation with senior Management. However, those who succeed do witness increased individual involvement and improved team performance.

3) Provide training in strategic sourcing and teamwork skills

Particularly for team members with no purchasing background, training in strategic sourcing is important. This enables all team members to participate actively, and results in higher quality teamwork. Managers should also not assume members have well-developed teamwork skills.

4) Balance the number of sourcing initiatives with the availability of human resources

Convincing management to allocate sufficient resources continues to be a challenge. An obstacle is often that the purchasing organization will often initiate too many sourcing projects, with too little time to implement, follow up and concluding these projects.

5) Develop a sharp eye for the quality of team processes

Purchasing managers should not take it for granted that sourcing team members will communicate sufficiently when assigned to a team. Internal and external communication should be monitored closely and stimulated actively by both management as well as team leaders.

6) Develop a structured sourcing process, clearly outlining the tasks and responsibilities of the team

A formal process enables a team to work autonomously. Moreover, internal stakeholders will more likely support team decisions based on a fair sourcing process. Though formalizing roles and responsibilities is a best practice anytime, the level of formality should fit the nature of the tasks assigned.

7) Develop information systems to the level that they usefully support team tasks

When systems provide easy access to accurate information, effective teams operate efficiently and are able to make adequate strategic choices.

8) Select only the best leaders

The study results show that sourcing teams demand great leaders. Sourcing team leaders should command a wide variety of leadership skills. It is therefore crucial not to select the best purchasing professionals to lead sourcing teams, but to select the best team leaders.

9) Create cross-functional teams whose members represent the different stakeholder groups

Purchasing managers tend to perceive functional integration as a troublesome process. However, those who have become closely involved are convinced of the benefits.

The implementation of cross-functional teams is also risky and should be managed cautiously. When products or services of a certain complexity are sourced, cross-functional teams will outperform teams staffed by purchasers only; providing the team is clearly briefed , well trained, enjoys a sufficient level of autonomy and has a competent leader assigned to it.

Source: Supply Management 15 April 2010

When making changes towards a cross-functional approach, we also have some useful research from R. I. van Hoek and A. J. Mitchell (2006). This provides the following summary of the action needed to ensure there is an internal alignment in organisations:

Checklist: Cross-functional Management Research

Peers
- Support exchange programmes and job rotations across functions
- Invest and understand each other's problems and build relationships: capture the voice of other functions and be able to articulate plans in their language, not our jargon
- Develop appropriate KPIs across functions; ensure that KPIs are linked or at least coordinated and are not driving conflicting behaviour
- Joint problem solving teams to tackle common issues

Individuals
- Trace and learn from the cause of lost orders; delivery time, price, specification

- Encourage open communication
- Avoid pointing blame
- Visit & "see, smell, understand customers, get under their skin"
- Create regular dialogue between sales and supplying units

Bosses
- Join sales on key customer visits to ensure you are close enough to the customer in driving the supply chain agenda and focusing efforts and service and be credible with sales when discussing service
- Align goals between functions and link these to incentives
- Encourage the use of the same language; avoid functional jargon and promote the use of business language (profit, customers, service etc.)
- Support appropriate forecasting tools

Teams
- Collaborate on common issues not functional pet projects
- Reach consensus on priorities; do not set a functional agenda but a company wide focus that will engage peers
- Work on improving accuracy of performance information and tell peers upfront of problems, do not surprise peers with bad events when they happen
- Awareness training in "natural" cross-functional process such as the supply chain and sales
- Improve the initiative planning process to focus on what essentials peers care most for (e.g. service, execution, price etc.) and articulate initiatives in those terms

Structure must enable the overall supply chain process; as structure influences behaviour and as structure and process make a system, then cross-functional management is one important way to enable efficient and effective procurement and supply chain management. Cross-functional management is also a fundamental part of "win the home games first" that should come before "playing away from home". When we do move externally, we need to ensure supply chain relationship management (SRM) and supply chain risk management (SCRM) are being practiced with the external team players.

Information Communication Technology and E-Procurement

Procurement and supply is an activity that has usually generated and employed large quantities of paperwork. This paperwork was necessary to communicate information from one function to another in order to facilitate action, to indicate requirements to suppliers, and to obtain the necessary goods and services on time and to specification.

The advent of information communication technology (ICT) and more integrated software systems has radically changed matters. Although the paperless office may still be in the future, and indeed may never materialise, simple transactions are today seldom paper-based. The Internet has provided further opportunities for electronic procurement, and has made new approaches possible, which can make added value contributions to procurement strategy. In the last few years, there has been an increasing universal acceptance of E-Procurement.

Organisations are realising that they have large opportunities to reduce their procurement processing costs and acquisition costs by revising their internal procurement policies and by fully leveraging their buying power using the Internet. This section will explore some of the electronic applications, which make up E-Procurement and how E-Procurement can assist procurement strategy.

What is E-Procurement?

E-Procurement is the term used to describe "the use of electronic methods in every stage of the buying process from identification of requirement through to payment, and potentially to contract management", or alternatively it is "A range of technologies that apply the speed of computer processing and the:

- connectivity of the internet to accelerate and streamline the processes of:
- Identifying and selecting suppliers of goods and services;
- Placing, receiving and paying for orders;
- Assuring compliance with procurement procedures;
- Consolidating purchases to achieve leverage :
- Providing visibility of information between collaborative partners"

Most E-Procurement models have the following key processes:

- E-Sourcing, covering the contractual processes where tools include E-Tendering, E-RFQs (Request for Quotations) and E-Auctions
- E-Procurement covering the transactional processes; tools include marketplaces using techniques such as e-Catalogues
- E-Payment tools include virtual or embedded PC (Procurement Cards) E-Invoicing and Self Billing

E-Procurement

The CIPS definition of E-Procurement is:

"E-Procurement is using the Internet to operate the transactional aspects of requisitioning, authorising, ordering, receipting and payment processes for the required services or products."

One of the keys goals of E-Procurement is to devolve buying to local users and covers the requisition against contract, authorisation, order, receipt and payment.

E-Sourcing

There is confusion about what is covered by E-Sourcing and how this differs from E-Procurement. The CIPS definition of E-Sourcing is:

"E-Sourcing is using the Internet to make decisions and form strategies regarding how and where services or products are obtained."

It therefore covers the parts in the buying process, which are at the discretion of the specialist buyers, which include knowledge, specification, and request for quotation/e-tender/E-Auction and evaluation/negotiation contract.

If E-Sourcing is to be implemented, a good E-Sourcing practice is essential to making E-Procurement work. If you do not make the correct strategic decisions, you will create a poor operational process.

E-Sourcing systems should enable the E-Sourcing team to:
- effortlessly analyse and model complex decisions in real time
- automate the contract lifecycle management including awards, rejections, amendments and renewals
- collaborate with the supplier, using a central system enables people to collaborate easily

E-Sourcing should deliver the following visible benefits:
- Real-time information as the E-Sourcing team get visibility on contracts and spending patterns. Any planned improvement must ensure reliable up to date information for analysis purpose. A system can provide pre-qualified information about suppliers.
- Integrated process automation where taking time out of the E-Sourcing process by reducing the amount of paper involved in the system. Typically, such systems can distribute all requirements electronically.

Another model of E-Procurement is provided by Gattorna, opposite. This model breaks E-Procurement into three distinctive processes, namely:

- E-Sourcing, which includes contracting, via E-Auctions
- E-Requisitioning
- E-Intelligence ,which is concerned with the collation of performance management information

The benefits of E-Procurement

According to Chin Nam (1998), the benefits are seen as follows:
- reducing purchasing cycle time
- enhancing budgetary control
- eliminating administrative errors
- increasing buyers' productivity
- lowering prices through product standardisation and consolidation of purchasing power
- better information management

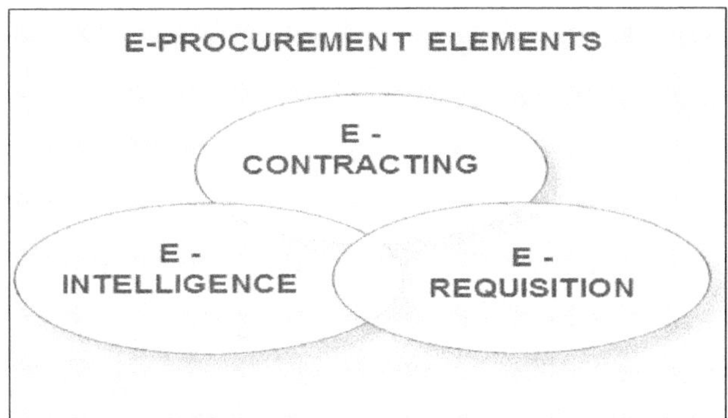

This can be expanded as follows:

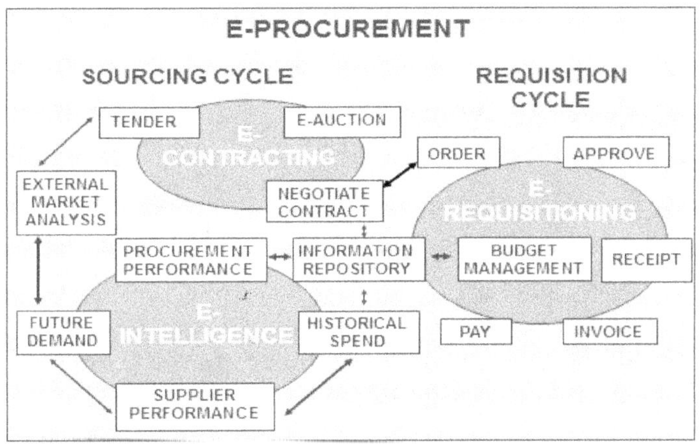

That is, it enables the E-Procurement process to be redesigned, taking out the slow, costly transactional work, resulting in faster cycle times.

As can be seen in the diagram below, many non-value added transactions have been eliminated, thus reducing the cycle times by several days.

EMPOWERMENT OF USERS - CHANGES IN WORK FLOW

OLD WORKFLOW	NEW WORKFLOW
PAPER REQUISITION TO BUYER	REQUISITIONER
TELEPHONE SUPPLIER	
ORDER NUMBER – ENTER DETAILS	HTTP://WWW.COM
PRINT ORDER - AUTHORISE	
SEPARATE ORDER COPIES	DELIVERY
COPY ORDER TO GOODS IN DELIVERY	
	CONSOLIDATED MONTHLY SUMMARY
COPY ORDER TO ACCOUNTS	
INVOICE MATCH	PAYMENT
CHEQUE PAID TO SUPPLIER	

This provides organisations with enormous efficiency improvements in how people work. It allows staff to concentrate their efforts on more strategic aspects of value-added procurement.

The improvements in information flow, especially with the improved sharing of sensitive information, allows for improved commercial relationships with suppliers

The Public sector has incorporated E-Procurement, as shown in the following case study:

Case Study: 2006 Public Procurement Update

Recent reforms give public sector purchasers wider scope to use E–procurement. EU procurement rules implemented in the UK by the Public Contracts Regulations 2006 extended the scope of E-Procurement. Contracting authorities may now purchase services, supplies and works under a number of E-Tendering processes such as E-Auctions and the more excitingly named "dynamic purchasing systems" (DPS) for common purchases.

The new rules also allow for framework contracts to be tendered with such systems. Over the past few years, there has been an increasing emphasis on E-Procurement from the European commission and the Office of Government Commerce, starting with the option for online tender submission, followed by online OJEU notices.

The incentives for contracting authorities to use E-Tendering methods include faster tender processes and more streamlined procurement, particularly for straightforward tenders where face-to-face contact with bidders is not paramount.

E-Auctions can also be used in DPS or mini competitions in a framework contract. The auction process starts with the publications of an OJEU notice, under the open or restricted procedures, and the purchasing authority setting out its specification requirements on line.

The contracting authority will invite initial bids and, after it has evaluated them against predetermined criteria, will then ask pre-qualified bidders to submit new prices. The E-Auction can take place over a number of phases, and, at each stage, bidders will be able to see their relative ranking and the number (but not names) of other bidders participating in the auction at that time. Bids may be adjusted until the closing date.

For contracting authorities, the other main development is the DPS. This is simply an electronic framework for commonly used purchases. The open procedure is mandatory, which enables any interest suppliers to bid. Bidders can apply to join the system at any point in its duration (as published in the OJEU notice). Bidders make indicative bids, which can be changed (if they are still compliant) throughout the system's lifetime.

When a contracting authority wishes to make a purchase, it will notify the bidders of specific contracts, for which they can submit their offer. Bids are then evaluated and a contract awarded. As a purchaser, you need to make sure your suppliers have considered the new regime because it can affect how they trade with you.

First, they must understand the rules and how they differ from previous tender procedures. Second, their pre-qualification submissions and tender responses will need to be streamlined and focused and to exactly meet the online requirements. Third, suppliers will need to speed up response times.

By using E-Procurement, contracting authorities can run the process more quickly than before, so suppliers need to note the key dates.

Lastly, IT systems and software will need to be secure and compatible with submission requirements.

Complex Procurement

E-Procurement programmes have also been successfully implemented to handle many indirect commodities. There are also opportunities for savings in the areas of direct materials and those commodities with more complex procurement processes. However, the spend in these commodities can be high with poor compliance to purchasing contracts on many previous occasions. Below is a typical profile of E-Procurement application across the four categories in the Kraljic Procurement Targeting Tool:

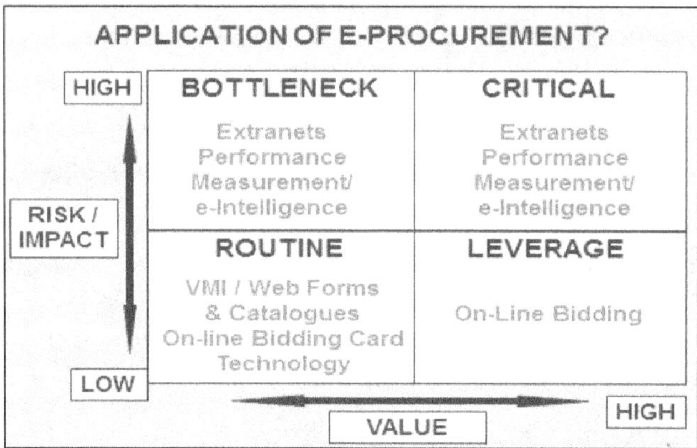

There appears to be no consensus across industry sectors about the correct application of E-Procurement to commodity groups. Some organisations say that it is too risky to use E-Auctions for critical and complex items.

Others state that they will use many of the applications for all of their commodity groups including bottleneck and critical items, by making it possible with robust specifications and processes.

Meanwhile IBM have identified the following benefits:

Value Drivers for E-Procurement	Problem highlighted	Savings from E-Procurement
Improved process efficiency	Long lead times from manual process	Time saved-70%-80% faster
Reduced costs	High transaction costs	73% reduction
Reduced prices	Maverick spending	Price reductions of 5%-10%
Improved compliance	Fragmented data and high off-contract spend	Maverick spending reduced by 50%
Reduced inventory costs	Long lead times resulting in high stock levels	Inventory level reduced by 25%-50% across categories

The following is another example of the application of E-Procurement in the public sector:

Case Study: Police E-Procurement

@UK PLC has further widened its customer base within public sector buying organisations by being selected to provide an E-Procurement and e-invoicing systems to Thames Valley Police (TVP).

TVP is one of the largest non-metropolitan police forces in the country, covering 2,200 square miles of Berkshire, Buckinghamshire and Oxfordshire and serving a population of 2.2 million people. The TVP area is policed by around 4,140 police officers, 350 special constables, 370 volunteers and 2,860 other police staff. The total spends by TVP on goods and services are over 400 million pounds per annum.

The @UK Supplier Management Systems (SMS) will enhance existing TVP Procurement systems by providing a mechanism to send electronic purchase orders to, and received electronic invoices form all their suppliers, no matter what their size or existing electronic trading capability. Stage one of the project will be creating a link between the @UK supplier network and TVP back office systems.

This builds on wide base of experience by @UK in linking to similar financial systems in other areas of the public service. Over the next 3 months, it is intended that the @UK PLC system will then be rolled out to the majority of the force's 1,500 suppliers.

TVP believe that the @UK system offers TVP an ideal infrastructure on which to build their futurE-Procurement strategy. It provides both TVP and their suppliers the ability to achieve real efficiency and process savings, eliminating time and the potential for effort right through the supply chain. The @UK e-invoicing capability for all of their suppliers is especially important part of this.

It establishes an ideal mechanism for TVP to achieve huge efficiencies in their backend processes. It is also a way for suppliers to reduce their costs significantly in dealing with TVP, with the ability for both parties to share those benefits.

E-Procurement Initiatives

Many successful E-Procurement initiatives have generally occurred in the E-Procurement of office equipment and supplies, using stand-alone desktop requisitioning tools. This category was driven by the technology focused office equipment suppliers and has been expanded into online ordering for simple services like business card printing, with basic integration into Finance and HR systems.

The focus has also been on simple, indirect materials like MRO goods (Maintenance, Repair and Operations or Overhaul) but in reality, many initiatives have looked only at the Operations elements, rather than Maintenance and Repairs, and generally start with the "create requisition" function.

Another successful E-Procurement initiative is with Strategic Sourcing using E-Requests for Quotation and E-Requests for Proposal (often jointly known as eRFX) as well as Online Auction tools. Most large organisations are using online auctions and E-Tendering systems to significantly lower the input cost of goods and services and the E-Procurement process costs. The key requirement here is that the goods and services can be uniquely defined and categorised. These tools are being used for both direct and indirect material procurement and in the final stages of complex procurements after a detailed specification had been prepared. Only now are organisations seeing the use of tools, such as E-Intelligence (which provides tailored Management and Market Information such as category level analysis to expedite E-Sourcing, collaboration and forecasting) in the E-Sourcing phases.

Procurement departments in most large organisations have also involved the process of developing global functions and strategies for the E-Procurement of key commodities. The direct contribution of an effective procurement strategy to the organisation's financial results can be extremely important, particularly in those sectors where revenue growth is flat or declining.

In the early days of E-Procurement, organisations focused on internal and external transaction costs. In many cases, the Business Case was based on cutting the cost of producing a purchase order. Although some improvements were made, suppliers found that their costs went up due to the cost of creating and maintaining catalogue content and marketplace transactional fees, and these actions were necessary if they wanted to continue to do business. Marketplaces put additional contracts implications in place and this, coupled with the higher level of costs needed via this medium, put some suppliers off using this route.

As far back as 2002 (a long time with fast changing ICT), a survey was conducted by AT Kearney (2002), when it was found that 96% of survey respondents used electronically enabled supply management (often referred to as "E-Supply") and this covered only 11% of their spend base. E-Supply Management was however found to have delivered measurable benefits such as 10% cost savings, up to 41% cycle time improvement and up to 10% head count reduction.

Therefore, there was clearly scope for most organisations to generate additional significant bottom line savings from E-Procurement. For those leading organisations, it is now time to expand their programmes into new categories. For those who have not yet started or have had limited success with their E-Procurement projects, now is the time to re-examine the business case.

Total Cost of Ownership, rather than simply process and purchase costs, becomes more important and sophisticated than for 'simple' commodities. The total cost model, however, needs to be understood if full advantage is to be made. This should take into account not just the E-Procurement costs, but also where relevant, maintenance, disposal, cost of managing the assets, cost of money etc.

Whilst, the scope for cost savings in complex procurement is large, it is more difficult to obtain than the simpler picking of the 'low hanging fruit' of ICT, office stationery and similar MRO categories. Careful planning is required and the payback period may well be longer. However, the ultimate value of savings can be greater.

Case Study: Lewisham gets its suppliers onboard

The London borough of Lewisham is making good progress in the recruitment of suppliers to its E-Procurement programme. Over 1200 of its suppliers have completed the first stage of the process by registering their details on the @UK website, a fifth of their whole target supplier vase. Each of these businesses will be contacted by one of @UK's 20 strong supplier advisory team to identify the most appropriate solution for them. This solution will differ according to the nature of goods and services offered: whether the organisation has a website already and if this site is able to receive orders and send e-invoices, although all options can be accommodated. The system will be fully integrated into Oracle iProcurement for the transmission of electronic purchase orders and electronic invoices.

Lewisham want the maximum available choice of organisations able to trade with them in a way that will cut costs. They are also giving every supplier the chance to; for example, receive "Requests for Price" for their services. This fits in with the latest guidance from the EU stressing equally opportunities for suppliers. At the same time, there are important local economic benefits as businesses linked to the @UK network are then able to trade with many other types of council, schools, plus other organisations and even individual consumers."

LB Lewisham has used the standard @UK supplier recruitment process, sending out their own tailored letter to each of their suppliers. Included in each letter is an individual reference code giving each organisation access to their unique record within the @UK national supplier database.

Their letter to their suppliers made it clear what the mutual benefits of E-Procurement were and why suppliers were warmly invited to participate. They have been happy to explain to suppliers who called them what the rationale was for this change, and exactly how both parties will benefit. They are finding the whole process of supplier recruitment getting easier as the number of buying authorities taking part increases. Of course, as some businesses are getting letters now from several of their local authority/hospital clients they are therefore beginning to understand that this is a real process that the public sector is committed to.

The Barriers

Organisations should try to choose software tools that are already integrated with their existing systems or which have configurable and quick to implement XML-based interfaces to enable linkages to demand and inventory management. Where possible, organisations should avoid stand-alone solutions which need bespoke integration work. Where appropriate, organisations should look to integrate with the Computer Aided Design (CAD) and Product Data Manager (PDM) software systems used to design complex products and with Project Management and Collaborative Working systems including suppliers' designs and configuration tools.

When organisations look beyond the transaction or purchase order cost for savings, this is the moment they begin to appreciate the full potentials savings and benefits from the implementation of E-Procurement. By producing an end-to-end value map of the supply chain for complex goods and services area in their operations, they can begin to look for opportunities to reduce the Total Cost of Ownership such as reductions in inventory, reductions in demand and supply lead-time and elimination of waste throughout the supply chain. Organisations can also look for potential savings in the costs of goods and services by internal aggregation of demand, the reduction of maverick, off-contract spend and simplification of the supplier base.

However, too often the current spend in some commodities groups is unknown – knowing this is essential if a company is to source effectively. Extending product classification definitions to cover all commodities, including services, ensures that all relevant spend can be measured. This process can start with spend by supplier and this can then be further broken down to identify the goods and services which are critical, together with major suppliers and frequency of purchase. This aim is to take an 80/20 approach rather than trying to tackle all items within a particular commodity.

Historically one cannot underestimate the difficulties in getting usefully accurate information, but such vital information is of paramount importance.

Measuring the Benefits of E-Procurement

As the first generation of E-Procurement projects have been starting to deliver measurable savings, the picture as to the real extent and value of these savings is still unclear. One explanation for this is that whilst project progress has been measured in terms of milestones achievement, relatively few organisations are accurately monitoring the real benefits achieved as the projects progress.

What to Measure

The principal metrics that will demonstrate a return on investment in E-Procurement are the hard (directly measurable) benefits:

- price savings
- process cost reduction (head count)
- reductions in cycle and lead times(hours/days/weeks)
- consequent reductions in inventory holdings(value/stock turnover ratios)

There are also the soft (indirectly measurable) benefits, e.g. individual time freed up through more efficient processes, enabling staff to be able to spend more time on value-added aspects of procurement such as :

- Supplier development
- Contract management

Soft benefits also provide important indicators of progress towards improvements in a measure that is beneficial and should not be ignored just because they are subjective or difficult to track.

Additionally there are a number of intangible benefits such as cultural change and broader staff efficiency savings delivered through training. These benefits are again difficult to measure, but may provide valuable support for a business case.

In order to identify E-Procurement cost savings as distinct from those achieved through other procurement best practice, the measurement system needs to discriminate between 'business as usual' type savings and those directly attributable to the implementation of the E-Procurement system.

A summary of the five main savings drivers for E-Procurement follow. Note that they are interdependent, as illustrated (overleaf):

A Summary of the five main savings drivers for E-Procurement

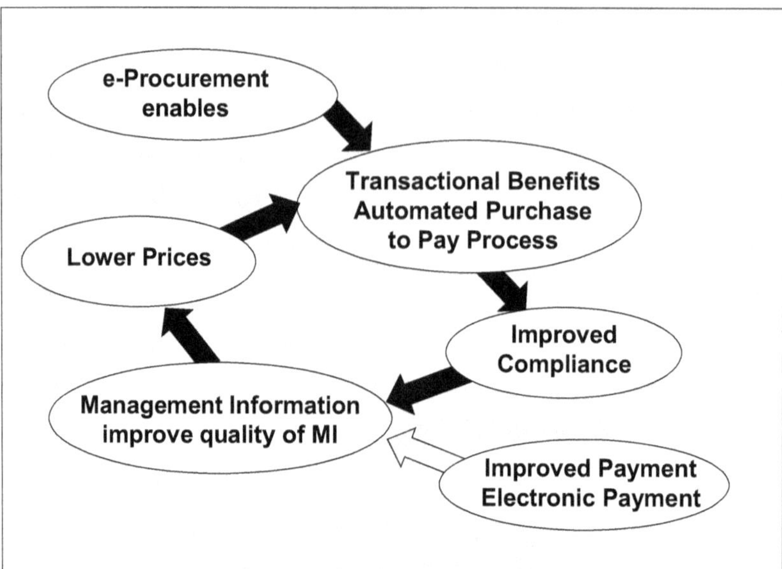

Case Study: @UK (the largest E-Procurement Marketplace servicing the UK Public Sector, offering 100% Electronic Options)

A free financial model has been constructed by @UK so that buying organisations can quantify their savings from implementing 100% electronic ordering and/or invoicing – both of which are now achievable using the latest @UK developments. The model combines the conclusions of organisations like the National E-Procurement Project (NEPP), @UK's own experiences with a number of clients and the expectations/situation of the particular buying organisation under examination. The model forecasts expected savings and Return on Investment (ROI) for any local authority, central government department, health authority, corporate body implementing E-Procurement completing any of the following stages:

Stage 1

Client has their back office finance system (or P2P system if present) linked to the @UK national supplier network and uses it to route all orders to suppliers electronically (with a Request for Price option for services).

Stage 2

All supplier invoices are received for processing in electronic format by implementing the @UK "@invoice" programme.

Stage 3

Client uses the @UK supplier recruitment programme to establish direct links for ordering and e invoicing to all significant suppliers, with correct terms applied to every order.

Stage 4

Client implements a change management programme internally to roll out full E-Procurement to all departments (with or without @UK implementation programme assistance)

Stage 5

Client adopts "strategic procurement" including e.g. buyer-neutral coding for all items, E-Auctions and e tendering, supplier pre-qualification etc as appropriate. @UKbelieve that most organisations have now gone way beyond the stage of thinking E-Procurement is some alien technology irrelevant to them. They know that their staff is confident buying from websites, so that 'ultimate user' is not a problem. It is the detailed implementation at procurement/finance department level to achieve bankable savings that is the issue now.

Electronic Auctions (E-Auctions)

E-Auctions initiated by the buyer use the internet to share communications, providing both buyers and suppliers, with visibility of bid status in real-time and allowing an instant response. If conducted properly, with adequate participant training, it creates a more level playing field for suppliers through increased transparency. An E-Auction allows for a bid on price and/or other quantitative attributes such as quantity discounts, delivery and quality.

E-Auctions should be considered as a tool in the buyer's E-Sourcing toolkit. They can be used to renew existing contracts or offer consolidated spend opportunities. They can also be used to negotiate significant spot purchases and to receive pricing on frequently tendered communications or service.

Types of E-Auctions

Electronic reverse auctions (ERAs) allow buyers to seek competitive pricing by inviting pre-qualified suppliers to participate in a real time dynamic online event. Usually the internet-based auction begins with the buyer posting his requirement for a product or service on an internet site; a reserve price (a price that suppliers must meet in order to be considered) is usually set. The buyer then invites suppliers to bid against each other.

The term 'reverse' simply refers to the bidding process as the participating suppliers submit successively lower priced bids during a specified time period. The key difference between an internet enabled auction and a traditional purchasing process is that all the suppliers can usually see their bid along with the current lowest bid, as well as having the opportunity to re-bid as many times as they wish.

If other quantitative attributes are included then the auction will be classed as a Weighted Multi Variable Auction. In the same way as an auction based on price along, suppliers know which rank their own bid is, and can usually view the other bids, but not the identify of the other suppliers. In this case, however, all bids are adjusted in real time from a range of variables from other attributes, which allows buyers to view a figure, which may make up the total cost of ownership. Other attributes may include carriage, discounts in price for quantities or for successive years, packaging, payment periods, quality, or guarantee periods. Switching costs could also be included in the non-incumbent supplier's calculations.

There are several types of reverse auctions. For example, it is not uncommon for buyers to use the terms "a bundled bid", or "cherry picked" or a "scorecard auction".

In the case of a **bundled** auction, the buyer usually bundles his requirements together into a single lot. Suppliers then bid for the total package. Usually they will submit a bid for each item, but these will be totalled up and one supplier usually wins the whole bid.

A **cherry picked** auction is slightly different. As the name suggest, suppliers have the opportunity to "cherry pick" certain lines from an auction and only bid for these. A buyer can then choose to award the contract to several different suppliers for different lots, or award to one supplier.

A **scorecard auction** is slightly more complicated in that the buyer can assign an internal scorecard to each potential supplier. Each bid a supplier submits is then recalculated against the values assigned by the value on the scorecard to produce a weighted bid. The buyer may chose to share the scorecard information with the suppliers, which may improve their performance, as they will know what they are up against and where they need to improve. This type is sometimes referred to as a **"transformation reverse auction"**.

Case Study: Schools to benefit from Local, Regional & National Savings

Schools will soon be able to benefit from a whole range of savings arranged across all types of goods and services. These will be available online and may have been set up nationally, by the schools' own local authority working with other neighbouring authorities or in some cases more local still.

Ina Taylor, Director of the FfES's new Centre for Procurement Performance said, "Many schools may have felt that they were struggling alone and have been crying out for better deals that reflect the purchasing power of the whole education system. This now becomes a practical possibility, using technology that is commonly available. The CPP is working closely with those local authorities, which have schools in their remit.

"First of all we want to ensure that the good deals which authorities or the local government consortia may already have set up are freely accessible to schools in a way which works with the schools' local administration systems, so the process is efficient and paper free. On top of this, we, the CPP and our procurement partners from local authorities, the consortia and from Universities and Further Education Colleges are working together to identify opportunities to combine our spending power to negotiate better terms from suppliers that can directly benefit schools. We expect real and significant results to start benefiting schools budgets during 2006."

Dudley George, Marketing Director of @UK PLC, a pioneer in this area with its @Schools online network, took up a similar theme.

"Our company objective is to cut the cost of commerce for buyers and suppliers. If we cut out the waste that is created for all parties by unnecessary paperwork, high levels of returns through errors and by delays in orders getting to suppliers, this allows everyone to benefit. Some arrangements, such as for instance plumbing, coach trips or grounds maintenance will probably be best set up at a local level, maybe a Local Authority on behalf of all or some of its schools, maybe by the schools themselves. Our organisation specialises in providing the facilities, to that even the smallest of suppliers can take part".

Other arrangements can be made at the level of groups of authorities, such as various Devon Procurement Partnership contracts now rolling out through that county. In other cases, of course the CPP may well be able to negotiate on behalf of all UK schools. This is not the end, because even when schools have had special arrangements negotiated, they may still want to put their high value and unique service needs out for quotation, for example using our "RFP" (Request for Price) facility.

The same written specification, plus any plans, schedules can then pass securely online to 3 or more possible providers. Replies are then all available for comparison and stored as electronic records should any audit issue arise, so no need for filing cabinets of old quotes."

Why organisations should be aware of E-Auctions

The benefits to buyers

Aberdeen Group research *(E-Sourcing: Negotiating Value in a Volatile Economy, April 2001)* supported the assertion that the internet provides a low cost and efficient mechanism for communications and negotiations between buyers and suppliers. Electronic auctions exploit technology to achieve real time market pricing, which generally results in significant savings for the buying organisation. First time savings of 10-20% are commonly reported using the reverse auction process. Other benefits include a reduction in the E-Sourcing cycle time (once the process is established), improved specification of requirements and increased transparency.

The IAdapt research found, using an auction to establish a new contract, the change in the five key performances factors as follows:

- Flexibility (i.e. Changing order quantities at the last minute + 22%
- Quality of the product or service +20%
- Delivery/reliability +12%
- Dependability (keeping promises) +11%
- Account or customer support +8%

There was an expectation that there would be at least no change or a reduction in at least one or two key factors, in particular it was expected that the 'soft' factors of flexibility, dependability and account management to deteriorate as the reduced supplier's margins led to a reduction in the level of support provided to their customers. It was surprising to see that this was not the case.

This may be because the supplier wants to please the buyer to avoid going through the E-Auction process again at the end of the contract, or to factor in an increases in switching costs against other suppliers if they E-Auction process is repeated at the end of the contract.

Motivation for using E-Auctions

IAdapt asked buyers what motivated them to choose an E-Auction as part of their purchasing process. The reasons for choosing an E-Auction were:

- To improve the cost of the product/service = 86%
- As a trial to experience the outcome of an E-Auction event = 69%
- Process improvement (including time/speed) = 67%
- Strategy for auctions is long term = 64%
- To ascertain current market conditions = 50%

- Told to use by senior management = 33%
- Competitors are using it = 22%
- Moving to a less personal approach to sourcing = 19%

Unsurprisingly the key reason for choosing an auction was to reduce cost supported by a need to reduce the process time.

Success criteria

Buyers were also asked what criteria they used to decide whether an auction was a success. The following are the results for the success criteria:
- To obtain the best market pricing = 91%
- Enabling software works satisfactorily = 94%
- Suppliers are able to bid satisfactorily = 89%
- Learnt from activity = 89%
- Time taken for negotiation significantly reduced = 69%
- Easy to repeat with other products = 63%
- Significant numbers of suppliers agreed to participate = 63%
- Suppliers agree to participate in future auctions = 60%

Obtaining the best pricing was the top criteria and also reported was that the software worked satisfactorily for both the buyer and the supplier.

Supplier Management Initiatives

When buyers were asked what specific Supplier Management Initiatives they were using in their E-Auction based procurement process, the following results were found.
- Developing supplier relationships = 90%
- Using a supplier reduction program = 70%
- Employing joint technological development = 53%
- Employing price as a primarily factor in your supplier selection = 33%

These results are surprising as auctions have not generally been perceived as encouraging the development of supplier relationships, yet this was recorded as a major objective.

Other Benefits to Buyers

E-Auctions will generally encourage:
- Competitive behaviour amongst suppliers
- Quick, efficient and paperless way of requesting pricing

- Use for catalogue items or spot shortages
- Identification of new sources of supply

Enablers and Inhibitors

Buyers found the top six key enablers to be:
- Comprehensive specification for product/service
- Supplier auction training
- Sound supplier pre-qualifying process
- Selecting suitable commodity
- Enabling software
- Clear auction objectives

Generally, the E-Auction process seems to encourage buyers to be more rigorous and thorough in the purchasing process.

The top barriers to successful E-Auctions were found to be:
- Lack of supplier participation; there is a community of suppliers who have a policy not to enter in E-Auctions, even though it may mean losing contracts to their competitors
- Unsuitable commodity/service; this might be an item where there is no competition in the marketplace, or that is too complicated to or cannot be largely specified.
- Lack of competitive supply base; if a product or service does not have at least three suitable suppliers, then the E-Auction process is not generally suitable.
- Poor training of buyer/supplier; getting things right first time is imperative to build trust amongst suppliers in your organisation's E-Auctions process.
- Auction timing; if you are inviting suppliers to participate from different countries and time zones, take into account if the timing chosen to run the auction is convenient to those suppliers, and also consider company shutdowns in the UK.

Supplier Adoption – Small and Medium Enterprises (SMEs)

CIPS has found that small businesses can miss lucrative public and private sector contracts by failing to conduct business online. 37% of small businesses tendering online for contracts and those that do, have noted the benefits of speed, savings, reduced paperwork, increased customer satisfaction and increased productivity.

The following research from CIPS indicates that many organisations share the same criteria for measuring the success of E-Auctions.

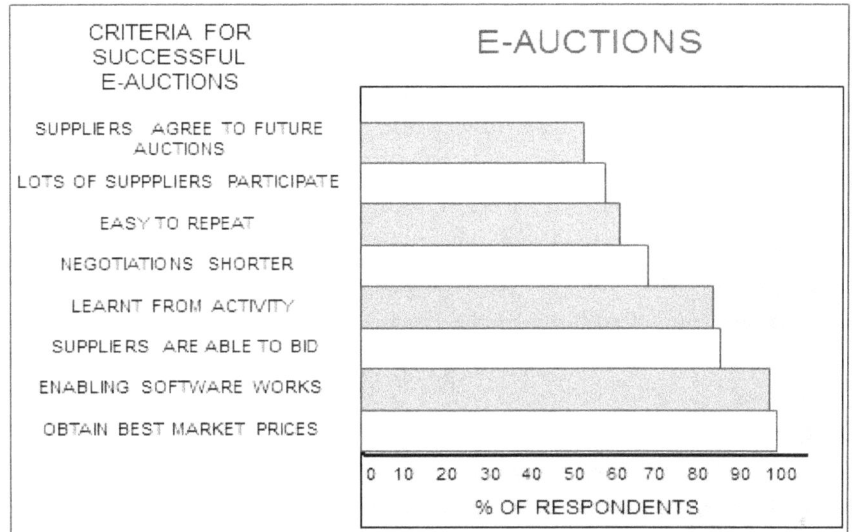

Mini-case study: Shell

Shell International's website states:

'When spending billions of dollars a year on materials and services getting the best deal is essential. By combining the needs of individual operating units, worldwide greater purchasing power has led to discounts as high as 55% over previous prices. Internet-based purchasing (E-Procurement) is also increasingly leading to significant cost savings. A combination of approaches has saved some $500 million in 2000 in Exploration and Production alone.'

Mini-case study: IBM

IBM encourages suppliers to use the Internet. The majority of purchasing transactions are conducted electronically. Suppliers must check that all their electronic transactions are correct; if so, payment is automatic and avoids payment delays. Late payment will only occur if the supplier's electronic documentation is not completed satisfactorily.

Mini-case study: Powerlink

Powerlink, an Australian power company, saved 41% of the originally projected cost of more than $2 million for fibre optic cable in an e-bidding event involving suppliers from four countries.

It can be argued that the use of reverse auctions is a price-focused approach to buying, and that other aspects of total cost of acquisition and/or ownership are placed initially in the background, but that these will then emerge later. The approach is attractive, in that it provides a very rapid and powerful way of meeting short-term price objectives and thereby providing apparent shareholder value. However, the approach is detrimental to the development of long-term alliances and relationships, and it does not fit well with supply philosophies where buyer and seller work together to drive out cost.

Perhaps the approach is not the panacea that some advocates claim, however it very clearly remains a useful addition to the range of methods available to the corporate buyer.

The Electronic Commerce (EC Directive) Regulations 2002

These regulations may apply to organisations within the UK if they:
- sell goods or services to businesses or consumers on the Internet or by email;
- advertise on the Internet or by email; or
- convey or store electronic content for customers or provide access to a communication network.

The key features of the regulations are:
- Online selling and advertising is subject to the laws of the UK if the trader is established here. Online services provided from other member states may not be restricted. There are exceptions, particularly for contracts with consumers and the freedom of parties to choose the applicable law.
- Recipients of online services must be given clear information about the trader, the nature of commercial communications and how to complete an online transaction.
- Online service providers are exempt from liability for the content that they convey or store in specified circumstances.
- Changes to the powers of enforcement authorities such as Trading Standards Departments and the Office of Fair Trading.

(This information is taken from A Guide for Business to the Electronic Commerce (EC Directive) Regulations 2002, published by the Department of Trade and Industry.)

Conclusion

There is overwhelming evidence from research that effective implementation of

E-Procurement, which actively involves all of the stakeholders can make a positive contribution to not only lowering total costs of ownership, but also to improvements in customer service and availability.

It is therefore essential to sustaining competitive advantage.

People Development and Learning

An organisation's capacity to improve existing skills and to learn new ones is the most competitive advantage of all. Therefore, as professional and personal development is somewhat important, organisations need to create opportunities for different types of experiences to ensure its people are educationally nurtured and continually being developed.

As people development involves change (in moving people from one position to another); this also means that learning is needed; as changing and learning are directly connected. However, one of the difficulties with learning is that many people think it is something they no longer have to do. This view is however an out-dated and dangerous one to have in times of change, continual challenge, and new developments. Learning is in fact not a passive activity or an automatic process. It may actually seem to be a passive activity, once you have learned something, but to learn anything genuinely requires an active approach. Learning involves activity, it needs thinking about, and it can be hard work. It is a very personal experience and fortunately, can be flexible and adapted to be fun and enjoyable.

We define learning as:

"Learning is the method and process which uses personal-power, knowledge and experience to:
- *Make sense of things (by thinking)*
- *Make things happen (by doing)*
- *Bring about change (by moving from one position to another)"*

Learning is our future

Everyone, especially including strategists, should be continually learning so they may keep up with the many changes and developments in the world and in business. The rate and speed of change is dramatic in a world of volatility and turbulence. Those who remain in the past can quickly have outdated knowledge and skills. Competence is not a constant. Development must be dynamic and not static; indeed the only thing certain about the future is that it will be different, so learning is very fundamental to our "tomorrow."

New developments need to be examined – often the "best" way may actually be the simplest way, but only if it has been examined, thought about and applied (i.e. it has been actively learnt).

We can and do learn anywhere and anytime, as learning activities can take place in many different situations. Strategists should consider all of the following opportunities for learning:

Informal (or unstructured) learning could be:

- work experience projects
- coaching and mentoring
- job rotation and work shadowing
- planned reading
- attendance at professional institute meetings
- using multi-media resources

Formal (structured) learning could be:

- attendance at courses, conferences and seminars
- distance learning with feedback or with some form of assessment
- studying for a qualification
- undertaking research
- coaching and mentoring
- job rotation and work shadowing

Learning does not always have to be with an outcome that is upwards and vertical, such as a job promotion; but it can be about horizontally broadening skills, knowledge and/or competence at any level. Learning can also result from making mistakes, ensuring we do not keep repeating the mistake, as then, we are not learning.

The Importance of the Learning Process

We have already noted that the ultimate organisational competence is the organisation's capacity to improve existing skills and learn new ones. Learning is the most defensible competitive advantage of all.

Of course, it is an individual that actually learns; therefore, each individual's ways of "learning to learn" (L2L) is critically important. The following sayings illustrate this:

"Those who are in love with learning are in love with life" – Charles Handy

"Learning is more important than knowledge" – Einstein

"All experience is learning" – Peter Vaill

"In times of change, it the learners that inherit the future" – Stuart Emmett

Contrary to many peoples' thinking (and actual practice), learning to learn is a skill to be developed. Yet how many of us, after having committed ourselves to learn; have never for example, considered how we could learn better? Many people have no idea how they "learn" and they consider it to be just common sense. Many others will only learn by "accident" and subconsciously, and whilst this is one way of learning, what more could be actually be learnt by actively considering how to learn more efficiently?

After all, just about everything we ever have done and do must have been, at some time, learnt. It is therefore useful and important to our learning, to have a healthy curiosity about the unique way we personally learn. Bear in mind though, that whilst "our way" will be unique to us, everyone will all go through the following stages:

- Motivation, by deciding "what is in it for me" (WIIFM)
- Obtain data and facts
- Convert this to information
- Get insight and hopefully that "a-ha!" moment
- This will give us knowledge, we have the "know how"
- When this is used, then we develop skills and the "know how to"
- Critically, we need at each stage to Reflect and Revise (discussed soon)

Another view of the above stages is as follows:
- Motivation is "I Will"
- Knowledge is "I Know"
- Doing is "I Do"
- Skills is "I Can Do"
- Reflect is "I Review and Re-connect"

The Learning Jigsaw

It is important for strategists to appreciate the way that individuals prefer to learn, as people will learn if they want to and in different ways. People have their own preferences, as well as already having different levels of competence and commitment.

- Competence being the knowledge and skills required to do something (the "know how")
- Commitment being the confidence and motivation to do it; (the "how to do")

Learning is therefore all about getting the "know how to do" something.

Learning is a cyclic and spiralling process and the stages in this cycle are as follows:
1. **D**oing
2. **R**eflecting

3. Reconstructing

4. Revising

We must go through these D3R stages at some time in our learning, however because of our personal preferences and personality; we may prefer some stages to others. For example, a "task orientated gets things done person", will prefer more hands on stage 1 doing, rather than spending time on the reflecting stage 2.

However, we need all of these stages when learning, they are like the parts of a jigsaw; all must fit together before we can see the overall picture.

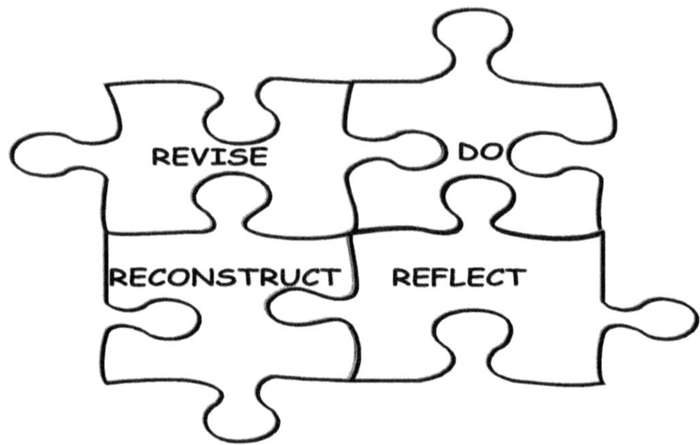

Doing

We start our learning process by gaining experience through undertaking an activity; we "do" something and this can involve the following.

- Experiencing
- Exploring
- Performing
- Trying
- Being Active
- "Hands on" learners
- Key point: Get a better "Awareness" about something

Reflecting

We then think on this experience and attempt to understand it through analysis and conceptualisation; we "reflect" and "think".

- Getting feedback
- "Tell me" learners
- Reviewing

- Reasoning
- Evaluating
- Conceptualising
- Key point: "Thinking back" is a critical skill and one that many leaders and managers need to acquire. Unfortunately, most people wrongly rush or totally ignore this stage.

Reconsidering

Next, we make choices based on analysing the implications of alternative options; we "reconsider and reconstruct."

- Realising
- Connecting
- Implications of alternatives
- Concluding
- Reconstructing
- Key point: "Understanding" and getting the "Know–how"

Revising

Then, we decide on the next steps to take; we "revise" or change our behaviour.

- Refining
- Planning
- Committing
- Deciding on the next steps
- Key Point: Determining "how to" and a commitment to "do"

The learning jigsaw demonstrates that learning starts with an awareness, then with thinking, before we can get the "know how to do" something. The D3R cycle is the means to do this and requires us to pass through all four stages. Then the cycle will start again with the next new experience and a new awareness; providing of course, that we continue, to be motivated to learn.

Thereafter, we will undergo another experience; we will "do" something again, but differently and better. This is then reflected on again, is reconsidered/reconstructed, and results in a revised way to do it.

All of this D3R process can be undertaken with help and feedback from others and is constantly repeated. It is a learning cycle of:

Doing – reflecting – reconsidering/reconstructing – revising – doing – reflecting – reconsidering/reconstructing – revising – doing etc.

"What we think or what we know or what we believe is, in the end of little consequence. The only consequence is what we do" – John Ruskin

"Those unable to change themselves cannot change what goes on around them"
"There can be no learning without action" – Reg Revans

"Learning to learn, is often about making the unconscious, conscious"

Helping People to Develop

All organisations must have people working in them with appropriate levels of competence and the following represents our view of competence development levels. As people develop, then they will pass through these different levels.

Level of ability	Objective	Tasks	Examples of questions
1) Knowledge	What you know	Arrange, define, recognise, relate, repeat , state	"Make a list"
2) Comprehension	What you understand	Classify, describe, discuss, explain, locate, review	"Communicate the key features of"
3) Application	Applying the knowledge	Apply, choose, practice, solve, use, write	"Apply the theory of x to y"
4) Analysis	Analyse what has been done/ applied	Analyse, appraise, compare, contrast, question	"Examine in detail"
5) Synthesis	Combining knowledge and application to create and plan	Arrange, collect, design, plan, organise, prepare	"Make justified proposals"
6) Evaluation	Evaluate, recommend and make decisions	Appraise, argue, assess, judge, evaluate, attach	"Assess the feasibility of x"

As we have explored earlier, learning is not always an automatic process and whilst an individual's personal motivation is a key aspect, people will often need help and support in their learning. A form of such help and support process is called by some, mentoring. However, the name used is secondary to the process involved; a process where organisations create opportunities for people to have different types of experiences where they can be nurtured (or mentored or supported), whilst they are learning and developing at work.

Learning Development Strategy

The myth exists in many organisations that the only way for anyone to learn anything is to send them on a training course. Learning however, will not always fully take place during the training course sessions. Certainly, most trainers will "plant seeds" and will work very hard to ignite the fire for continued growth and development when the learner returns to their work environment.

However, there are some necessary and needed conditions for learning and development to happen in the workplace. These conditions are often about giving support, this effectively being where managers will "water the planted seeds." If this does not happen, then the applied learning opportunities are missed, "the seeds die" and the training event time/cost will be wasted. For example, many UK public sector organisations have recognised the need to change and have collectively spent many millions of pounds on training on skill updates. As many trainers have subsequently reported, such training seems wasted, as most delegates on training courses constantly reported they are unable to implement the changes needed. No thought had been given at all on how to implement the changes, this reflecting a poor initial training design (from both the training supplier and the buying organisation).

This can be avoided when people are being developed; by recognising that they need to get:

- Identification of development needs
- A development programme
- A learning culture at work which fully understands:
  - how people learn
  - how to give support/coach/mentor

However, having a learning culture that practically works is unfortunately a rare find in many organisations, as they just simply fail to include the important support, before and after a development programme.

What do we mean by support? Well the following support is needed:

1) The set up and support, before a development programme:
- Think what work-based projects can be used to apply learning and benefit the organisation.
- Ask the learners to seek feedback on their current performance so that they come up with specific learning goals in this work based area
- Let them do a pre-task
- Meet and finalise learning goals
- Stimulate interest in the programme within the organisation
- Put learners into learning sets/buddy groups
- Arrange a mentoring scheme/programme(see below)

2) The set down and support, after the development programme:
- Ongoing mentoring support
- Evaluate by the success of the work based project
- Ensure specific opportunities exist with 2 days of the end of the programme
- Discuss learning
- Reinforce learning by letting them teach others
- Publicise the success
- Link rewards (and these involve more than financial rewards) to the transfer of learning into the workplace
- Continue with successful learning sets by transforming them into improvement teams

Only when the above, set and set down, is successfully considered, can the crucial transfer take place into the workplace and become effective applied learning. In turn, this will work towards creating high performing organisations. These have the following characteristics:
- Opportunities for continuous learning
- Information sharing
- Employee participation
- Linked personal compensation and performance
- Flat organisation structures with cross-functional working
- Supportive work environments

Learning support and behaviour change
All regular habitual behaviour patterns become hard-wired in the neural pathways of the brain. Behaviour patterns create neural connections in the brain and eventually,

with repeated behaviour, these will reinforce the behaviour. As the behaviour pattern is now automatic at the brain cell level, the result is that these ways of behaving will now feel natural, easy and comfortable.

Introducing a new required behaviour can therefore now be often extremely difficult, because it means replacing the old pattern. As this existing behaviour pattern exists in the brain cell level, any new pattern will often seem to be extremely awkward; even if the new pattern makes sense and is desired. The brain is not like a digital computer, there is no "delete" key.

The only way therefore to replace an old behaviour pattern is to establish a new pattern that will prove to be more satisfying than the old behaviour. With an adequate period of reinforcement, there is a chance that new connections are made, as this new pathway can then become the preferred wiring. Over time, the old habitual pathway will eventually fall into disuse. However, without reinforcement, the pathways will not establish themselves and then people will fall back on their old, comfortable habitual patterns.

The only thing therefore that can create permanent behavioural change is frequent reinforcement over the long term. This means receiving support, for example by ongoing feedback, guidance, praise and encouragement. This support can be internally done (DIY), or can be provided externally, from others, such as a learning supporter or mentor.

The Learning Supporter/Mentor

A learning supporter or a mentor is someone who is involved in:
"A one to one contact of equals, in a defined and agreed relationship; with the aim to learn and to improve, personal and professional effectiveness."
This is therefore someone who:

- Helps another person through a learning experience
- Gives help which can be informal (such as seeking advice), or the help can be more formal (for example, with an organised organisation mentoring scheme):
- Gives one to one attention
- Is totally focussed on learning potential
- Can be removed from organisation politics, when using an external mentor.

Having access to such learning supporters is important part of a learning and development strategy.

Individual Development and Continuing Professional Development (CPD)

It is widely recognised that an individual must undertake, continually, personal development. This so-called Continuous or Continuing Professional Development

(CPD) is defined as:

"The systematic maintenance and improvement of knowledge, skills and competence throughout a professional's working life."

"The process by which a professional person maintains the quality and relevance of professional services during their working life."

CPD is an individual's commitment to ensure that their knowledge and skills are maintained at a suitable level, in a changing world. CPD is therefore all about maintaining standards of competence and professionalism. It puts the emphasis on the individual taking responsibility for developing and directing their career. It is practically the conscious updating of professional knowledge and the improvement of personal competence throughout their working life.

Indeed, many professional career development standards require people to be able to explain:

1. How wider environments affect their career
2. The relationship between their aspirations and the labour market
3. The external sources of support that are available
4. The role of outplacement and support
5. The importance of self assessment
6. The differing and changing career needs
7. Mechanisms for evaluating career management

As major professional institutes also have a responsibility to maintain standards and to ensure public and environmental safety; then employers, clients, and the public will all require, better standards, faster and at a lower cost. CPD will help people to prepare for and cope with, the challenges that they will face in the future world of work.

With Procurement there is excellent support from the UK Chartered Institute of Procurement (CIPS), indeed the authors of this book are not only Chartered Members, but have also been involved in the CIPS qualification programs as trainers/lecturers and examiners.

Not only would we wish to encourage all procurement people to be members of such an Institute, we also note that people in accountancy and legal sectors are required to be qualified members of professional institutes. This should also be the case with Procurement and with all of the supply chain functions.

Measuring Supply Lead-Time

This is an important component of inventory management and stock holding, yet it is one so often not understood by procurement people. However, the holding of stock follows on from procurement activity to satisfy a need/demand; a classic example of functional silos and a lack of cross-functional understanding.

The four key concepts in inventory are as follows:

- Demand analysis
- Demand forecasting
- Supply lead-time
- Costs balanced, with the benefits of holding and carrying inventory,

Full coverage of these concepts is found in *Excellence in Inventory Management* (Emmett and Granville 2007), with the supply lead-time issue being a fundamental aspect for procurement, as they have initially sourced the supplier from whom the orders are subsequently placed.

Whilst understanding demand is an essential first step in inventory management, and the time spent in determining the underlying characteristics of demand behaviour will seldom be wasted, once this analysis is complete, attention can be switched to the other side of the balance – the supply.

Our ability to be able to balance supply and demand will ultimately determine how much inventory will be required to act as a buffering mechanism. The key aspect about supply is the lead-time. Unfortunately, the term lead-time is interpreted to mean quite different things by different people so we will begin by explaining exactly what we mean by lead-time and how it contributes to inventory management.

For many organisations, supply will necessitate acquiring products from another organisation, typically referred to as a supplier. For others, particularly manufacturing organisations, the supplier might be a different part of their own organisation. In either case, the supplier can be asked how long it will take to receive the goods, following from when the supplier has received the order. The response is the supplier lead-time.

Supplier lead-time

It is important to understand that the starting point for the supplier lead-time is the time that the supplier receives the order. The exact end point will depend on, for example, Incoterms, such as whether the customer purchases the product to include delivery (say Delivered Domicile duty Unpaid (DDU), then here the end will be when product arrives at the customer's warehouse.

Sometimes however, the customer will buy the product ex-works (EXW) in which case the supplier lead-time will end, when the product is available at the supplier for despatch.

Of course, it will immediately be apparent that the mode of transport selected will have a defining effect on the length of the lead-time. So will the location of the supplier in relation to the customer. If customer and supplier are separated by long distances and sea transport is used then the final transit leg of the lead-time can be quite long. In the event of international transport, it is probable that customs clearance will also be involved, which can also add extra time into the calculation.

Impact of order processing

Supplier lead-time is not, however, the full picture. Before the supplier receives the order, the customer must place it. These days most orders are placed using some form of electronic transmission, such as the Internet, EDI, fax or phone and in these circumstances time between the customers placing the order and the supplier receiving it is in effect zero. However, for those organisations that sends orders by post, there will be delays before the supplier receives them. Additionally, for other organisations, there may be some time involved in getting approval to place an order.

Before an order can be placed, a decision has to be made to order product. Often as decisions are made, orders will be raised and transmitted to the supplier immediately, thus minimising this time. However, this time may be considerable when a procurement tendering process is used with tender boards meeting infrequently. In addition, if decisions are made through the week to place orders but then all orders are placed on the Friday, a further delay will occur.

Impact of Receipt operations

At the other end of the supplier lead-time there can also be further time added. When the customer receives the product, they may perform inspections and quality checks, these will also add time. It may also be that product is received and put away but delays occur in entering the receipt into the system.

The Supply Lead Time

The total of all the above times, from when the decision is made to order until the product is available for issue, represents the supply lead-time. It is this supply lead-time that is important in inventory management and it is used, as we shall see later, as a key component in the replenishment decision of when and how much to order.

The supply lead-time is the major multiplier of inventory risk and hence it is very important that its make up is fully understood. Too often buyers and customers take the lead-time provided by suppliers as given and do not attempt to challenge it or indeed to understand how it has been derived. This can be dangerous as the following story illustrates.

When working with one client that had 300,000 SKUs and very demanding inventory availability targets, the supply lead times were both long and unreliable. This gave birth to a project to work with suppliers to improve the situation. During the discussions with one supplier, they were asked if it would be possible to reduce the current 20-week supplier lead-time. The supplier responded that it would be and asked what they would like it to be. The client tentatively suggested 18 weeks, which received a positive response. Somewhat surprised by the quickness of the response, the supplier was then asked, what they could provide. The supplier stated that they could achieve 2 weeks.

This begged the question of why 20 weeks was being used when 2 weeks could be achieved. The supplier stated that they had never been able to understand why the customer gave them 20 weeks notice, because all they did with the order was to place it in a drawer for 18 weeks before processing it!

Together they explored how the situation had been created and discovered that when the initial relationship had been set up, the customer's buyer had dealt with the supplier's sales manager. For the supplier this was a new account and a significant one. Hence, the initial order was larger than they could supply from stock. A lead-time of 20 weeks had therefore been quoted to allow sufficient time, for the supplier to manufacture the order and deliver the goods. However, no one had then thought to ask what the lead-time would subsequently be, when it was planned for the supplier to satisfy the replenishment orders from stock. If they had asked, they would have been told 2 weeks!

For several years, our client had been using a longer lead-time than necessary and consequently was carrying more stock than was needed with the obvious financial penalty. Whilst this true story may seem unbelievable, it does demonstrate many issues that can arise when lead times are defined in an arbitrary fashion.

Frequently, when inventory problems exist, people believe it is because forecasts are inaccurate. In our experience, it is more likely to be the result of lead times being wrongly or inaccurately defined. Consequently, analysing lead times can be fertile improvement territory.

Lead Time Summary

We trust by now you will have appreciated that lead-time is a critical component in making inventory decisions. The following over-simplified example will serve to illustrate the importance of lead-time:

If demand is 70 items per week, and supply LT is 2 weeks. Then the quantity to order to cover the demand during the supply lead time (called the lead time demand), is 140 items. However, if the supply LT is variable by +/- one week, then, the maximum order is 210 items and the minimum order is 70 items. However, we may also decide to "play it safe" and order 210 items.

This is not the best decision but maybe an understandable one for those who are left to base replenishment decisions on protecting against personal "noise" factors when past stock outs have occurred. In such cases, then clearly inventory management is also not understood or involved both strategically and operationally in the business.

One of the main issues therefore to be resolved with lead-time therefore is not the length of it but the uncertainty and variability that can occur. Consider another simple example:

Supply Lead time (SLT) is halved from 12 to 6 weeks but the supply lead-time variability (SLTV) stays the same at 4 weeks

	Current SLT		**New SLT**
	SLTV SLT SLTV		SLTV SLT SLTV
	-4 12 + 4		-4 6 +4
Total LT	= 8 to 16 weeks		= 2 to 10 weeks
	(Index 100 to 200)		(Index 100 to 500)

Therefore, if SLTV stays the same and only SLT is reduced, then there is actually a higher disruption factor.

Types of Lead Time

As we have explored above, lead-time covers many aspects. The following is a comprehensive view of lead-time.

Lead Time	Action	By
Pre-order Planning	User	Customer
Procurement	Order placing	Customer to supplier
Supplier	Order despatching	supplier
Production	Making to order	supplier
Warehouse	Supplying from stock	supplier
Transit	Transporting	supplier
Receivers	Receiving	customer
Payment	Paying	Customer to supplier

To repeat, the Supply Lead time used in inventory calculations is not the same as the supplier lead-time. The supply lead-time is the total time taken for deciding to order to the time it is available for issue.

It is therefore made up of many parts both "internally" within the business and "externally," with the supplier and transit lead-time; these "parts" are shown below.

Components of Lead Times

Lead time	Lead Time Stage	Steps, by date
Pre Order Planning	User Need	Analysing status to determining need to order
	User Requisition	Need to order to date of order requisition
Procurement	Order preparation	Order requisition to order release date
	Order confirmation	Order release to date of confirmation
Supplier * see also the production and warehouse lead times	All the stages here are in the production and warehouse lead times	Confirmation to order despatched date
Production (e.g. made to order)	Order processing	Date of order receipt to date order accepted/ confirmation
	Preparation	Order accepted to date manufacture starts
	Manufacture (Queue time, set up, machine /operator time/inspect/put away times)	Start of manufacture to date it finishes
	Pack/Load (to the Warehouse or to Transit LT)	Finished manufacture to date order despatched
Warehouse (e.g. available ex stock	In stock	Date goods arrived to date of order receipt
	Order Processing	Order receipt to date order is accepted or confirmation
	Picking	Date order accepted to date order is available/ picked
	Pack/Load (to Warehouse or to Transit LT)	Order available to date order despatched
Transit		Date despatched to date order received

Receiving		Date order received to date available for issue/use
Payment	Credit	Date invoice received or of other "trigger," to date payment received
	Payment processing	Date payment received to date cash available for use

These lead times need to be examined using real examples to ensure that all appropriate stages and steps are included. There may even be some additional stages, with for example on imports, the customs clearance lead-time.

After each stage has been quantified, each stage will then need analysing to ask, can we do things better? By understanding the processes first, then rationalising them, supply lead can be dramatically reduced.

Who controls Supplier Lead Time?

As shown above, one part of the overall Supply Lead Time is the Supplier Lead time; this is an important lead-time as it is often the longest lead-time. Supplier lead-time therefore must be actively set up, then maintained, monitored and controlled with suppliers. It should be a critical aspect of Supplier Management.

In one of our books, *Excellence in Supplier Management* (Crocker and Emmett 2009) we noted:

"Unfortunately, we are both of the opinion that many organisations, especially those serving internal customers, often fail or perhaps, stumble, in managing their suppliers. This is because the internal customer, or worse, someone else, is left to manage the selected suppliers, without perhaps realising, that they have to!

The internal customer will often provide the kick-start to a procurement department (with the need and the specification), who then takes over by sourcing a supplier and the eventual placing of the order/contract.

After this, however, procurement departments so often "wave the order goodbye" leaving the internal customer to continue with the procurement process cycle. This is sub-optimal; it is a classic example of a cross-functional dependent process failing at the interface between interdependent departments.

There is therefore often little accepted practice of just how a procurement department relates to, or gets involved, with the post order supplier management."

Whilst above we have referred to the post order process of supplier management, traditionally, contacts with suppliers are undertaken by procurement. Therefore, in the absence of any other clearly defined organisational responsibility for inventory controls, it seems logical for procurement to be involved with suppliers on inventory aspects. Indeed, it is a fair contention that as procurement effectively source and deal with suppliers on essentially the five Rights of quality, quantity, time, place and cost, then the lead-time aspect should also be part of procurement.

The control paradox we commonly find, however, is also illustrated by looking at what often happens after the eventual receipt of products from suppliers into the organisations store or warehouse.

Here, assuming a contract for delivered domicile terms has the delivery made to the right place; products will be checked for quality and quantity, with the cost being verified from the invoice against the purchase order. Should there be any discrepancy between what was ordered/confirmation/agreed, then this is taken up with the suppliers.

In our experience, so often the supplier lead-time is not checked for conformity to expectations. It is not unusual to find orders being placed for a specific quality (e.g. as per the sample received etc) and a specific quantity (e.g. 10 tonnes net weight) at a specific price (e.g. £1000 per tonne net weight) and for a non-specific delivery time of 10 to 12 weeks.

In such circumstances, we fail to understand why the time aspect is agreed as a variable, when all the other "rights" are fixed; indeed, as we have yet to see an order being placed for 10 to 12 tonnes at £1000 to £1200. Supplier lead-time must therefore be negotiated, fixed, monitored and controlled, exactly as is done with the quality, quantity, place and cost.

However, commonly time conformity is not even recorded because it is not a part of KPI reporting/examination on the Actual/Standard expected. Whilst it often is common practice that following the receipt of products from suppliers, any variation with the expected quality, quantity, place and cost is reported to suppliers for remedial action; time variations can be the missing element of the Five Rights.

The result of failure in monitoring and controlling supply lead-time, and specifically the supplier lead-time element, will systematically lead to inventory over or under stocking. In turn, this has impacts to customer service, availability and excess cost.

"Frequently, when inventory problems exist, people believe it is because forecasts are inaccurate. In our experience, it is more likely to be the result of lead times being wrongly or inaccurately defined. Consequently analysing lead times can be fertile improvement territory"

Source: Excellence in Inventory Management (Emmett & Granville 2007)

Outsourcing of non-core activity

The Outsourcing Institute has defined outsourcing as:

'The strategic use of outside resources to perform activities traditionally handled by internal staff and resources.'

Therefore, outsourcing is not a synonym for procurement but is concerned with the external provision of functional activity. Thus outsourcing decisions are strategic in nature as it impacts upon the nature and scope of the organisation. As such, they are not taken at the operational level, but involve top management, with the consideration of a great variety of variables such as:

- Do we have candidate functions for outsourcing?
- How do we select?
- How do we assess ourselves?
- Who are the potential providers?
- How do we assess them?
- What sort of relationship will we form?
- How will we manage it?
- How do we ensure efficiency?

Outsourcing is, essentially, the contracting out of non-core activities with a difficulty of course, that a decision has to be made as to what really is core activity, and what is not. That is not to say that the activities are unimportant; for example, the government has outsourced much of the computing activity required by various Civil Service departments and the NHS has outsourced logistics and the purchasing of consumables covering food, bed linen, cleaning products, stationery and some surgical and medical equipment.

Pralahad and Hamel wrote that business development would depend on an organisations ability to identify, to cultivate and to use its core competencies. These are prophetic words. Many organisations, large and small in both manufacturing and service operations, have invested, and continue to invest, great amounts of effort in attempting to do just this. The fundamental questions of 'What business are we in?' and 'What business do we want to be in?' are at the root of corporate strategy.

No single commercial or public sector concern can undertake all the production of goods and services necessary to the business, and decisions of a strategic nature will need to be taken and adopted as a matter of policy for the concern in question. Decisions on which classes of goods and services to outsource, are about those core matters which define what the business is actually all about.

Major issues of investment, location, planning and direction are, largely, dependent on the make/do-or-buy decision. These strategic decisions have informed many considerations, amongst them:

- Financial constraints; if we cannot invest in everything connected with supplying the needs of our organisation, which factors do we invest in, and which do we outsource?
- Which of our capabilities provide competitive advantage? Should we outsource those that do not provide competitive advantage? Once, outsourcing meant handing over functions such as catering and security to third-party specialists, allowing organisations to better concentrate on their core competences. Many of the deals being announced these days come dangerously close to having an impact on organisations' critical competencies; for example, handing over the entire ICT function, or passing over the full responsibility for warehousing and distribution.
- Will integration (vertical or horizontal) bring benefits to our organisation? If so, how do we pursue this?
- What services, goods or commodities are difficult to acquire externally? Should we develop our own capability?
- If 'downsizing' seems to be an option for us, which parts of our operation do we shed, and which do we retain?
- Are we in the right business? Are we making things when selling them is what we are good at, or are there opportunities to become producers of the goods or services that we sell?

Some organisations have brought back in-house activities that were formerly outsourced. For example, RMC, a cement company that had outsourced transport in the expectation of cost reduction, found that costs were going up instead, and decided to improve their control by reverting to an in-house provision.

Nor is the improved service that organisations expect from outsourcing necessarily the service they receive in practice. Many organisations report that rather than improving control, they are actually losing effective control.

One common problem is outsourcing for the wrong reason. If the company is already efficient and effective then it is unlikely that the desired cost savings will be achieved. If the objective is cost savings, or improved service, or being better able to cope with flexible demand, then outsourcing offerings should be evaluated and monitored in that light.

The reaction of far too many organisations is to 'outsource and forget' when instead it should be 'outsource and manage'. Within the contract, a number of specific key performance indicators should be made explicit, and the results to be both produced and reviewed in a timely manner.

> ### Mini-case study: Vita phone
>
> At Vita phone, a German company producing mobile phones for medical and emergency applications, the decision to outsource the making of the devices to US based contract electronics manufacturer Flextronics was based partly on the supplier's commitment to provide such metrics. However, more importantly, was Flextronics's parallel commitment to engage with Vita phone to review, interpret and use the figures to drive improvements.
>
> They have a regular schedule of monthly meetings, where issues such as quality, cost reduction, adherence to delivery schedules and other measures are reviewed.
>
> What is important to them is to be able to see trend information. How long is it taking to process a claim? How many claims are processed per employee?

It is often said that the secret of successful outsourcing is a solid relationship between the two parties. Original contract negotiations often failed to fully appreciate the links between pricing, the required service level measurements and the specified scope of the services provided. Both sides also often fail to fully define the process.

Most outsourcing agreements do not incentivise the correct behaviour from the outsourcer. "Risk and reward" contracts, in which both parties to the deal share the risks and the rewards have been found to achieve mutually acceptable levels of performance.

A Team Approach

The cornerstone of a successful outsourcing project is the creation of an effective team, one that provides a pool of talent and represents all the stakeholders. KPIs relating to quality, speed, flexibility, dependability and cost frequently form the basis for continuous improvement plans. They provide a measurement system for management to gauge the effectiveness of the outsourcing decision and communicate results to a wider audience.

Conversely, they also help to increase expectations over time, with pressure to meet tough new business goals, stretch service performance and improve business growth. Plans are not complete without a termination clause and an exit strategy with clearly identified switching costs, allowing an efficient switch to an alternative supplier or in-sourcing with minimal disruption to the buyer's business.

Why outsource?

The main driver of outsourcing is the need for focused competitiveness therefore, simply:

- Outsource where others can do it better
- Outsource to focus on core business
- Outsource to reduce cost base

However, there are many considerations that might influence an organisation, such as the following:

- External supplier has better capability
- External supplier has greater or more appropriate capacity
- Freeing resources for other purposes
- Reduction in operating costs
- Infusion of cash by selling asset to provider
- Reducing, or spreading, risk
- Lack of internal resource
- Desire to focus more tightly on core business
- Economies of scale

Unfortunately, rarely is there a clear organisational focus for determining which activities are 'core competences' or, for determining strategic impact. Therefore, the most important contributors to success are as follows:

- Activity is well defined
- Roles and responsibilities of all parties are clear
- Good relationship with the supplier
- High quality of the supplier
- Effective contract management/monitoring

An important part of managing outsourcing is the consideration of potential exit strategies. Indeed, as mentioned earlier, there are instances where outsourced services have been taken back in-house; clear evidence that even if organisations outsource, they must retain long-term control.

Best practice Contract Management skills

Buyers need to carry out better planning and post contract management to prevent outsourcing ideals collapsing, according to outsourcing advisory organisation, Orbys. In a report, *Managing Outsourcing for maximum value*, Orbys found nearly a quarter of the UK's biggest organisations have brought an outsourced function back in-house after failed expectations.

According to interviews with 82 manufacturing, financial services and retail organisations with a UK presence, including Kellogg's, Selfridges, Dixon's, Boots and Citibank, 43% said their supplier had failed to meet expectations and 23% have brought work back into their own business as a result. Traditionally procurement focuses on the P2P source/evaluate/order procurement cycle, rather than the planning and post order/contract management, which is where real benefits and value can be identified.

Contractual relationships

Outsourced functions normally lead to relationships where the supplier is providing services on a continuous basis. The determination of an appropriate relationship in which this continuous service is provided, is likely to require a very great investment of time and effort at the planning stage. Additionally, of course, as with all relationships, there will be evolutionary change; change which will itself need to be managed.

Good practice is to:

- Reward good performance
- Share the risk and reward
- Perceive the contractor as a potential partner

Most of those who are looking to make increased use of open book mechanisms or performance-based contracts will of course, currently have very little experience of doing so. The level of skill and sophistication necessary for effective monitoring is clearly increasing beyond the current capability of many organisations.

Strategic buyers will manage relationships as well as contracts. It is as important to manage the relationships between the customer and the supplier as it is to manage the contract. In pursuit of this, strategic buyers are more willing to share risk and reward and less likely to rely on penalising poor performance. This is in line with a greater use of partnership-type contracts, where incentives and the sharing of risk and reward are features that are more common.

There is a demonstrable correlation between the adoption of a strategic approach to outsourcing and the achievement of satisfactory outcomes.

An approach to market testing

In making the decision as to whether to outsource or not, it might be helpful to undertake a market testing exercise, whereby one's own commercial and technical capabilities are benchmarked against providers in the external market. This process requires:

- Some analysis and evaluation of current and projected needs and capabilities

- The reduction of the product of this analysis to a clear specification
- The invitation of external providers to bid against this specification

Analysis of supplier bids might result in a decision not to proceed, but if it is determined at this stage, that outsourcing might be appropriate, then a thorough but conventional supplier selection and evaluation exercise will follow.

Important considerations

It is essential that both the client and the supplier under consideration have a clear and shared understanding not only of the specification but also of goals and objectives, and that this understanding is translated into a workable strategic plan.

Following the careful and rigorous procedures necessary for appointment of a supplier, there will need to be a well-designed and mutually acceptable contract and an open and continuous working relationship underpinned by senior management support from both organisations.

Best Practice on Outsourcing: The Long View

A Dun & Bradstreet global outsourcing survey of 1,000 organisations on its database reported that a quarter had terminated at least one outsourced relationship before its due date. Dataquest also reported that more than 50% of oursourcers surveyed had renegotiated a contract mid-term, resulting in 25% of the incumbent providers losing the account.

Why?

What we can be said with some degree of certainty is that if the needs and expectations have been clearly defined, communicated and understood during the selection process, the execution, measurement and subsequent review would have been far more focused and cohesive.

The value proposition for outsourcing must be to shift the business's focus from managing its own resources to one of managing the provider's results. This demands a more advanced approach to selecting the right partner and performance management of the contract with the business needs, the desired results, being defined in clear and measurable terms. This needs to be done in conjunction with all interested parties (or stakeholders).

The required results must reflect the time requirements of the business and as importantly, they must be owned, measured, reported and modified, as a business needs change.

However, performance is two-way, and the customer will also have to meet obligations in terms of 'owning' the relationship.

There is also a strong correlation between the (good) performance of outsourced service providers and clear lines of responsibility, authority and accountability being established for the outsourced relationship.

There must be an ability to amend or change the outsourcing requirements over time. It must be recognised that there will be cost and performance factors associated with such changes. Include provisions for external benchmarking to stimulate the opportunities for continuous improvement.

Warwick Business School research study found that 4-8% of internal management time is applied to managing relationships.

Focus on soft skills such as mutual problem solving, listening, error-cause removal, force field analysis (the factors in favour of and against change) risk and vulnerability analysis.

Clear escalation and resolution procedures for conflicts should be developed.

Regular (an action orientated) quarterly or six monthly reviews of key performance indicators might be one feature linked to target settling, continuous improvement activities and resource planning to achieve goals and deliver improved performance. Measurement of benefits is essential to ensure value is delivered and recognised.

Source: Hunt.P (2004) "Outsourcing – The Long View" Supply Management Sept 2004

Checklist: Key Contractual Elements
- Comprehensive service definition = just what is actually required?
- Process for service evolution and the ongoing continuous improvement
- Ability to add/delete service
- Volumetric change
- Service levels (meaningful measure/targets)
- Service credits/bonuses (shared risk and reward)
- Objectives to be delivered by both sides
- Supplier responsibilities and contact management
- Customer responsibilities and the partnership concept of win-win
- Force majeure

- Change control processes
- Avoid undue 'lock-in' to
- Particular technology
- Particular solution/service
- On-going market testing/benchmarking
- Dispute resolution
- Termination procedures

Outsourcing Methodologies

Lonsdale and Cox (McIvor 2000) revealed that outsourcing decisions are rarely taken within a strong strategic perspective, with many organisations adopting short-term solutions for cost reductions. Other research demonstrates the same phenomenon.

Many organisations have no formal outsourcing process, and make short-term decisions based on reduction of head count and costs, rather than managing the risks and securing added value and continuous improvement.

The Outsourcing Process

Here we highlight three methodologies for effective outsourcing, all of which involve examining risks at each stage of the process in terms of a decision tree approach, which allow organisations to consider the full implication of their actions.

The first of these was introduced by Lonsdale and Cox (1998) below:

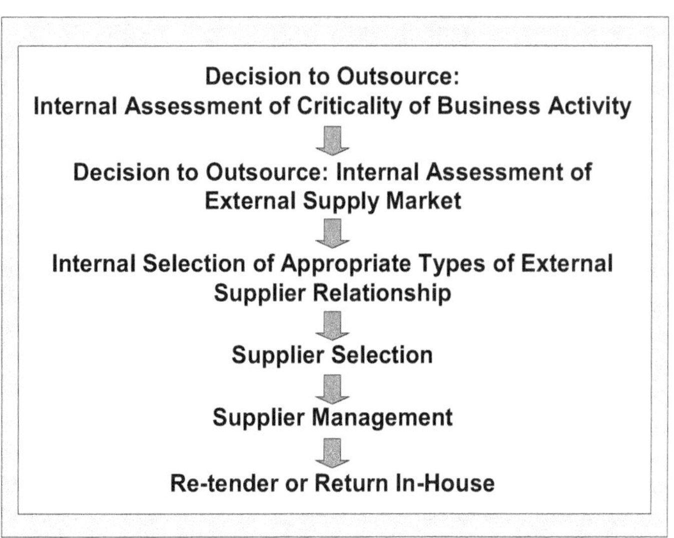

Source: Lonsdale & Cox 1998

This very useful model allows organisations to assess the risks of outsourcing in terms of non-core/core competencies and criticality of the activity. Organisations must have a clear understanding of what business they are in, how value is sustained and therefore, what activities are non-core and low risk in terms of outsourcing.

Moreover, the model indicates the importance of assessing the supply market, as it is imperative that the selection of suppliers/providers is of those who have more specialist knowledge in order that they can provide superior levels of service and continuously improvement. If the market is not sufficiently 'mature' in that there are many providers, but there is a lack of a sufficient level of competence, then clearly it may not be appropriate to outsource at this stage.

Supplier management in the form of effective contract management and performance monitoring with appropriate partnership/collaborative approaches is imperative if benefits of outsourcing are to be realised. Finally, any re-tender or return in-house decision must be managed effectively as badly managed termination of provision can cause interruptions in service levels and an unprofessional reputation in the marketplace.

McIvor (2000), again in the form of a decision tree involving four key stages, provides a second outsourcing framework and if organisations follow such an approach, they will better manage the risks associated with outsourcing more successfully.

Stage 1: Define Core Activities

It is essential to distinguish between non-core and core activities, those adding value to the customer and therefore key sources of competitive advantage. Organisations such as Honda, Apple, IBM and Digital build their strategies around their core activities and outsource as much of the remaining as possible.

Stage 2: Evaluate relevant value chain activities

This involves analysing the competence of the company compared to those of the potential providers, comparing the ability to add value and the implications for the total cost of ownership. Activities for which the company has neither a strategic need nor special capabilities can be outsourced to more competent providers who have a lower cost base.

Stage 3: Total cost analysis

At this stage, if after analysis of total costs, the organisation is more capable than the supplier is, then they should retain in-house capability. If a number of capable suppliers exist, then move to the final stage.

Stage 4: "Relationship analysis"

At this stage, organisations are attempting to select suppliers who have the ability to initiate and develop suitable relationships that will add value and provide continuous improvements. Again, elsewhere in this book, we demonstrated the importance of relationship management. If no suppliers are suitable, then again, the risk is too high and therefore the decision should be to retain in-house capability.

Finally, Galetto, Pignatelli and Varetto (2003) provide a third framework. Again, there are several stages associated with the following:

- Core competency evaluation
- Identification of process to be outsourced
- Types of relationships
- Prioritisation of activities to be outsourced (Criteria at this stage are capabilities, total cost and control)
- External benchmarking
- Supplier selection
- Establishment of service level agreements and suitable relationships, involving future targets for continuous improvements
- Management of the outsourcing process.

Essentially, this highlights the importance of on-going contract management and regular reviews. Again, this was found to be most important to users in research findings elsewhere in this chapter.

In summary, if organisations adopt such formal strategic thinking as outlined in the above three frameworks, it is likely that the percentage of successful outsourced contracts reported would increase dramatically.

Mini Case Study – Goodyear

The Goodyear Tire and Rubber Company in North America is outsourcing more than 40 indirect spend categories in a drive to cut costs.

A Goodyear representative claimed the deal "will help save $1 billion by 2008 and allow buyers to focus on strategic and direct spending."

Outsourced categories included:

- Transportation
- Distribution
- Maintenance

- Repair
- Operations
- Packaging
- Energy
- Marketing services

Outsourcing – Pitfalls

A study from PA Consulting found 58% of clients carried out no due diligence on potential suppliers, 44% admitted to under estimating the effort involved in managing their supplier and half of the lawyers believed less than 10% of their clients understood what partnership meant.

A study by outsourcing adviser, TPI said outsourcing a function saves on average 15%. However, there is a need to retain a small team with the commercial and technical credibility to manage the contractual relationship and manage supplier performance over the life of the contract.

Clients also have to specify what services they need. They need a format that sets out qualitative requirements combining outputs, measurable results, and key inputs. Often, specifications are a wish list of outputs that bears no relation to current performance. This may result in the contractor having to improve the service from a low starting point without adequate resources or time. If can also increase costs beyond the means of the client organisation. There is a need to specify "fit for purpose" service requirements just as with any other purchase.

It is also often the case that clients do not know the true cost of current services, as costs are hidden, delegated or not reported accurately.

Only 21% of suppliers in a survey (2006) felt that clients communicated their objectives well. With a figure this low, it is no wonder that their expectations are failing to be met. 44% of clients surveyed underestimated the effort involved in managing a supplier.

Both customer and providers fail to appreciate the complexity of contract and resources needed to effectively manage a structured relationship. Effectively this demonstrates a lack of meaningful engagement between suppliers and clients.

Ongoing contract management is often, either non-existent or far too simplistic. Success lies in a tailored deal that is flexible to meet changing business models over the life of the contract.

Active management of performance, service and relationship, and measuring them against the market performance are vital to ensure that mutually acceptable objectives are met.

Outsourcing – How to avoid pitfalls

More often than not, outsourcing contracts collapse because of a lack of communication between suppliers and buyers. Two out of three clients said they wished they had focused more on their supplier's ability to deliver on their promises.

Many of the problems that arise during the course of a contract could have been readily resolved at the outset. This is why buyers and suppliers need to agree exactly what the supplier will deliver, the time frame for delivery and targets that need to be met. A key performance indicator (KPI) of 20% savings, for example, is not enough; buyers need to be explicit about the benefits they want to achieve, the risks involved and the scope of activities covered.

The buyer needs to be aware of what level of service the end user expects and ensures this is part of the service procured from the suppliers.

Outsourcing deals are more successful when the buying team works closely with the department being outsourced to agree equally beneficial KPIs. This is crucial when outsourcing areas of the business that cannot always be measured in hard metrics, such as with HR or training.

Once the KPIs are agreed, discussions between buyers and suppliers should continue through monthly reviews, with agreed delivery dates and escalation processes should anything go wrong. It is the supplier's responsibility not just to meet the terms of the contract, but also to prompt the buyer on measuring its success at meeting KPIs.

Taking a partnership approach can reap dividends in this respect. One strategy we take is to outsource work in stages. This way, a relationship is established, the supplier gains an understanding of the buyer organisation and its needs whilst the buyer learns how outsourcing works.

Transfer of Undertakings Protection of Employment (TUPE)

Transfer of Undertakings (Protection of Employment) Regulations 1981 (TUPE) requires that, where an undertaking is transferred from one employer to another (i.e. outsourced), the following, with the exception of pension rights, are taken over by the new employer.

- The contracts of employment
- The rights and obligations arising from these contracts
- The rights and obligations arising from the relationship between the transferor and the employees working in that undertaking
- Any existing collective agreements

Employees who are employed by the original employer at the time of transfer automatically become employees of the new employer, as if their contracts of employment were originally made with the new employer, service is counted as continuous from the date on which employment commenced with the first employer.

All employees transferred must, under TUPE; retain all their current employment rights and conditions. The employees cannot be dismissed for a transfer related reason without such dismissal being ruled by an industrial tribunal to be automatically unfair.

However, new employers can change the workforce numbers and/or conditions of employment for economic, technical or organisational (ETO) reasons.

The virtual organization

Some organisations are using outsourced services to the point of retaining control, but in an almost 'virtual' capacity. Until recently, functions, services, products and processes that were considered core to the success of a company, such as customer care, remained in-house to maintain control, maximise potential advantage and minimise risk. Many of these areas are now emerging as potential candidates for outsourcing, for example, Ford considers virtually anything outside design and final assembly as non-core.

Procurement; a candidate for outsourcing?

A number of authorities have argued that if an organisation is to concentrate on its core competencies, then procurement activity may well not be one of them, and the activity might itself be placed in the hands of an external agency. A number of contributors to the 1996 International Procurement Education and Research Association (IPSERA) conference presented papers suggesting or predicting the end of 'purchasing' in the traditional or established sense.

Benmaridja and Benmaridja (1996) suggested outsourcing the non-critical part of procurement, and suggested a methodology for determining exactly what the non-critical parts are.

Stannick and Jones (1996) argued convincingly that purchasing as defined by Burt (1984) as "the systematic process of deciding what, when, and how much to purchase, the act of purchasing it and the process of ensuring that what is required is received in the quantity specified on time" was dying. They saw this was to be replaced by 'the assessment, management and monitoring of supplier behaviour to optimise organisational inputs'. Compelling though the arguments put forward by Stannick and Jones are, the fact remains that at least some the operations need to be undertaken by somebody somewhere. Perhaps this somebody might be a specialist services contractor, or a supplier rather than a buyer, and perhaps the somewhere will be remote from the customer's place of business.

Evans (1996) reported the case of an organisation, which developed its interface with suppliers to such an extent that it, had a small cadre of well-regarded suppliers who worked strategically in alliance with the company. Supplier appraisal or sourcing work was no longer necessary, negotiations no longer took place, and the routine requisitioning, ordering acknowledgements and payments work took place electronically and automatically. Procurement had improved to such an extent that there was no longer a need for the function. The quality department resolved quality issues, manufacturing teams met regularly to discuss initiatives, and the accountants worked closely with their counterparts at suppliers where prices were concerned. Therefore, with no more need for a procurement department, the staff was redeployed and the department closed. Of course, this does not mean that the activities that many regard, as being part of the role of procurement had all been rendered obsolete, but rather those they had been relocated in a more appropriate place in the organisation and its interface with suppliers. Direct supplier/customer linkages at the appropriate level and between appropriate managers had obviated the need for procurement in an intermediary role.

Many commentators report benefits of outsourcing procurement such as:

- Improved return on investments through improved use of resources
- A focus on core competence
- Access to greater economies of scale

Others point to the negative effects such as:

- Conflict of interest
- Loss of control
- Outsourcing core activities by mistake

Mini case study – Roadchef Motorway Services
In 2004, Roadchef outsourced both direct and indirect spend.
Shortage of internal category knowledge prevented the company from realising its true purchasing leverage and potential.
Benefits have been-reduced costs, simplified processes, best practicE-Procurement, quality products, and improved KPIs overall.

And finally...

Organisations must have a robust contract with their service providers which contains such provisions as:

- Prescriptive arrangements relating to the sharing of gains
- Commitment to realising and capturing real savings
- Agreed processes
- Clear scope of work for the services to be provided

If not, they may find that many of the expected cost savings do not materialize and that the outsourcing is actually unsuccessful.

Of paramount importance is the safeguarding of quality by ensuring satisfactory provisions for supplier selection and maintenance of quality standards whilst producing year on year total costs of ownership reduction.

Summary checklists for outsourcing – key aspects

What is involved?
The transfer of selected services/activities to a third party, not the transfer of control

Enables concentration on core business

Normally multi-year agreements

Contractually linked to targets, such as minus cost, plus service etc.

Geared to set/step performance improvements

Levels of outsourcing
1. Migration of infrastructure (people, technology, systems, supplier management)
2. Assume responsibility for some process
3. Offers added value functions such as strategic sourcing, supplier relationships
4. Formulation of strategy

Why outsource procurement?
- For same reasons as would outsource anything
- Enables core concentration by the business
- Increase efficiency due to economies of scale of people, systems etc.
- Reduces, commonly, costs by up to 15%
- To drive change and to introduce new technologies more easily
- Connect to a larger supplier base

How does it work?
- Aggregate spend by pooling requirements
- Access higher levels of expertise
- Tap economical labour sources in transactional processing by "off shoring"
- Operations after the transition are more "self-service"
- Adjustments needed to now being more automation intensive

- More centralised purchasing contact
- More use of operating performance matrices
- More formal service level agreements (SLA's)

Going forward
- Needs a careful consideration of current circumstances. it may not suit everyone
- Executive team decision is due to: need for change, merger activity, urgency for cost reduction, ability to change, reducing fixed costs
- Scope for savings/need for capital/prioritisation/sharing of benefits
- Future vision/capability/investment needed/strategic nature

The secrets of outsourcing have been identified in "Supply Management" 29 June 2000, as follows:
- Concentrate of what do well and allow specialists in other areas to handle the non-core services
- Adapt to new ideas and developments, as, what was acceptable in the past, may not be so in the future
- Choose a provider who understands all your needs
- It is crucial to fully know the current costs and service levels
- Ensure outsourcing delivers, planned benefits such as cost/service/time targets
- Acknowledge that information equals power in areas such as service level requirements
- Develop a strategic alliance with the provider, based on mutual trust
- Start with a phased controlled service with monitored cost/service levels at all stages
- Develop the right company culture which supports outsourcing
- Monitor the outsourced function with regular performance measurement

The important questions a business will need to consider, before outsourcing, can be asked as follows:
- Is it a non-core activity
- Can we release some capital
- Will we retain some operations in house
- Will we retain management expertise

- What increased monitoring will be needed
- What are the risks of committing to one contractor
- Will flexibility be increased
- Will costs be reduced, whilst service is increased
- How will we account for future changes
- Are there any implications on the Transfer of Undertaking, Protection of Employment (TUPE) legislation

Continuous Improvement

One of the major problems with continuous improvement in organisations is the all too frequent practice of only looking at and using some of the superficial improvement tools and techniques and thereby, ignoring and understanding the "deeper" thinking that is behind, and is also supporting, such tools. To use one TQM principle, the tool may not be actually "fit for purpose", therefore, its application can be dangerous and actually counterproductive.

Unfortunately, though, choosing to use only the tools to get a quick fix is too common a practice. When this is done, what happens next is analogous to what happens when people 'blame a computer' for mistakes or for the computer being unable to do something. Such a failure, shown by the software output, follows from the software being programmed to work in specific ways.

As most people have become merely computer keyboard operators/superficial users, they will effectively ignore "what goes on behind the screen" in the computer program. Whilst we would not expect all computer operators to be software programmers, the contention here is that, without an understanding of the software key drivers and their impact on the program's output, there is effectively little knowledge of what really has gone on behind the screen.

Therefore, any changes in the key drivers are not acted on and the software's default settings remain unchanged. When the programmed rules and procedures are out of date and old default settings are being used, failure will be a consequence, albeit this is often shown in a disguised and an unexpected way (at least to the keyboard pressers).

This is not to say that all keyboard pressers must have the knowledge of the key drivers – however someone in the organisation must have this knowledge, along with a structured review process for the software program.

There are real dangers here when, for example, a new starter is shown only what keys to press and how to use the screen display answer. They then continue on perhaps into more senior positions, yet when they remain armed only with their basic starter knowledge; the result can be that, over time, an organisation is left only with an army of keyboard pressers and with no "behind the screen thinkers". Additionally, there is now no one around who has any knowledge of the original program, let alone the key drivers. Consequently, we now have a situation that when any key drivers change, these are ignored. In turn, this knocks onto the program output/decision.

Whilst tools, like computers, are very worthy means to an end, by choosing to make only the tools the end, then really we have forgotten to use all of the correct means!

Such thinking is wrong, but is very common and is often compounded by organisations deciding to follow trends and adopt a "mob culture". This has happened with some ERP implementations, indeed, we can now see many disappointments. This is not to criticise or decry ERP which, correctly used, has transformed some organisations from the Stone Age to rocket science in a few years. However, with successful ERP applications, we would expect to find that a correct study and implementation has been undertaken. The blind following fashion or a mob culture type of approach is one where an organisation has:

- Done it because others are doing it
- Done it because the boss has been to a conference and instructs it to be done and report back in three months on its success

Wrong implementation can also follow when any of the following occurs:

- Introduced too much, too soon and at the same time (the reality is an over run and over time project)
- Guessed what the costs would be (the realty is over budget)
- Allow consultants to have ownership (and contracted out the control)
- Have the wrong balance between "passion" and "reality"
- Give up when have problems; (when these are "opportunities to be overcome" and real learning lessons are often only to be found whilst on the journey)

Continuous Improvement as the norm

As explained above, there are dangers in only looking to use the "superficial" tools and techniques and in ignoring, or not understanding the "deeper" thinking that is behind, and "invisibly" supporting, the tools.

In recent times, we have seen a reincarnation of the Toyota Production System (TPS) as "lean". TPS in turn, has its foundation in Japan from work that developed into Total Quality Management (TQM) that was started in Japan by the American W. Edwards Deming in the early 1950s (it was originally developed by him in the USA in the late 1930s, but was largely ignored in the USA during the Depression).

One thing is very clear about such initiatives – that improvement is part of the normal job, for example, "everyone has two jobs: one, what is says on the job description and two, to improve it". Consequently such enlightening approaches are worthy once again of looking at.

Quality and Total Quality Management (TQM)

Lean (simply meaning thin with no waste) is one aspect of Quality, but what is Quality? This means different things to different people, as Quality is not necessarily "luxury"; e.g. quality car, designer clothes etc. but is actually something that:

- meets customer requirements
- is fit for purpose
- delights the customer
- is of value to the customer

TQM is the integrative management philosophy used for continuously improving the quality of products and processes. It involves the following three fundamentals:

1. Quality control: on the work undertaken, for example inspection, checking, removing the scrap etc.

2. Quality assurance: on the way the work is done; for example, systems, procedures, designed in methods, consistency and conformance etc.

3. Quality management: on the results of what is done; for example, everyone responsible for quality of their own work, right first time every time, the standard is set by the customer etc.

Using these fundamentals enables doing things, exactly how we want them done as Quality is all about continually satisfying requirements, which involves, satisfying the need plus, where possible, adding value at little/no extra cost. Total Quality is then continuously improving customer satisfaction, whilst simultaneously improving margins and gaining everyone's commitment and involvement.

Other Quality definitions/sayings:
"Doing the right things right, first time, every time"
"100% customer satisfaction"
"Zero defects, error free"
Note:
- Good quality does not always mean high quality.
- Good quality means a predictable degree of uniformity and dependability.
- Good quality means the quality is suitable to the market.
  Source: After Deming

Q principles are common sense, but whilst recognising that Quality is 'sense', it is so often not very 'common'. This is especially so for those who have an "I want it and want it now" approach, and for those who make comments like "just give me the tools" (effectively also saying, "And stop me having to think about it").

However when Q principles are ignored, this can mean there is going to be ignorance about:

- What actually results with the customer, e.g. how are they really treated and what are their points of view
- What the flows and processes are (that give customers what they want)
- How their own staff and people who do the work can make improvements

The connections with these three aspects are well noted by Toyota who has observed that:

"Brilliant process management is our strategy. We get brilliant results from average people managing brilliant processes. We observe that our competitors often get average or worse results from brilliant people managing broken processes"

Let us simplify this, as it is somewhat important:

- Toyota has brilliant processes using average people, and gets brilliant results
- Others have broken processes using brilliant people, and get at best average results

TQM is therefore, fundamentally, a state where we no longer carry on doing those bad habits, which have "always been done" that have all too often followed from years of:

- Bad management of people
- Wrong measurement processes, procedures and systems
- Buying cheap and making cheap
- Failure to recognise what customers need

Checklist: TQM

TQM is:
- Customer setting the standards; Never forget that the customer is internal as well as external. The external customer is however the final "arbitrator"
- Reducing total cost
- Continuous improvement
- Strategic change lead by managers

- Doing the right things that add value
- Everyone is involved
- Avoiding waste/eliminating errors

TQM is not:
- Luxury
- Meeting only own standards
- Quality Control experts checking what is done
- Using only "Quality experts" or "Six Sigma Black Belts"

Many recognise the importance of TQM, for example, Japan dominates many markets and they use TQM. Many markets now have customers who have become more demanding; for example, the growth of "consumerism" that has created changed demands. In turn, suppliers can be under pressure; this can lead to reduced supplier bases, which in turn can mean a requirement for consistency/reduced costs and working differently with fewer more vital suppliers.

For many organisations, TQM is also a necessary condition and an entry condition for some markets, this being in addition to the usual requirements to win business on price, delivery, reliability etc.; this being a continual activity, as competitors are also "continuously improving". Therefore, the goal posts keep shifting globally and locally, and "getting better at being better" becomes the ongoing challenge.

Checklist: TQM means:

- Broad organisational and culture change
- Empowerment of staff; as people are released to use their natural energy and ability
- Continuous improvement
- Delighting customers
- Changing from old ways to new ways
- Changing from quick fixes to "right first time every time"
- Changing from making only major breakthroughs to making continuous small improvements

Employees in TQM organisations will become more involved and in turn, are commonly found to become more motivated/productive/effective. What surprises many managers, is that this often happens with people, who before TQM, were seen to be not like this. Here the managers own thinking has changed, reflecting, "as a person thinks, then so they are" (where they thought people were not capable)" and also, "if you think you can or think you cannot, then you're right" (where they thought before, they could not change).

Quality and the Toyota Production System (TPS)

With traditional production methods, we find the following:

- there are only rigid fixed procedures,
- quality problem checking is done at the end of the production line by "inspectors"
- this is accompanied by an additional, "this cannot be changed" management approach, with
- only the "top" authority allowed to change things and with
- a classical "do it by the book only" approach, that is so reminiscent of Adam Smith (1778) in the "The Wealth of Nations".

Fortunately, things have moved on in enlightened organisations since 1778 with the fundamental ideas on TPS being as follows:

- Processes and flows must follow precise rules. For example, the process rules include built in tests, that will immediately signal and flag up problems.
- Every input and process method is rigidly scripted (e.g. in the supply and all the other processes)
- Problems are responded to, by testing solutions, by taking action (sometimes called JDI or Just Do It).
- These continuous creative responses to problems give flexibility, and are therefore more immediately responsive to problem correction.

In TPS, all processes are seen as a continuous series of controlled experiments. In this regard, whilst the origin of TPS is in the 1950s, it displays attributes of what would be called in the 1990s 'a learning organisation'. Whilst some would see a paradox between being rigid yet flexible, there is no doubt that TPS does work. Indeed, it is this paradox that makes it different, as TPS is the outworking on Quality into production methods; but it also has wider applications beyond manufacturing of products and the provision and supply of services.

Checklist: False Views of TPS

The following 3 myths have been noted by Spear and Bowen (1999):

Myth 1. Tools are fundamental e.g. Kanban, Quality circles.
• Toyota do not believe this and see that such explicit tools are merely temporary "countermeasures" and are eliminated, once improvements work.
• Therefore it is only solutions, that are the permanent resolutions

Myth 2. Must have zero inventory
This is an ideal. In practice, the following types of inventory are often held:
• Supply: to give time for suppliers to make changeovers in setups
 - Work in progress: to cover unpredictable machine downtime
 - Finished goods: to cover variable mix and volume of demand
• The appropriate process owner always owns inventory and therefore they "pay" for deciding to hold inventory. (This is a basic sound business practice where, the department or person who creates a need, actually pay for all costs associated with satisfying that need.)

Myth 3. It does not always work. For some this is true but this is usually because "Many are unsuccessful with TPS as they concentrate on the explicit tools and not on the implicit principles; they want the easy tools but not the thinking behind them". The implicit principles of TPS are in the use of the Scientific method that uses a hypothesis that is tested to show the gaps between what has been predicted/expected and the actual.

There are 4 implicit rules that underpin TPS:
1. How people work
2. How people connect
3. How the process/production line is constructed
4. How to improve

Let us look at these further to enable you to draw parallels with good procurement and supply chain processes:

TPS Rule 1) How people work; every part of work shall be highly specified as to the content, sequence, timing and outcome; this means:

- Getting into the details of work content, sequence (with dependencies and interfaces), outcome, timing etc.
- Everything is specified, exactly
- Removing those work variations that hide poor quality and also hinder learning and changing

TPS Rule 2) How people connect; every supplier/customer connection must be direct with unambiguous communication:

- All connections on who provides what, when and to whom, are standardised and are made direct
- Clear and unambiguous details are needed on the numbers of people, goods, and services required and the timescale to meet these requirements (e.g. the quality, quantity, place, time and cost)
- Those needing help, can request help directly from those who are providing the supply (e.g. if need help then are able to ask immediately, there is no hiding, no waiting, and can solve issues, "here and now" where it happens)

TPS Rule 3) How the production line is constructed; every route must be simple and direct:

- Simple direct specified smooth flowing paths, with no loops or forks; (flow being the operative word here)
- Once the path is designed, it stays, unless a total redesign is undertaken

Rules 1 to 3 will require that all work shall be highly specified as to content, sequence, timing, and outcome. Every customer-supplier connection must be direct, and there must be an unambiguous yes-or-no way to send requests and receive responses. The pathway for every product and service must be simple and direct.

The results from Rules 1 to 3 is better productivity, quality and cost, plus the design of the work is continually being tested to create the expected (and often frequently changing). outcome. This means that it is very clear when work is being done correctly or not; for example, if work is running over time, or there is poor quality, then this means it is being done wrong, which in turn, means we need to redesign the work process, or, the workers need retraining. Rules 1 to 3 therefore identify any problems and the following rule 4, covers the solutions and making improvements.

TPS Rule 4) How to improve; improvements use the scientific method, with guidance and improvements undertaken at the lowest level possible.

- To make changes, people need the know-how and who is responsible; they may need to be taught to do this
- Any changes to the work, connections, pathways etc, are made by doing it under guidance from a teacher/coach/mentor and this is done, at the lowest level possible. Clearly here people are empowered to make changes as they are encouraged to do so, are supported and provided with feedback in a conductive work environment
- People also present ideas that are persistently positively challenged. A view here is that everyone has two jobs, one to do the work as per the job description, secondly, to improve it
- All are motivated towards improvements, and these go beyond what is needed to met "just" the current customer needs
- All involved share a common goal with a common sense view of what the ideal can be

TPS is all about applying the above principles to fit your ways. It is not at all about blindly copying others or about only using the tools.

Effectively, TPS is not an abstract approach but a very simple one that sees, for example, the "ideal" or best or the ultimate end goals are as follows:

- Defect free to met required customer requirements
- Batch size of one
- Supply on demand the version/variety required
- Delivered immediately
- Produced with zero waste of resources
- Produced in work environment that is safe physically and emotionally

Checklist: The Learning principles of TQM and TPS

Both TQM and TPS represent for many, deciding to take a new way and therefore involve change that in turn, requires learning. The learning points here are as follows:

- Managers must be able to do the work of the people they supervise. This applies from the "team leader" right up to the organisations leader.
- Managers must take time to "work through" from "bottom to top" . This takes many years, and they will fully "work through on the job"; therefore,

- a "blind" fast tracking of managers is not seen as being effective.
- Managers are enablers, not fixers, e.g. they must coach/mentor/enable others
- There is no substitute for direct observation
- People are not told 100% "how to do it"
- They use trial and error on the job in a supportive and safe (physically and emotionally) environment with changes structured as experiments undertaken as frequently as possible
- Secondments are made to a "consultancy school" for leaders-teachers-coach-mentors, to learn how to facilitate and to work on the "higher level" problems.

(We can see here the problems for some organisations in TQM and TPS, problems especially for those who use a management model of being overtly directive, who have managers without the knowledge of the work done by the people they supervise, and with a preference for developing managers by fast tracking).

Above all, we can see that TQM and TPS use supported learning and practical doing with:
- "Discovery by solving problems"
- "Discovery by asking questions" (e.g.5W2H; see the following checklists)

Checklist: 5W2H

We must ask questions to get an answer.
"The problem with western managers is the emphasis on finding the right answer, rather than finding the right question" – Peter Drucker
- Who? Identifies e.g. a person
- Why? Beliefs/Values e.g. purpose
- Where? Environment e.g. the location, place
- When? Environment e.g. the time/sequence
- What? Behaviour e.g. objects
- How much? Costs
- How? Capabilities e.g. the method

With TQM and TPS, we therefore have capable people who are responsible for the actual doing of the work, and are also responsible for improving their own work. Standardised connections exist with the resolution of any problems undertaken at the lowest level possible in an organisational structure that becomes a "nested modular" structure. This enables implementing change in one area, which will not necessarily affect the other parts. Changes are therefore made without any disruption.

TQM and TPS are essentially about having a system, which creates thinking "on the job" people at all, levels.

Suppliers have needs

Information has to be gathered on the supplier market conditions, as the available options for sourcing will be affected by the product or service availability, location, number of suppliers and competing buyers along with the growth/decline in the market.

We must also consider the satisfaction of need, this being the starting point for procurement from the users/customers perspective. This is actually a "two-way street" as suppliers are also looking to have their needs satisfied.

A buyer's ability to influence a supplier to do something is largely dependent on the buyer's perception of the supplier's willingness to meet the buyers need. The opposite is also true, where a buyer's ability to influence a supplier is also dependent on the supplier's perception of the buyer's willingness to help the supplier met their needs.

Finding ways to ensure both parties' needs are satisfied is therefore an issue to be considered and this will influence the behaviour patterns between buyers and suppliers.

First, therefore, let us consider the balance of power between suppliers and buyers.

Power and Kraljic

Procurement is influenced by the relative power of buyers and sellers, therefore, the power of each party has a part to play; an overview of this is provided below:

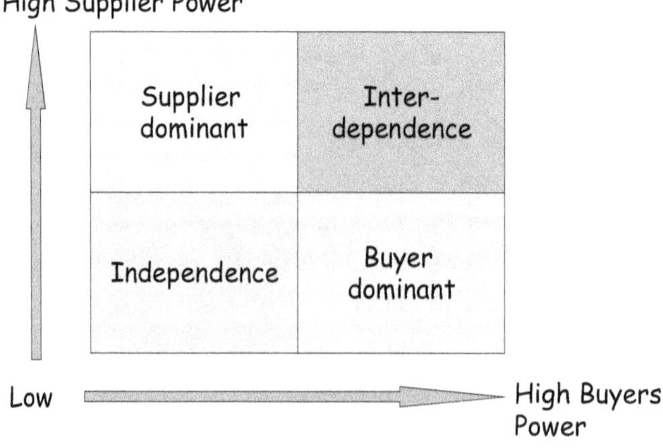

Power is not therefore going to be equally distributed and the relationship of the Kraljic portfolio and procurement strategy can be seen as follows:

1) Buyers are dominant on Leverage items as there are many competing suppliers of standard commodity goods that the buyer purchases in large volumes. Therefore, this is an attractive proposition to those suppliers who see attractiveness in volume sales at low price. Buyers can therefore easily exploit their buying advantage by "playing the market." When the buyer is dominant we will therefore find:

- A small number of big buyers with a large market share and a high spend and influence
- They buy a large percentage of a seller's output
- It is easy for the buyer to switch suppliers, creating a "take it or leave it" view from the buyer
- There are many sources of supply giving a highly competitive supplier market
- Low transaction costs

2) Suppliers are however dominant on Bottleneck items as they have a bespoke product, often branded, which the buyer has to purchase; so buyers must ensure and secure supply, whilst searching for alternatives. When suppliers are dominant we therefore tend to find:

- A small number of big sellers
- Supplying to many buyers
- Difficult for buyers to switch
- Few sources of supply as suppliers have "unique" products. For example, OEM spare parts
- High transaction costs
- An "enforced" view from the supplier
- There are barriers to entry for other suppliers into their market, for example, requirements for specialised research and development

3) Buyers and suppliers are interdependent on Critical items where for example, alliances enable sharing and collaborative working for mutual benefit.

4) Buyers and suppliers are however independent on Routine items as minimal effort is needed for sourcing these items due to the relatively little impact procurement can make to reducing costs. Buyers therefore look for reliable and efficient supply and once this is found, they can "let it go", for example, the outsourcing of stationery supplies to

just one supplier with who, those who need stationery, will then make direct contact to place an order.

It cannot therefore be assumed by buyers that every supplier is "desperate" to supply them with products or services; indeed this may only occur with Leverage items and even then, with the low price on offer, some suppliers may not be interested in the business.

Power and Economics

The type of market and its association to power exists in economics, as can be seen below:

Aspect	Monopoly markets	Oligopoly markets	"Perfect" competition markets
Supply & Demand Control	Statutory controls and checks exist in the UK	Fewer organisations, with the possibility of market collusions	Few controls, most things are open
Barriers to entry	Retained and suppliers look to maintain the "status quo".	High costs to enter the market for any "new" suppliers.	Few to no barriers of entry with low costs to enter.
Market view	Focus and concentrate.	Large and valuable markets. Possible cartels.	Customers can easily "switch." Continual customer searching for a better deal.
Customers' view	No really considered as the customer has no choice.	Sometimes considered, possible competition between suppliers.	Customer "rules" and drives the market.
Prices	Can charge, "What the market will bear."	Stable and related to costs and desired profits. Possible price fixing.	Demand driven, possible cost plus provision.

Arguable Examples	Oil production, although some alternatives do exist	4 UK Supermarkets control over 60% of consumers spend, but there is some competition	Consumer goods for example, cars, electronics.

Links to Kraljic's bottleneck and leverage items may be especially noted in the monopoly and perfect competition markets.

Supplier's views

Suppliers will have also have a view of their market and this will affect a supplier's positioning towards their customer's buyers, for example:

Suppliers View

Source after: Steele and Court (1996)

So for example, suppliers may be seen as exploiting when they are the sole providers of a buyers bottleneck item. Suppliers may also view some buyers as a nuisance when the buyer is seen to be very demanding and unreasonable.

Clearly then, not every customer is going to be seen by the supplier as being a key account or a "core customer".

In turn, we can see that the supplier's objectives may be as follows:

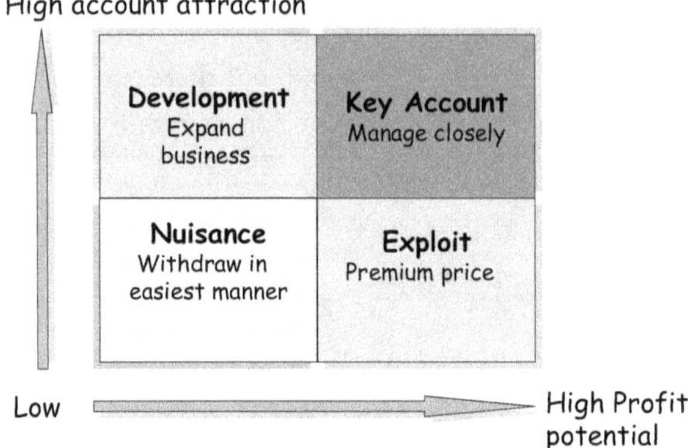

Suppliers' and buyers' views

For effective supplier relationships, then the above four supplier's objectives can be matched to the earlier four Kraljic buyer's objectives. This gives rise to 16 options, so let us start by looking at leverage items and see how this fits with the above suppliers objectives:

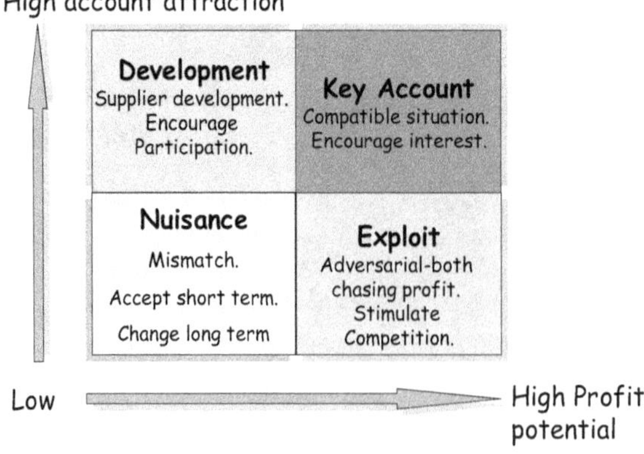

If the supplier sees the buyers leverage items as a key account then this is a very compatible position, as indeed is the supplier's development position.

However, the other two supplier's objectives are not computable, with the buyer's options for supplier management effectively changing, and looking for alternatives.

Suppliers & Routine Items

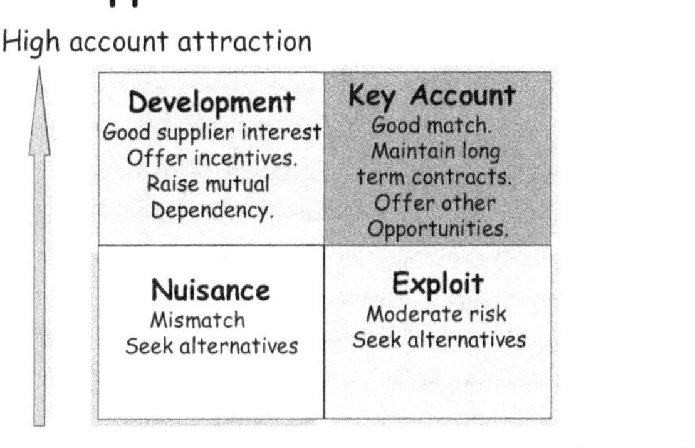

With a buyer's routine items, again the key account and development objectives of suppliers enable a good match for both parties, with the other two options requiring buyers to seek alternatives.

Suppliers & Bottleneck Items

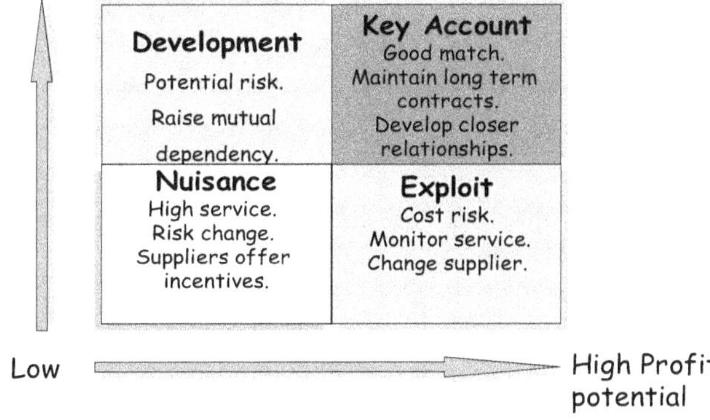

Here the buyers may have to risk making a change on three of supplier's objectives, with only the key account one fitting.

Finally, for the buyer's critical items we can see the following:

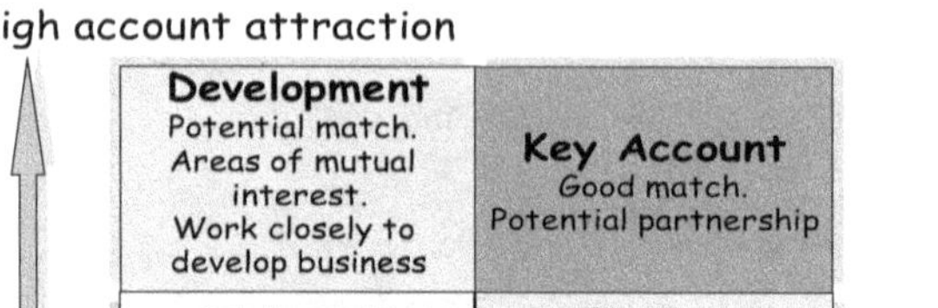

With critical items we find buyers needing to seek competition, with a potential match requiring closer working for the development supplier's objectives, whereas, the key account objective clearly fits.

Getting the best from suppliers

What happens therefore when a buyer is not actually a key account of a supplier? The question from the above analysis shows the following two options:

- **Change the suppliers.** This is clearly a risk for bottleneck items and will involve the subsequent time spent in searching, sourcing and evaluation.
- **Develop the suppliers.** This is fine as long as the supplier also has this as their objective.

Efforts therefore can be appropriately directed, including of course, efforts to find and encourage those suppliers who see the buyer as a key account. However, having suppliers who see buyers as a key account will not automatically happen. Indeed, as the above simple analysis shows, this will only clearly happen in four out of the 16 permutations.

Therefore asking, finding and searching for the true realty of how a supplier views you, is important. This must go beyond asking just say the salesperson, who may be be somewhat biased. Honest conversations between the right people are needed as "whilst the Supply Chain is driven by flows of materials, information and money, it also needs people working together in flow – that special state when people are connected and think together; when we have a positive relationship with no separation; when we have connected our hearts and minds. Only then, can we realise supply chain success." – ***Source: Emmett, SAPICS 2007***

The only way to find out what suppliers think of you is to ask them how happy they are; just we would normally do with customers. The following survey methods may therefore be considered:

1) Face to face/telephone

- Ask open questions = expansive answers
- Tell me = ask directly

2) Questionnaires/hard copy/electronic/web based

- Yes/No/rate on 1-5 point scales
- Rate also against the competition

Questions to ask suppliers:

- How often do we do things right the first time?
- How often do we do things right on time?
- How quickly do we respond to your requests?
- Do we keep commitments we have made?
- Do we pay you on time?
- How accessible are we when you need to contact us?
- How helpful and polite are we?
- How well do we speak your language?
- How hard do you think we work at keeping you a satisfied supplier?
- How much confidence do you have in us?
- Overall, how would you rate how we compare to others you supply?
- How willing would you be to recommend us?

Many buyers will be surprised by responses to such questions. Some buyers are actually staggered when they find out they are not being viewed as core customers. The writers have many times experienced a buyer's surprise when a supplier has told them that they no longer wish to deal with them and that their business is no longer important to the supplier. However as it becomes more important for buyers to be a supplier's customer of choice; the days of endlessly playing one supplier off with another are ending for some buyers; indeed a survey of buyers has reported that:

"72% believe becoming a customer of choice will be important in the future" and continues "As long as procurement demonstrates professional and ethical behaviour then suppliers are more likely to engage with them. Follow this with fair contracts and incentives and you will be top of their list of favourite clients". – ***Source: Supply Management 27 March 2008; Power and control.***

Additionally here, a few aspects about working together better may be helpful:

Some Lessons from Experience on working together better

1. The case for it

"The only way forward is to get players working to a common agenda – the collaboration agenda. We have been taught to compete: nobody has taught us to work together. The need and awareness is there but still nobody has taught us how to do it" – Professor Alan Waller

2. Some things to consider:

"Personal relationships that bridge former gaps in communications between supplier and retailer are what can really spell success".

"It changes the paradigm. It is definitely a different type of relationship with your customer. It's based on mutual trust and it's got to be there to succeed".

"On paper, the process seems simple to implement, but in the real world of personalities and professional relationships, there are many obstacles to climb. Trust is very important for success".

"You have to interested in being criticised"

3. The benefits found:

"Benefits of our Collaboration programme include:

- *Improved service levels.*
- *Faster flow of product through the supply chain.*
- *Rational use of resources and more effective promotion planning.*
- *Synchronisation of production to better match supply with demand.*
- *Shared responsibility and mutual trust"* – ***Source: FMCG Retailer and Supplier***

"A real focus on joint and collaborative planning has been critical. It's all very well putting in great capability and structurally changing our supply chain but at the end of the day you can't make it happen unless you work together." – ***Source: Logistics Manager June 2004***

"Key suppliers work collaboratively, ensuring efficient processing and best practices, driving our competitive edge" – ***Source: IBE Report 2006***

Behaviour

The above supplier relationship approaches will very likely require a behavioural change; indeed as already noted in this book, some observers readily note that better supplier relationships is all about 70-80% behavioural change and only 20-30% on process change. Additionally, in January 2007, a procurement manager, when asked for his predictions for 5 years forward, said that then his job title would be 'relationship manager.'

There may be much to do here, especially when comments like the following are reported:

"The Mail of Sunday alleges the Retailer was asking 700 of its suppliers for a contribution from their contracts and the company was to lengthen its payments terms from 60 to 90 days"

(Supply Management 18 January 2007)

` *"The Company is locked in a bitter dispute battle with its suppliers over attempts to extract cost savings from its supply chain…One supplier claimed the company were arrogantly out of touch"*

(Sunday Times 11 February 2007)

In both of these reports, it would seem the buying organisations have suppliers of leverage items as they are displaying buyer power, interpreted by one supplier, as arrogance.

Another description of behaviour, between buyers and suppliers, is revealed by the following examples of sales and buyers evaluating each other.

What a supplier needs from buyers can be seen by the traits of a good buyer as seen by salespeople. These are as follows:

- Does not act aloof towards the seller
- Does not try to get a lower price to be used as leverage against the existing current supplier
- Assists in contacting appropriate people in their company when they find they lack knowledge or authority. They also explain the buying process in their company
- Allows adequate time for a presentation
- Has a working knowledge of their company's products
- Maintains good credit standing and pays invoices promptly
- Have good relations with their company's top management
- Follows ethical procurement practices

From this, it would that a poor buyer is one who is aloof and arrogant, is secretive about internal contacts, hurries presentations, has poor knowledge of their company, and does not pay promptly.

A good supplier can be seen by the traits of a good salesperson from the buyer's perspective, as follows:

- Offers a thorough presentation and a good follow through
- Has a good working knowledge of their product line
- Is willing to go "into bat" for the buyer within the suppliers company
- Shows knowledge of the market and a willingness to keep the buyer informed
- Has a good working knowledge of the buyer's product lines
- Uses imagination in applying their products to the buyer's needs
- Uses diplomacy in dealing with operating departments
- Follows ethical sales procurement practices
- Prepares well

From this, it would appear that a poor supplier is:

- one who is not thorough or prepared well
- has poor knowledge of their own company
- will not look after buyers interests in their own company
- has poor knowledge of the market and the buyer products
- is not diplomatic when dealing with other departments in the buyers' organization and uses unethical sales techniques.

Using the above lists to measure or view the actual behaviours can be revealing. This will indicate what actually does take place and perhaps lead us to conclude that the following style of negotiations and discussions are preferable:

- Participants have a problem solving approach, where wise outcomes are reached amicably and efficiently
- Separation of the people from the problem, by being soft on the people but hard on the problem
- Exploring and focusing on interests and not on positions
- Avoiding having a bottom line
- Developing options for mutual gain
- Insisting as far as possible on objective criteria
- Listening and being open to reasons
- Yielding to principles and not to pressure

Behaviour displayed during meeting, discussions and negotiations, will most definitely, affect all of the parties involved. Consider the following comparison on negotiation behaviour styles.

Adversary negotiation style	**Collaborative negotiation style**
Compliant supplier	Partner supplier
Supplier is unsure of the buyers or customers/users real needs	Work together to agree needs and the means to satisfy them
Supplier maybe closed and hostile	Supplier is open and friendly
Cold contractual issues are discussed	Warm and "how to improve" issues are discussed
Each side tries to minimise risks for themselves	Risks and prevention measures are explored
Each side tries to pass risks onto the other	Sharing of risks is allocated by agreement
Each side tries to score off the other	Each side tries to find benefits
No risk taking, growth or development	Innovation and assured quality with expansion and growth

The inevitable win-lose adversary style will however be often defended as being appropriate, as this prevents the other side from attacking them first (what was called by the British Lions Rugby team in the 1970s, as getting your retaliation in first). We seem also to be back here to Professor Alan Waller's view, that suggests we have been taught to compete and not to cooperate.

It seems paradoxical that people consciously reflect their own concerns and do not anticipate their behaviour pattern will be shown back to them; this may be done covertly or be remembered until some future "payback time".

The reality can also be therefore, that whilst people will recognise that trust is needed between suppliers and buyers/customers, they will actually exhibit a lack of trust. Well known expressions again say that; what you see is what you get (WYSIWYG) and that people believe what you, actually, say or do, and not what you say you *want* to do.

Behaviour patterns also occur outside of negotiations and are displayed in normal communications; behaviour therefore continues beyond negotiations and a specific pattern usually emerges; often this maybe framed by the E-Procurement strategy and/ or by the individual personalities of influential people. This behaviour will therefore influence the responses received from suppliers.

Such responses from supplier's can also affect the prices quoted to buyers; please consider the following:

Exercise: Supplier Pricing

Imagine you are a supplier; not a buyer and that your company has a good reputation for supplying high-end specialist IT services to a specific market sector. You have a history of supplying the two major customers in this market sector. Currently you are not supplying either of them. They are both large and important and look good on your customer list. They provide you with a good springboard for more business with other customers in the same market.

Almost at the same time, they both ask you to quote for a new project with the same specification for each one. At present, you do not have the capacity to supply them both. Your average quote-to-sale conversion rate is typically one in three. So you decide, on this occasion, to quote for both jobs and pull out of one if the other gives you the go-ahead. This is not an unreasonable strategy since, with a conversion rate of one in three, you might not get either of the projects, and there is only a one in nine chance that both will say yes.

Customer A

- Likeable people who are enjoyable to work with
- Prompt payers
- Give clear specifications
- Demanding
- Set very high standards
- They regularly visit to check what you are doing
- They understand your problems and often sit down with you to help sort them out
- They demand fast service, sometimes quicker than you can provide
- They are open to explanation if you have genuine reasons for failing to meet their deadlines
- In short, they are your preferred customer; a joy to work with.

Customer B

- Some likeable individuals with whom you get on well

- They are poor payers - sometimes invoices are 'lost', and occasionally they have taken 90 days to pay up
- Different departments contact you separately, often with different messages
- No one function seems to be in overall control
- They keep changing the specifications
- On the last contract you thought you had provided exactly what was required, but they weren't happy and forced you to make changes free of charge
- They are unhelpful, do not like answering questions and rarely return calls.

The Project
- Cost of £400,000 in time and materials
- You normally add 10% contingency to cover unforeseen charges, taking the cost to £440,000
- Then you usually add a 10% profit margin, taking the cost to £484,000
- Finally, on goes a bit more to allow for negotiation after the quote has gone in. The size of that 'bit more' is up to you.

Task
- As the supplier, decide what you are actually going to quote to customer A and customer B to win the business.
- Think about it carefully as the way you think, and the decisions you make, will be very instructive.

Source: after Will Parsons. www.qualitair.co.uk

In considering this exercise "live", then inevitably the lower price goes to customer A, the one who is "tough but fair". Meanwhile, customer B gets the higher price as they show poor behaviour, is a poor payer, sometimes losing invoices, occasionally takes 90 days to pay up, has different departments/different messages, keeps changing specifications etc.

The facts are clear: buyers/customers who treat suppliers poorly, will pay a price. Regrettably, many buyers do not realise this and remain with their own perception; one that lacks empathy.

Behaviour and power on leverage items – a special word

What also surprises some buyers is that this single-sided view can also happen with leverage items (buyer power). Here poor buyer behaviour will also affect suppliers and may negatively affect the buyer.

Suppliers do have the choice to refuse orders for commodity leverage based work from some customers, for example those like customer B above who pay poorly, delay payments, change specifications and requirements at short notice, do not provide updates on changes etc.

However, such customers are often then upset when such shortcomings are pointed out to them. They may then rationalise the comments as "you are the only one", "take it or leave it" and "no one else has a problem" etc.

The reality however is that the buyer's behaviour does more than likely actually cause these others to have a problem, but these others have chosen to "keep their heads down". In so doing, they have therefore blocked any chances of open communication and continuous improvement between what could be, cooperating players who are aiming for their own versions of "win/win".

The view however here from buyers, with leverage items, is there is always someone who can do it cheaper and that perhaps, doing things better is maybe not needed, or at worst, is not even considered.

From the supplier's perspective, "putting their head about the wall", when they are viewed as a leverage item, may be seen as a risky strategy for them to use. When the supplier has the customer as a core or key account, then maybe they see it is best to keep their head down and practice a negative form of compliance. However they then effectively camouflage any chances for improvement in their customer's organisation; effectively a "win/lose" that is not apparent to the customer!

Conversely, where suppliers of leverage items have just the one customer, or where a customer accounts for a significant part of their turnover, some forward-looking buyers do realistically appreciate this can be dangerous for both parties. It can lead to having suppliers who are submissively compliant and display non-challenging, negative and passive behaviour.

In this regard, Miles Davis, jazz man extraordinaire, once noted that he preferred to play with musicians who challenged him, as he got something extra from them that changed and improved what he did.

Challenging is important for change and improvement, please see the following checklist:

Checklist: Change and Challenging

This involves conflict and compliance; however, these words can be easily misunderstood. To give clarity, we have explained the positive and negative sides of both conflict and compliance.

Positive conflict

This is constructive as it enables new learning through an open disagreement and discussion on ideas between people. The outcome is either a full agreement about the others position (there has been a "We" view and a "walking in each others shoes"); or finding a new "third" position, this is through taking an emotional detachment and an objective "helicopter view". All those involved believe they have gained something from the conflict process.

Negative conflict

This is destructive as it inhibits new learning through creating personal tensions among people. The outcome is on "one" position only; "I", which sees this "own" view only. The position taken is essentially founded on an emotional subjective response. Those involved are usually divided, as whilst one may feel they have gained, the other feels they have lost something.

Positive compliance

This open challenging encourages positive conflicts and recognises these are needed for effective learning and changing. People are actively involved in shaping the outcome from a mutual awareness and understanding of the differences. They can change their position in the process.

Negative compliance

This encourages blind or forced agreement, which hinders effective learning and changing. It is effectively closed challenging as it discourages any open challenge and positive conflict on any differences from the "status quo". One party remains uninvolved and keeps quiet with "unspoken disagreement". This gives a "false" agreement, which can encourage mistakes to be repeated, and little change brought to the "status quo". People will internally remain with their own position, even thought this will not be externally expressed in their "false" agreement.

Meanwhile those organisations that choose to ignore supplier-suggested improvements and therefore refuse to consider change, may then find they continually have a fast rate of "supplier churn" (which may be costly to them), but it will also likely lead to stagnation in the medium term and therefore bring them a very visible "lose".

Those however, who choose to listen and discuss, will gain and "win".

A parallel here can be drawn about managing and handling one's own employees where two questions can be asked of the behaviour used in these circumstances:

1. "Is the 'stick' or the 'carrot' used when we manage our people?"
2. "Which of these, over time, gives us the best results?"

For the writers the answers to these two questions are so clear that this leads us to ask, 'why should our behaviour with suppliers be any different?' so that we can then get the best from suppliers. Why some buyers ignore such simplicity is frankly, most amazing.

Many organisations must therefore remember that they are only as good as their suppliers. Additionally, in times of increasing outsourcing, supplier relations become "mission critical". After all, what comes in to an organisation does eventually create what goes out; the "rubbish-in/rubbish-out" scenario. This means therefore that relationships with suppliers need managing effectively, if they are not, the very business itself may be at risk.

Behavioural understanding and meeting needs

It is increasingly the view of many observers that behavioural understanding is going to be increasingly important in procurement. For example, "the [London Heathrow] T5 contract took technical competence for granted and focussed as much on the behavioural competence of both organisations and people". – *Source: Riley, 'Flying in Formation', Supply Management, 13 March 2008.*

Building trust, respect and integrity is vital for a sustainable deal, but knowing how to achieve this, without being seen as weak, and without being exploited, is not always going to be easy or straight forward. Monitoring relationships and the ensuing performance is therefore critical, as shown in the following case study:

Case study: Philips

Philips is a global operator in the electronics market with factories all over the world. In order to compete and to ensure customer satisfaction, Philips has to manage its quality and procurement strategy very carefully. The company recognises that customer satisfaction depends on the quality of what happens on the production line, which in turn depends on the performance of suppliers. If any of the links in the chain break down or fail to meet the required standard, then all the glossy advertising in the world is not going to make up for the customer's disappointment in a product that is unavailable, or does not work properly, or fails to meet their technical expectations.

Total quality, therefore, is an ingrained philosophy throughout Philips' operations, resulting in better products and better processes. 'Philips Quality' has five simple, but important principles:

(a) Strive for excellence
(b) Customer first
(c) Demonstrate leadership
(d) Value people
(e) Supplier partnership

Directly or indirectly, many of these principles could not be properly implemented without good relationships with the right suppliers. Philips cultivates supplier relationships based on trust and co-operation, sharing experience and expertise to benefit not only the buyer and the supplier, but also the end customer. Together, Philips and its suppliers develop technology, solve problems, learn from experience and try to avoid errors and misunderstandings.

Clearly, Philips cannot develop and maintain deep relationships with every one of its suppliers. Instead, it assesses its suppliers to discover which ones are the most important in terms of their strategic significance to Philips' business. These receive the most attention and investment in relationship building. Philips has three categories of supplier:

1. Supplier-partners: this might be the smallest group, but these are the most important suppliers and Philips builds intense, involved relationships with them. An important focus of the co-operation is innovation, the development of new expertise and new opportunities. These suppliers might well have essential knowledge and/or expertise that Philips could not otherwise access or develop for itself. This makes these suppliers extremely significant strategically as their loss could seriously undermine Philips' current business and future direction.

2. Preferred suppliers: these suppliers are less important, but there is still good reason for Philips to work closely with them on issues such as quality, logistics and price to gain mutual benefit. The supplier does adapt itself to suit Philips' requirements, to some extent, but there is not the same mutual dependence as in the first category.

3. Commercial suppliers: these are the least important suppliers and although Philips will encourage better performance in terms of quality etc, it is unlikely to get involved in helping the supplier to achieve it.

Philips also emphasises the importance of supplier evaluation as a basis for improving future performance. A supplier's actual performance is measured against mutually agreed targets in terms of quality, logistics, costs and responsiveness.

Behavioural and cultural understanding must also include mutual understanding and empathy, which leads to a level of satisfaction existing between suppliers and customers. As the following diagram shows, there can be varied positions found in the satisfaction of needs between suppliers and customers.

Position	Suppliers perception	Customers perception	Action needed
Success	Satisfied	Satisfied	Build/develop on these strengths and look for new ventures together
Satisfaction/ Dissatisfaction	Satisfied	Dissatisfied	Discuss issues and determine corrective actions needed
Dissatisfaction/ Satisfaction	Dissatisfied	Satisfied	Discuss issues and determine corrective actions needed
Separate	Dissatisfied	Dissatisfied	Negotiate out of any deal, part and say goodbye.

Where dissatisfaction occurs, poor communication is often a result, mainly because understanding the other party's supply chains and organisation is likely to be missing.

Communication must therefore be regularly "health checked" and examined – the following questions may be considered:

- Are there any agreed clear milestones/review points?
- After every meeting/communication, did we agree the time/place for the next one?
- Do we record by email but use also the phone (as this gives intimacy/personal communication)?
- Do we have regular face-to-face meetings?
- Do we separate the person from the problem?
- If we clash, is this on ideas and not on personalities?
- Do we work on interests not positions where we try to satisfy the underlying need and not the stated position?
- Do we generate a range of options and work towards a shared search and evaluation of solutions that uses measurable objective criteria?

Poor communications will systematically always lead to poor results. Indeed, communication must itself be a budget item and needs to be costed with an appropriate time allocated. The cost can be calculated on a simple basis related to either the contract time (for example, at a ratio of 1 day to 10 days) or by spend (e.g. at 10% of spend).

The main point here is that the effective management of suppliers, costs, and communication must be budgeted for and whilst there is a cost associated with doing this, there are certainly higher costs if it not done. For example, a comparison before the successful construction of London Heathrow Terminal 5, found that the average out-turn contract performance for similar projects was an overrun of 40% on time and between 15-23% on spend. These enormous unanticipated costs can be avoided by taking appropriate steps.

At the beginning of this part of the book, we noted that the buyer's ability to influence a supplier to do something is largely dependent on the buyer's perception of the supplier's willingness to meet the buyer's need. The opposite, however is also true, where a buyer's ability to influence a supplier is also dependent on the supplier's perception of the buyer's willingness to help the supplier met their needs.

Finding ways to ensure both parties' needs are satisfied is therefore necessary, for, as we have seen, this will influence the behaviour patterns between buyers and suppliers.

Supplier Development

One option used on the supplier side to obtain benefits is the formally labelled process of supplier development where the wide range of supplier development activities involve varying degrees of procurement input and resource.

Definitions

There are many versions of definitions for supplier development, but as you can see below, they all contain the similar means to achieve the same objective.

"Supplier development is the process of working with certain suppliers on a one to one basis to improve their performance for the benefit of the buying organisation."

"Supplier development is supporting the supplier in enhancing the performance of their products and services or improving the supplier's capabilities."

"Supplier development is a long term cooperative effort between a buying organisation and its suppliers to upgrade the suppliers' technical, quality, delivery and cost capabilities and to foster ongoing improvements."

For the purposes on this book, Supplier Development will be defined as:
"Any effort of a buying organisation towards a supplier that will increase the supplier's performance and/or capabilities, to meet short and/or long-term needs of the buyer."

Reasons for Supplier Development

There are very good and sound reasons for embarking on a supplier development process and these are as follows:

- Improving supplier performance
- Reducing costs
- Resolving serious quality issues
- Developing new routes to supply
- Improving business alignment between the supplier and the buying organisation
- Developing a product or service not currently available in the marketplace
- Generating competition for a high price product or service dominating the marketplace

Supplier development should therefore lead to improvements in the total added value from the supplier, in terms of:

- Product or services offered
- Business processes and performance
- Improvements in lead times and delivery

Approaches

There is no single approach to supplier development. Procurement professionals must select the most appropriate approach to suit their relationship with the supplier that they have selected for development. There are therefore different types of, and approaches to, supplier development, and these are appropriate for different supply markets.

Supplier development involves embracing supplier expertise and aligning it to the buying organisation's business need, and, where appropriate, vice versa. The objectives for development can be relatively minor, such a slight adjustments in staffing levels, or very substantial such as the appraisal and re-launch of an entire range of critical products.

A supplier development project might involve developing a supplier's business such as helping the supplier to evaluate and redesign their corporate strategy. The purpose of this might be to align the supplier very closely and on a long-term basis with the buying organisation in a strategic alliance or joint venture. A case study will provide an example of this:

Case Study: BAE Systems

A development for BAE Systems when building navy submarines is their Performance Partnering Arrangement (PPA). This has improved deals with major suppliers by providing more certainty for longer-term contracts and a gain share/ pain share deal.

Pre-PPA supplier relationships were more adversarial. The problem was that suppliers were competing for contracts on the basis they would work, for instance, on one project but maybe not on the next. Inevitably, this pushed up costs. It took time to convince the suppliers that BAE would use their equipment on future boat building work.

For the suppliers working under PPA, the situation changed as BAE commit to a supplier for the duration of the class of boat this is being built. As long as they hit quality, cost delivery and technical innovation targets, mutual gains are shared.

The transformation in supplier relations came about suddenly and urgently. Previously, contracts with suppliers had been completed five or six years earlier and their focus had been on delivery. After speaking to suppliers, they identified three market trends:

- That some manufacturers were going out of business
- Others were leaving the market
- Costs were increasing

To find out what was causing these things, they devised a questionnaire for existing suppliers. The results were alarming and revealed BAE was not the customer of choice it believed it was. The research concluded that unless the submarines business was attractive, then:

- a significant number of critical suppliers would not have any incentive to continue production of key equipment
- a lack of continuity of work would give rise to skills retention issues and a loss of capability
- a significant number of critical suppliers were at the risk of business failure

The answers revealed 64% of suppliers gave BAE cause for concern and there was a risk that the next boat would be unaffordable. Because of closer collaboration, boats now cost less. BAE also were able to take out 30% of the material prices. A change was the introduction of supplier forums, where the top 10 suppliers cover 70% of spend. These forums are held every eight weeks and enable regular communications with suppliers. The consensus among the buying team is that these meetings are successful because they instil trust.

Whatever the form of supplier development, the process may be a highly resource intensive exercise and involve for example, a steering group and various action teams, each with action plans for allocated projects and formal reporting procedures against time scales. Both organisations must share a mutual understanding, appreciation and desire to achieve the objectives of the supplier development project.

Such a project would involve change and require a visible commitment from both parties' top management teams with identifiable sponsors and champions of change. It is critical to involve people with vision, imagination and commitment; to keep these involved and to ensure the project is not damaged by a change in personnel.

It is also important to ensure that there is a smooth decision making process and that, where appropriate, those involved in the supplier development project from both organisations are empowered to make decisions. Another approach to supplier development is "Reverse Marketing". One example of which is where a buying organisation encourages a supplier(s) to enter a new market. This might, for instance, involve the supplier developing its operation or introducing a new range of products.

Selection of suppliers

The selection of suppliers for development should be dependent on the procurement strategy related to the:

- Scale of value/improvement opportunity
- Cost, complexity and duration of value attainment
- Supplier co-operation

Supplier development is normally undertaken with existing suppliers that can be and agree to being, improved. The supplier's performance against agreed criteria must be measured in order to identify the scope for development at the outset and, once the development process has started, to monitor and manage improvements.

As supplier development can be a resource intensive process, it should be undertaken only with selected suppliers. It should only be undertaken with those suppliers from which real business benefit can be derived. Therefore, supplier development can be a one off project as well as on going activity that may take some years to come to fruition. Additionally, supplier development is a two-way process and should be thought of as a joint buyer/supplier development activity.

Incentives need to be given to suppliers to encourage their commitment to supplier development, such as, a reward of shared benefits, or "preferred supplier" status. In many cases, the development of the supplier will be of benefit to the supplier's other customers, some of which may be the buying organisation's competition. This in itself may be an incentive for the supplier to participate in a supplier development project, i.e. they can improve relationships with all their customers consequently.

Activities

The main purpose of close, long-term relationships with suppliers is the achievement of high quality products and services that satisfy customer needs. Often, suppliers lack the abilities and competencies required to deal with the different or special standards that are now required by their buyers, therefore, supplier development is necessary. This may vary widely and can include:

- Raising performance expectations
- Education and training on quality requirements and know-how for supplier personnel

- Recognition of supplier's achievements and performance in the form of rewards
- Placement of engineering and other buyer personnel at the supplier's premises
- Direct capital investment by the buying organisation in the supplier.

We shall explore this range of activities in the following sections.

Supplier Development Categories

The following diagram summarises some key categories of supplier development:

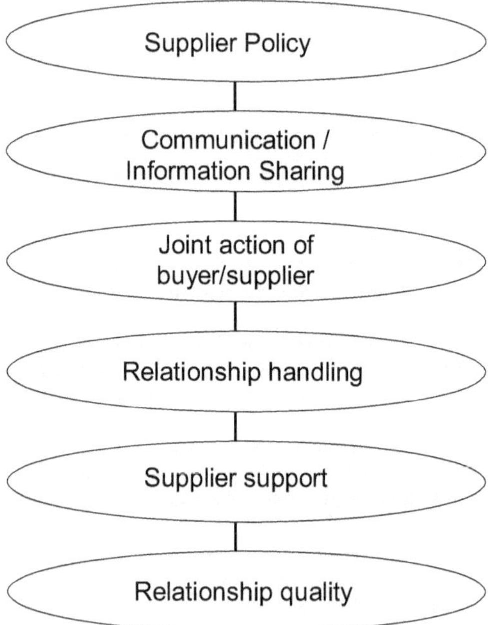

Questions can be posed in each of the above categories to form a useful survey/audit of existing supplier development activities, as follows:

Supplier Policy
• Buy – make decision
• Establishment of long term relationships (over 5 years) with suppliers
• Supply base reduction during the last 10 years
• Supplier's performance formal evaluation
• Benchmarking of other suppliers

Information sharing/Communication

- Frequent and informal exchange of information
- Communication includes many inter organisation contacts
- Electronic data change
- Supplier's knowledge of his products specifications
- Supplier's knowledge of his product use in buyer's final product
- Timely feedback of supplier's mistakes
- Feedback of supplier's evaluation
- Timely planning and communication of purchase programme
- Supplier certification programme

Joint action of supplier/buyer

- Joint quality planning (e.g. product specifications, quality requirements
- Joint production planning (e.g. JIT system)
- Supplier involvement in product development process
- Joint workgroups
- Held meetings on a regular basis to solve problems
- Conflict resolution techniques

Relationship handling issues

- Systematic contact with supplier to know what is going on
- Use of formal contract
- Clear delegation of responsibilities
- Feedback from supplier regarding complaints and suggestions
- Acceptance and implementation of supplier improvement suggestions

Supplier support

- Placement of buyer personnel and facilities at supplier's premises
- Advice and suggestions to supplier according to quality results
- Recognition of supplier's performance in the form of rewards
- Training/education of supplier in quality requirements, know-how

Relationship quality
• The relationship is considered as a partnership • Priority is given to quality • Mutual trust between buyer and supplier • Mutual awareness of other party's needs • Goal congruence between supplier and buyer

Partner approach

As a company's needs, supplier goals and objectives change constantly, it is unlikely that the capabilities of a supply base and the requirements of a client organisation will naturally align for any prolonged period of time. Supplier development aims to create and sustain alignment between an organisation and a supplier for the benefit of both parties.

However, effort should be focused on those key categories of spend that are most likely to deliver significant additional value to the business, as developing current or potential suppliers can be resource intensive. Using portfolio analysis to segment spend, it is relatively straightforward to determine the most appropriate categories and therefore, which suppliers to engage in a supplier development programme.

At this stage, two further factors should also be considered:

- The expected benefits from supplier development for the buyer and the supplier's ability to develop and change
- The cost of development for both the buyer and the supplier to ensure that there is an acceptable return on investment for both of them

Buyers will need to protect themselves from any supplier power on bottleneck items, and long-term relationships built up through supplier development programmes may be a way of achieving this. This is because the expenditure is large enough to encourage supplier participation and the category's supply market is difficult to buy in, so the relationship tends to be seen as long rather than short term.

Generally, supplier development is used where there are tangible value benefits to be gained over using other suppliers in the long term, potential supply vulnerability or where suppliers are believed to have the power.

The objectives of any programme will be based largely upon the gap identified between existing supplier performance and the standard required now and in the future. The style of development can be coach, mentor or challenger, depending on the balance of expertise that exists between the buyer and the supplier.

Progression in relationships

When there is a clear commitment to supplier development, this means it is likely the relationship between buyer and supplier will then make progress up a relationship spectrum; for example, from being competitive leverage or preferred supplier, to becoming a performance partner or even strategic alliance partner. This relationship progression being illustrated below:

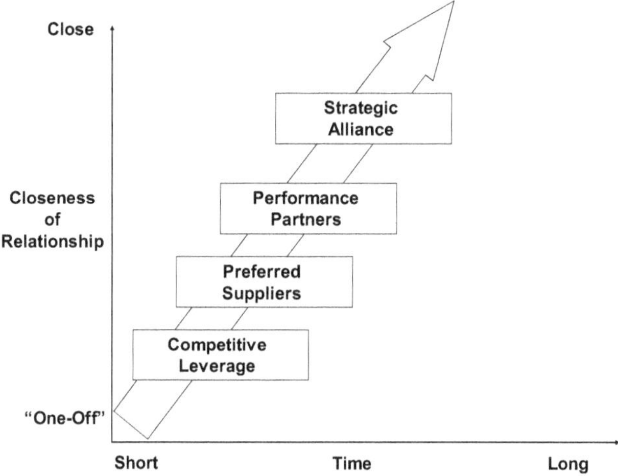

However, this progression should not occur by default. A well-structured supplier development programme should link the achievement of specific performance deliverables to discrete "steps" in this relationship progression, where suppliers receive benefits for delivering on their commitment to change and develop.

A structured approach that could help to achieve such a progression could contain the following drivers:

Checklist: Creating success in relationship progression

1) Define and develop a strategy to meet the business and end customer needs.

2) Secure agreement between both parties on how the supplier can help achieve these needs.

3) Establish clear measures to gauge the supplier performance.

4) Ensure regular, detailed and action focused feedback to the supplier.

5) Agree on the supplier's current performance gap and expected performance requirements.

6) Obtain acceptance and commitment from the supplier's senior management.

7) Develop and agree a time plan with the supplier to close the performance gap.

8) Get commitment on the part of the buyer to transfer knowledge and potentially best practice to the supplier.

9) Get commitment to invest significant procurement resource in the programme.

10) Establish a multifunctional customer team that will a) adhere to a common sourcing strategy and b) share knowledge.

Some suppliers may retain fundamental objections to the more open methods of the relationship philosophy and prefer not to change their ways, or are unable to. Meanwhile a number of different offerings can add value to the relationships, and could help to compensate for any price increases or offset them. Examples here include the following:

- Joint focus on identifying and solving the shared problem together
- Incentivised performance and shared risk and reward
- Product innovation, assistance with research and development, or even out sourcing responsibility for development
- Scheduling delivery in order to support product availability
- Consignment stock or simplified ordering and invoice processes
- Packaging waste reclamation, reduction or both
- Improvements and developments in product yield
- Higher quality levels

There are many ways to increase the value that suppliers can deliver. These will now be explained in the following sections.

Supplier Development Practices

Buying organisations faced with problems of deficient supplier performance, can implement a wide range of supplier development practices such as, supplier evaluation and feedback, supplier recognition and supplier training. These will work towards upgrading the performance and/or capabilities of the weakest links in the supply chain.

Such activities require different levels of involvement by the buying organisation and are characterised by different levels of implementation complexity. Therefore, it could be useful to characterise supplier development activities according to their level of involvement and implementation complexity (i.e. skill, time and resources required to execute successfully a particular activity).

As supplier development broadly involves any effort by a buying organisation to improve a supplier's performance to meet the buying organisation's short and/or long-term supply needs, then buyers can make use of a wide range of supplier development practices to improve a supplier's performance and/or capabilities, as shown in the following checklist:

Checklist: Supplier development practices
- The predominance of quality over cost in selecting suppliers
- Buying from a limited number of suppliers per purchased item
- Sourcing from a few dependable suppliers,
- Providing education and/or technical assistance to suppliers,
- Long term contracts with suppliers
- Clarity of specifications provided by the buyer Supplier performance evaluation and feedback
- Parts standardisation
- Supplier certification
- Supplier reward and recognition
- Plant visits to suppliers
- Training to suppliers
- Intensive information exchange with suppliers (i.e. sharing of accounting and financial data by the supplier and sharing of internal information such as costs, quality levels, by the supplier)
- Collaborating with suppliers in materials improvement and development of new materials
- Involvement of suppliers in the buyer's new product development process

There are three other supplier development practices to be considered: direct involvement, incentives and enforced competition.

Direct involvement includes such practices as formal evaluation of the suppliers, supplier certification, site visits, supplier recognition, feedback to suppliers, training, information evaluation of suppliers, inviting supplier's personnel to the organisation's facilities, and verbal or written requests to improve performance.

The incentives factor includes the promise of current and future benefits to the supplier if performance was improved and enforced competition includes using two or three suppliers per purchased item.

Since the availability of resources is always a constraint for organisations, there are different levels of supplier development practices, characterised by their degree of company involvement and amount of resources required.

Supplier development phases

The supplier development practices shown in the above Checklist can be grouped further into three sets of practices according to the level of organisation involvement and implementation complexity (i.e. skill, time and resources required to executive successfully a particular activity). These three sets are shown in the following checklist:

Checklist: Reactive, Proactive and Strategic Supplier Development Phases

Reactive Supplier Development
- Reporting of supplier evaluation results to suppliers
- Sourcing from a limited number of suppliers
- Parts standardisation
- Supplier qualification process

Proactive Supplier Development
- Plant visits to suppliers
- Supplier reward and recognition
- Collaboration with suppliers in materials improvement
- Supplier certification (ISO 9000)

Strategic Supplier Development
- Training to suppliers
- Supplier involvement in the buyer's product design process
- Sharing of cost and quality information by the supplier
- Sharing of accounting information by the supplier
- Supplier Co-ordination

We will now look closer at the reactive, proactive and strategic development phases.

The Reactive Supplier Development phase

The Reactive Supplier Development phase relates to those supplier development practices that require the most limited organisation involvement and minimum investment of the company's resources (i.e. personnel, time and capital) and thus, are likely to be implemented first in an effort to improve supplier performance and/or capabilities.

These supplier development practices include evaluating supplier performance, providing feedback about the results of its evaluation and sourcing from a limited number of suppliers. Parts standardisation complements sourcing from a limited number of suppliers by increasing the volume orders with specific suppliers.

Supplier qualification is generally considered a more informal and less stringent programme than supplier certification; consequently, it was included as a basic supplier development practice. Therefore, the Reactive Supplier Development phase included measures of evaluating supplier performance and providing feedback to suppliers, sourcing from a limited number of suppliers per purchased item, parts standardisation, and supplier qualification.

Although improvements can be made, it has been found that superior levels of service and response can be achieved by investing more time and effort in the following phases.

Supplier Rationalisation: A process of elimination
Supplier rationalisation is the process that organisations use to identify the optimum number of suppliers needed to fulfil their business goals. The result can either be an increase or decrease in the number of supplier used, depending on the nature of existing supplier relationships and market conditions in which they operate.

The first stage of the rationalisation process is a detailed analysis of how much is spent which each supplier. Organisations can bundle goods together to create an attractive package of potential bidders. In addition, introducing online catalogues, where end users ensure business compliance with the supplier, reduces the risk of maverick buying, which leads to fewer suppliers on the database.

However, when using supplier rationalisation, organisations should take the following three factors into consideration:
- Contractual obligation
- Location
- Specification

First, many organisations are not fully aware of their contractual obligations and may not know that they are locked into contracts and unable to delete suppliers from their lists.

Second, in terms of location, many suppliers maintain they can offer countrywide service and support, even though the reality can be quite different. Where speed of response is a crucial business requirement, the premature elimination of a supplier before another can be validated may prove a costly mistake. Therefore, an investigation of the supply market is essential.

Lastly, the specification of a product or service is a key facet of what determines high or low market difficulty on the portfolio matrix. The onus should therefore be on the owner of the specification to create a brief that can be fulfilled by a number of suppliers to create competition. The impact of specifications written in favour of one solution or supplier will reduce the opportunities to change them easily.

Rationalisation Process

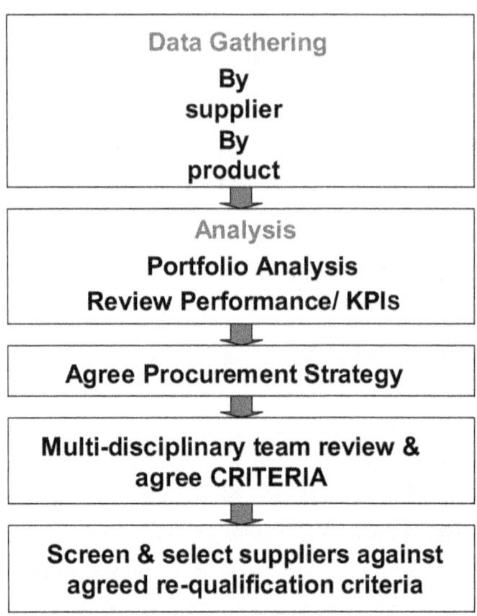

Source: Roberts, G (2003)

Case Study: Laing O'Rourke cuts supply base

Construction organisation Laing O'Rourke cut its suppliers from 2,000 to less than 500.

It saw the move will improve relations with a smaller group of suppliers so it can drive competitiveness and improve standards of service. It also wants to target environmental issues in its supply base and reduce waste.

The organisation will give suppliers the opportunity to get involved with projects at an early stage. It hopes they will influence design and the choice of materials and demonstrate their capabilities directly to the company's clients.

The construction industry is starting to realise the benefits of tighter management of the supply base, but explained selection is important. "We need to be consistent. We need to ensure the suppliers we select are the best fit for our ongoing business requirements. Though this we will have a greater opportunity to manage the supply base to ensure we have competitive supply conditions, greater certainty of project timing and excellent health and safety."

Supplier base reduction: Research

More than three quarters of buyers are looking to use fewer suppliers, according to a "Supplier Management" poll. In a survey of 100 buyers, 77% said they were looking to make cuts to their supplier list.

Buyers considering reductions said consolidation would make the supply base more manageable and cost effective.

Supplier reduction is a legitimate activity enabling aggregation and optimisation, leading to cost reduction.

The benefits of having fewer suppliers are:

- Less administration time
- Less logistics time
- Smaller carbon footprint
- Less reactive buying

Becoming a bigger fish in a few suppliers' ponds rather than a small fish in a large organisation's ocean.

To rationalise, procurement must have a good understanding of what each of their suppliers provide. The challenge in supplier rationalisation is not so much in reducing the suppliers, but in developing the category management strategy so that you are clear on what kind of suppliers you want to be left with.

The Proactive Supplier Development phase

This phase refers to supplier development practices characterised by increased yet still moderate levels of buyer involvement and implementation complexity, therefore requiring comparatively more company resources (personnel, time and capital) than the Reactive Supplier Development phase.

The supplier development activities considered in this phase have moderate levels of involvement and implementation complexity including visiting suppliers' plants to assess their processes, reward and recognition of supplier's achievements in quality improvement and supplier certification.

We refer to Supplier Certification (see below for further amplification) as suppliers having ISO 9000 registration, a practice accepted by some organisations. The collaboration with suppliers in the improvement and development of new materials and components is another practice involved in this phase.

This practice contrasts with the involvement of the supplier in the buyer's new product design process that requires a higher level of involvement and implementation complexity and therefore is considered in the Strategic Supplier Development phase below. Hence, the Proactive Supplier Development phase include measures of visiting suppliers to assess their facilities, rewarding and recognising supplier's performance improvements, collaborating with suppliers in materials improvement and certification of suppliers through ISO 9000.

Supplier Certifications

Supplier Certification is a comprehensive process designed to ensure that a supplier's products or services are planned, procured, processed, prepared, packaged, documented and delivered under controlled conditions to meet or exceed an agreed set of requirements. The result of a successful Certification programme will be consistent quality with reliable on time deliveries from the supplier.

The goals of Supplier Certification in the purchase of goods and services can be stated as follows:

- To maintain consistent quality in conformance with specification
- To improve quality over time
- To control processes rather than identify defects
- To control the cost of quality
- To support and optimise customers operations, for example assembly/ productions
- To improve communications between supplier and customer
- To minimise lead times (both external and internal)
- To remove inventory from the supply chain

Supplier Certification Process

Preliminary Stage
Establish objectives

Stage 1 – Supplier Selection

Stage 2 – Preparation for the Certification Audit
Review quality performance gaps

Stage 3 – Conducting the Certification Audit
Technical/Commercial/Quality Management/Managerial

Stage 4 – Review of Audit Findings & Corrective Action

Stage 5 – Certification complete with ongoing programme for improvement

Stage 6 – Periodic Audit to maintain Certification

Source: Evans, P (1998)

The Supplier Quality Assurance Process

An overview of this process is provided below:

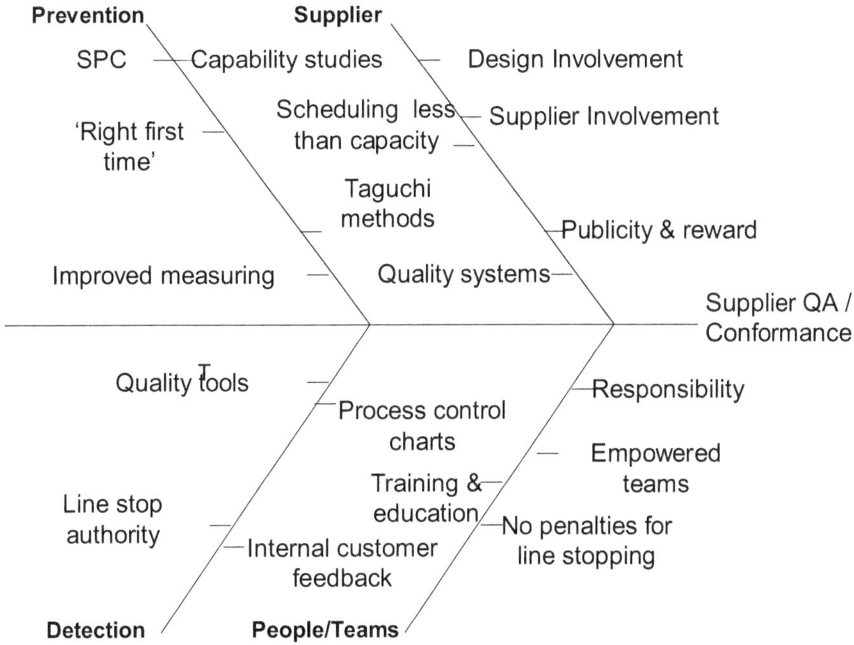

Source: Ellison, H (2003)

Checklist: The benefits of effective quality assurance

- Goods or services delivered within the agreed parameters to meet or exceed requirements
- Conformation to specification
- Control of processes rather than reaction to defects
- Minimisation of lead times
- Hidden costs of quality identified
- Improved communication between supplier and customer
- Inventory reduction
- Facilitates joint cost reduction and benefits to supplier and customer

---

As a starting point, reviewing current practices is essential to identify hidden costs of quality and where duplication may exist with a supplier. This should include:

- Assessing inspection practices and looking for unnecessary or indiscriminate

testing, backlogs of items awaiting inspection and goods held in quarantine.
- Reviewing performance measures and their effectiveness. For example, is the unit of measure (parts per million or percentage, say) sufficient to avoid a defect causing a significant problem? Is the supplier actively engaged in solving the problem and is quality performance measures fed back to the supplier consistently?
- Evaluating the supplier's audit practices.
- Reviewing how the buyer organisation audits its supplier and what follow up action is taken.

A supplier quality assurance programme must form part of the overall supplier management strategy and the appropriate analysis applied before individual supplier are selected for implementation. Involving suppliers in the development of the relevant quality processes and ensuring implementation is focused on results will deliver significant value in not only preventing costly defects, but also in delivering opportunities for continuous improvement.

The Strategic Supplier Development phase

This phase relates to those supplier development practices characterised by high levels of implementation complexity and buyer involvement with suppliers, therefore, requiring a greater use of company resources (personnel, time, and capital) than either the Reactive or Proactive Supplier Development phases.

Supplier development practices that have shown high levels of implementation complexity include training suppliers and involving suppliers in the buyer's new product design process. Supplier involvement in the buyer's design process is also linked to other supply practices, in particular, a collaborative atmosphere. Intensive information exchanges such as suppliers releasing internal information (e.g. costs, quality levels) and buyers having access to a supplier's accounting and financial data can achieve a cooperative climate between suppliers and buyers. This type of communication with suppliers requires a high level of inter-organisation involvement and consequently we have included it in the Strategic Supplier Development phase.

In summary, the Strategic Supplier's Development phase therefore includes:
- Measures of training provided to suppliers
- Supplier's involvement in the buyer's new product design process
- Sharing of accounting information by the supplier
- Sharing of cost and quality information by the supplier.

Connections among supplier development activities

Sourcing from a limited number of suppliers can be the first step towards the implementation of more interactive and closer supply chain practices. This is because practices requiring closer interaction between buyer and supplier, such as involving the supplier in the product design process, are not feasible with a large supply base.

Supplier evaluation allows the buyer to identify what supplier performance indicators and/or capabilities need to be improved. Using this information enables the buyer to make a better decision about the kind of supplier development activity that needs to be implemented. For example, if the quality of materials needs to be improved, the buyer could collaborate directly with suppliers in materials improvement, or provide training on quality management to suppliers.

Similarly, if the focus is to improve on time delivery, the buyer could share production information with suppliers. Additionally, the reward and recognition of supplier performance improvements is not possible without continuous supplier performance evaluations. Supplier development activities are not independent, but complementary and, in some cases, they are a requisite for adopting other supplier development activities.

Procurement managers interested in enhancing Strategic Supplier Development practices (such as providing training for suppliers, involvement in the buyer's product design process and sharing of confidential information with suppliers), would benefit most by adopting Proactive Supplier Development initiatives. For example, rewarding and recognising supplier's performance improvements, visiting suppliers to assess their facilities, and collaborating with suppliers in materials improvement, as well as Reactive Supplier Development activities, such as sourcing from a limited number of suppliers, supplier quality qualification, supplier performance evaluation and parts standardisation.

Such a cumulative response will be more effective in providing continuous improvement.

Maximising Supplier Performance

As we have seen above, there are many approaches available to increase supplier performance contributions and capability improvements. The overall effect is that organisations pursue tactics which:

- Emphasise the direct and immediate improvement of supplier performance contribution towards a buying organisation's overall performance, and then possibly move on to:
- Focusing on the direct improvement of supplier capabilities which then increase supplier performance contributions more dramatically into the longer term

We can further differentiate these approaches as those which move performance steadily along a conceptual supplier performance contribution or capability improvement curve (the steady approaches) and those which actually shift the performance curve (the proactive approaches). Shifting the performance curve upward supports increased supplier performance contributions and capability improvements at an accelerate rate.

Certain strategy approaches have the potential, over time, to increase steadily supplier contributions and improvements. Examples of steady approaches to increase supplier performance contributions include:

- Electronic data interchange with suppliers
- Longer term contracting with co-operative efforts
- Supplier councils
- Supplier rationalisation

The viewpoint for example of Bournemouth Council, is that a long contract duration that does allow for performance to be monitored, managed and leveraged, with the relationship worked for the benefit of both parties, wins every time over short-term contracts.

Supplier Development Methodology for local suppliers

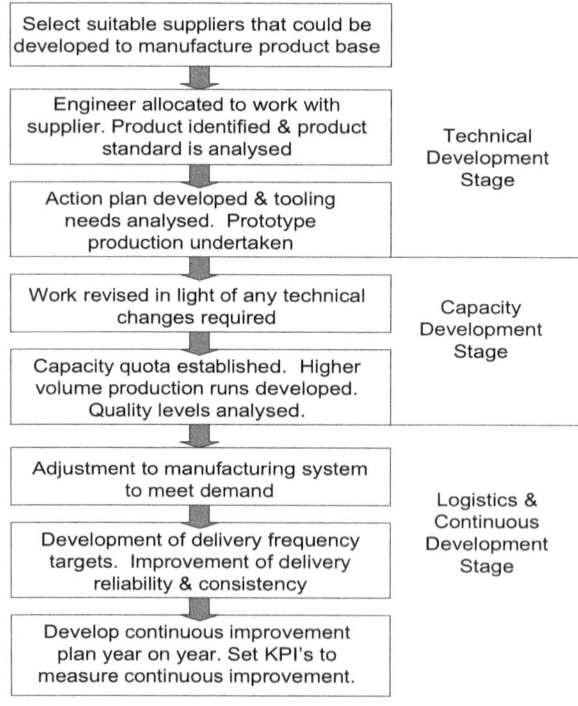

Source: Thomas, A and Barton, R (2007)

Increasing Supplier Performance

Successful implementation of proactive procurement approaches can accelerate supplier performance contributions and capability improvements in a shorter period of time, compared to the use of steady or traditional approaches.

Given the importance of suppliers along with their limited performance improvement response over time, senior management must take action that is proactive and direct to improve supplier contributions and capability improvements.

Supplier's performance can be improved as shown below:

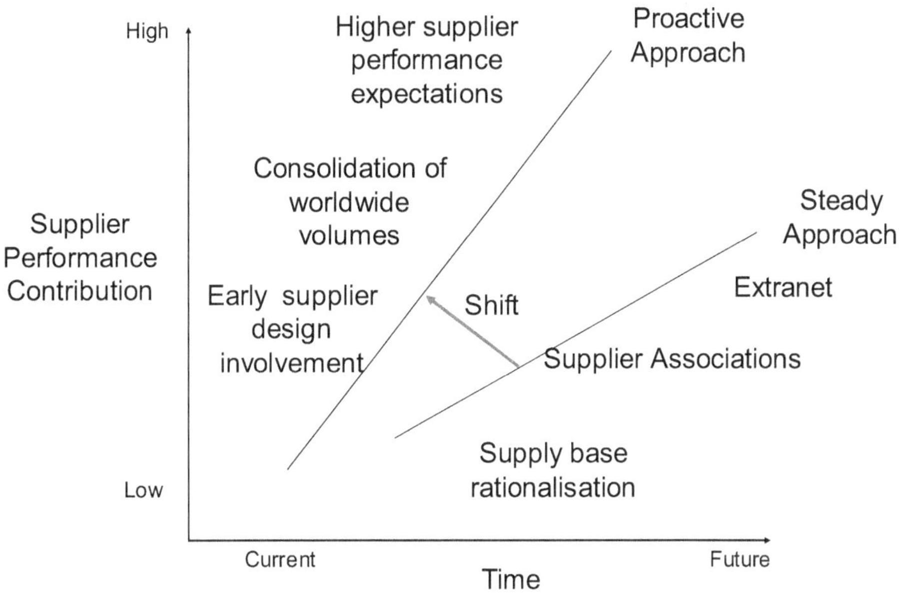

Source after Monczka, R.M and Trent, R.J and Callaghan, T.J (1993)

Examples of steady approaches to improve supplier capabilities include:

- Setting higher supplier capability objectives
- Statistical process control (SPC)
- Supplier certification
- Formal education and training programmes

Each of these activities, when carried out properly, can increase supplier contributions and improvements at a relatively steady rate over time.

The supplier's capability will be improved, as shown overleaf:

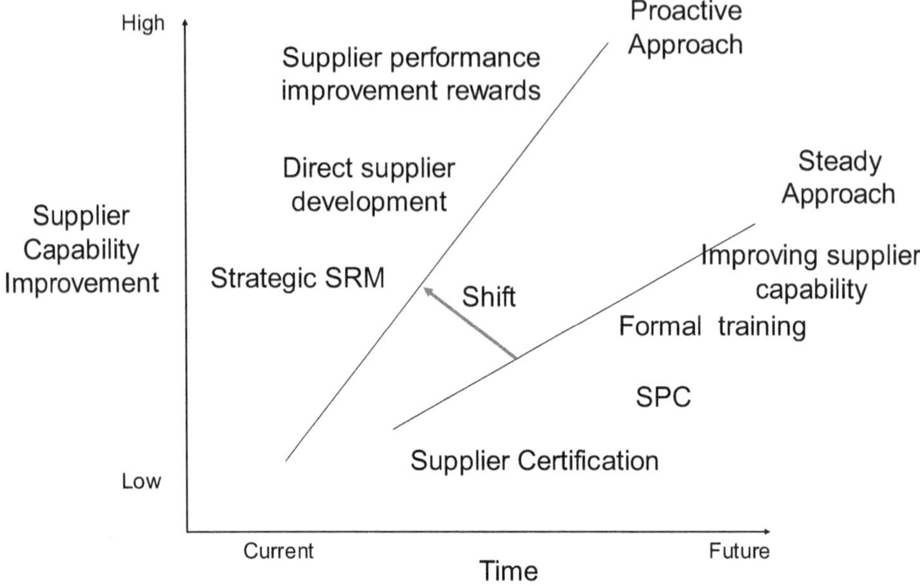

Source after Monczka, R.M and Trent, R.J and Callaghan, T.J (1993)

Many organisations have yet to realise the total performance contributions that a world-class supply base can provide. For an organisation to develop a competitive advantage from its sourcing process and its suppliers, it must take more strategic actions that focus specifically on increasing supplier performance contributions.

Purchasers must also begin to challenge proactively and increase the performance expectations of suppliers. This recognises that increased supplier performance directly affects a buying organisation's competitive position. By proactively increasing supplier performance expectations, a buying organisation expects supplier contributions to increase at an accelerated rate. Eventually, organisations must maintain only those suppliers capable of satisfying higher performance expectation levels.

Case Study: Motorola

Suppliers must satisfy stringent performance expectations in at least four critical areas. These include:

- Keeping pace in attaining perfect quality
- Remaining on the leading edge of technology
- Practicing just in time manufacturing and delivery
- Offering a cost competitive service

Consolidation of purchase volume

The objective of purchase volume consolidation is to maximise an organisation's buying leverage. The result should be not only lower purchase prices for commonly purchased items but also the selection of suppliers that provide consistent excellent quality, delivery and support to each buying location. Consolidation can involve combining separate purchase agreements for the same supplier into a single, larger volume agreement or eliminating multiple suppliers of a common item by establishing a single company-wide source.

Worldwide co-ordination of purchase strategy

Systematic co-ordination of procurement strategy can also increase a supplier's performance contributions. This approach requires procurement centres or business units located throughout different geographic regions to develop jointly regional or worldwide procurement strategies that maximise the total contributions of best in class suppliers.

Traditionally, many manufacturers have decentralised the materials and production function to the division or business unit level. While this may contribute to procurement responsiveness, it also contributes to inefficiency and lost opportunities. Uncoordinated procurement strategy results in lost purchase leverage opportunities worldwide. It also lowers an organisations overall procurement effectiveness as they are not able to share material expertise between buying units.

Organisations can benefit directly from the coordination of procurement strategy, product design, supplier performance information, suppliers, and common purchased items between business units or procurement centres. Worldwide integration and coordination represents a proactive and strategic approach to accelerated supplier performance contribution because organisations coordinate and manage supply base strategies at a highly visible, executive level. Additionally, the procurement function, usually through cross-functional sourcing teams, searches for the best suppliers world wide to provide common purchased times or families of items.

Early and continuous supplier design involvement and selection

Early supplier design involvement and selection requires key suppliers to participate at the concept or pre-design phase of new product development. Supplier involvement may be informal, although the supplier may already have a purchase contract for production of an item. Early involvement will increasingly be through participation on cross-functional product development teams.

Early involvement recognises that qualified suppliers have more to offer a buying organisation than the basic production of an item according to established specifications. Early supplier design involvement, part of a simultaneous engineering approach between buyer and seller, seeks to maximise the benefit received from a supplier's engineering, design, testing, manufacturing, and tooling capabilities. It can also help ensure that suppliers can reliably produce a designed part with existing processes.

This approach represents a direct effort to reduce total product development cycle time by using key suppliers early in the design process.

Some organisations have yet to develop a closer, trusting relationship with their suppliers and do not have the appropriate confidentiality agreements to maximise the benefit of early supplier involvement. Greater trust and commitment between buyer and seller, however, has always been a stated goal of the supplier rationalisation process.

Direct supplier development

Direct supplier development involves the commitment of resources by the buying unit for the improvement of an existing supplier capability, or, the development of new performance capability. Direct support can involve providing capital, equipment, technology, or the assignment of support personnel to a supplier's facility. This differs from indirect supplier development that stresses supplier encouragement, training, and self-improvement.

Direct supplier development efforts are critical for effective supply base management. Once a company reduces its supply base and assures itself that it has best in world suppliers, supply base improvements will occur primarily through the development of existing supplier capabilities and not through large-scale supplier switching.

Often organisations develop supplier capabilities primarily through increased supplier performance goals and formal education and training programmes. Many organisations stress these two activities are overwhelmingly beneficial, over the more direct activities of providing support personnel, capital, equipment, and technology, or the direct involvement with suppliers in identifying and eliminating non-value added costs, processes and time. The actions required to accelerate supplier capability improvements, however, are those emphasised the least, for example, providing personnel, capital, and equipment resources to accelerate development with resulting preferential treatment expected from the supplier.

An example of a systematic supplier development effort is Toyota and Nissan; who send teams of engineers directly to suppliers to help adopt lean and efficient production methods. The programme is open to suppliers of all types of purchased materials that can benefit from direct assistance.

Checklist: Ranking for Developing supplier capabilities
1. Increase supplier performance goals
2. Conduct education and training programmes
3. Provide technology
4. Provide support personnel
5. Provide equipment
6. Provide capital

Such supplier development requires a mutual recognition by the buyer and the seller of the need for continuous performance improvement. Executive management at the buying unit must commit the time, personnel and financial resources to support the suppliers who are willing to participate.

A successful programme requires a proactive attitude that moves well beyond increased supplier performance goals and education and training programmes. This approach, however, requires very close monitoring of the supplier development effort, as well as of each supplier's actual improvement over time.

The need to develop, maintain and manage a supply base, which performs at world class levels, must not only be of interest to functional procurement management. Indeed, management must begin to link closely corporate/business unit, product and procurement strategy. The ability to compete rests, in part, on the development of proactive strategies, which recognise the critical contributions of procurement and the supply base towards achieving over all corporate objectives.

Besides recognising the critical role of procurement during the development of corporate/business unit and product strategy, management must take other steps to maximise procurement performance contribution. Only by working with suppliers can a company hope to remain at the forefront of technology and hence protect its share of the market.

Supplier Co-ordination and Associations

Kyoryoku Kai or "Supplier Association" is a concept which was first developed in Japan, and uses study groups where new production techniques can be learnt, such as Lean and/or Agile Supply, Statistical Process Control, Just in Time (JIT) delivery, Value Analysis, and Sustainability techniques. Essentially such supplier co-ordination is a technique to add value as well as remove waste. It involves buyers identifying its most important suppliers and bringing them together on a regular basis for the purpose of mutual benefit and in particular:

- To devolve strategy and policy throughout the chain to create a sense of common purpose
- To strengthen trust and the relationships of the members
- To share knowledge and expertise
- To facilitate joint development and learning
- To jointly identify ways of minimising waste

The process of learning for member suppliers does not merely depend on technology transfer from the client company to its suppliers, but also on mutual teaching among member suppliers. This might be through mutual factory visits, to offer constructive criticisms and suggestions on factory layout, process technology, or quality control procedures; all of which tend to lead to enhanced efficiency and effectiveness.

It is important to select suppliers that are in synergy with each other as there would be little point in the selecting suppliers if there were no inter-relationship between them. This means that suppliers should be grouped into categories in which they have something in common, e.g. a glass bottle supplier, a bottle top supplier, and a packaging supplier. Another way of grouping would be into supply chains so that the first, second and third tier suppliers of a vital supply chain can be brought together for the supplier co-ordination and mutual benefit.

Trust is absolutely critical to the success of Kyoryoku Kai, between all those participating. In some cases, it may be necessary to have confidentiality agreements in place. Additionally, all suppliers must be able to benefit from Kyoryoku Kai. The buying organisation must ensure that they do so; otherwise, the forum will not be sustainable. Ideally, the forum should be a long-term arrangement with the objective of continuous improvement.

There are alternatives to Kyoryoku Kai that can achieve similar ends – such as an eSupply Hub that is a virtual meeting place in which suppliers can air issues, and share experiences and problems. However, Kyoryoku Kai is a way of solving problems and bringing about improvements but procurement and supply chain management professionals need to deploy the necessary hard and soft skills to determine whether, or when, circumstances are right to ensure success.

Supplier Development Positioning Matrix and Model

Another range of supplier development approaches is given opposite:

Supplier	Criteria		Strategy
To provide mutual competitive advantage	Maximum network benefits	Stage 4	Network Development
To continually improve technical/competitive advantage	Maximum mutual benefit	Stage 3	Systematic Development Programme
Supply goods customer does not want to make	Lower cost	Stage 2	Reactive Problem Solving
Supply goods customer does not make	Lower cost	Stage 1	External Accreditation

(After Hines, James & Jones (1995) Supplier Development Positioning Matrix)

Again, we see the gradual progression towards greater co-ordination of supply chain networks and systematic supplier developments programmes, to give greater mutual advantage to buyers and suppliers. This is further outlined in the model by Massey and McCartney below:

Checklist: Supplier Development Model

Stage 1: **Individual**	• Cheapest price • No TCO • Little performance monitoring • Short term relationships
Stage 2: **Fragmented**	• Supplier rating • Lack of supplier information • Short term focus • Vision is not communicated
Stage 3 **Integrated**	• Cross-functional teams • Policy communicated to suppliers • Jointly agreed KPIs • Open communication • Risk sharing

Stage 4 **Networked**	• Supplier associations (Kyoryoku Kai) • Kaizen • Trust • Shared information • Aligned processes

Source: after Massey L and McCartney L (1998)

Longer-term deals are better than shorter contracts

More than three quarters of buyers prefer long-term contracts with suppliers, according to a Supply Management poll. The survey of 100 buyers found 83% in favour of longer-term relationships, while 17% preferred shorter deals. Most respondents said providing contracts are maintained and managed properly, having longer-term relationships with suppliers is beneficial to both parties.

Case Studies: Long-term contracts

Tetley

Tetley believe the benefits of long-term contracts include "price and supply stability, the ability to get the supplier properly tuned into their needs and for Tetley to tune in to their strengths, and the ability to develop products, services or systems".

Kronospan

Believe long-term contracts have greater rewards, and that they "encourage suppliers to provide added value initiatives and ideas that may produce greater cost reductions, not just short term price reductions that result from constantly changing suppliers and contracts".

Continuous improvement and Kaizen with suppliers

Effective leaders and managers should attempt to nurture a culture of continuous improvement/Kaizen from key trading partners. Therefore, this section will provide a brief summary of how Kaizen operates and how it can assist in developing supplier's performance.

Kaizen is a word meaning "continuous improvement" and comes from two Japanese words; Kai meaning transforming and Zen, meaning worth/value.

Everyone is encouraged to come up with small improvement suggestions on a regular basis. This is not a once a month or once a year activity. It is continuous and in Japanese organisations, such as Toyota and Canon, a total of 60 to 70 suggestions per employee per year are written down, shared and implemented.

In most cases, these are not ideas for major changes. Kaizen is based on making little changes on a regular basis: always improving productivity, safety and effectiveness whilst reducing waste. The Kaizen philosophy is to "do it better, make it better and improve it even if it isn't broken, because if we don't, we can't compete with those who do."

In Supply chains, Kaizen encompasses many of the components of Japanese organisations that have been seen as a part of their success. Quality circles, automation, suggestion systems, just-in-time delivery and Kanban are all included within the Kaizen system of running a business. Kaizen involves setting standards and then continually improving those standards. To support the higher standards Kaizen also involves providing the training, materials and supervision that is needed for suppliers to achieve the higher standards and maintain their ability to meet those standards on an on-going basis.

Kaizen and Supplier Relationship Management

In terms of supplier relationship management, as shown by the Relationship Positioning Tool (RPT), this approach emphasises actions and attitudes of both sides of the contractual relationship, which must change in order that there is a culture of continuous improvement.

> ### Case Study: BMW
>
> BMW are continually consulting with their key suppliers in an effort to reduce costs by four billion over a four-year period.
>
> Teams of Procurement, Logistics and Quality experts consult with suppliers during workshops to evaluate areas of improvement. BMW believe that large cost reductions can be made throughout the supply chain.
>
> By encouraging improved efficiency and effectiveness throughout the supply chain, BMW hope to continually improve workflows and significantly reduce supplier lead times.

The following outlines some of the key philosophies of a Kaizen approach.

- The consequences of change cannot be predicted = We are all learning together; we being our company and our suppliers
- Without shared vision there can be no shared goals = Sharing our objectives with our suppliers

- Vision is constant = Mutual objectives and goals, are developed, which are continually shared with the suppliers.
- Alignment can only be achieved through empowerment = Empowering our suppliers

Case Study: Dairy Crest

Dairy Crest have introduced three key targets for Procurement:
- Greater Supplier Innovation
- Increasing the influence of Procurement over the total spend
- Improving Supplier relationships

Their approach is centred on Procurement unlocking expertise both within their company and within their suppliers. Their overall spend of 400 million is expected to reduce as they look to the supply chain to encourage innovation.

An increased focus on supplier relationships will seek to improve sustainable procurement.

Continuous Improvement, or Kaizen, involves the improvement of all aspects of an organisation's interfaces with suppliers. Suppliers are an asset and innovative suppliers are potentially very valuable in terms of value-added. The authors have experience of procurement functions that have actually been seen as blockers when it comes to harnessing innovation.

If Procurement departments wish to continue to grow their influence, it has to be more forward-looking and open-minded in terms of driving innovation. It is not just the coming up with new ideas, which are important, but also being the facilitator for channelling alternative ideas from the supply chain. This not only requires more internal collaboration, but also improved supply chain relationships. Small continuous changes, like the following, are easier to make and less daunting than single major improvements.

- Puts the "customer" and" supplier" at the forefront of the organisations activities
- Identifies both the "internal" and "external" customers of the organisation
- Aims at constant improvements
- Involves a cross-functional approach
- Utilises techniques such as the tools of TQM/5S/6Sigma
- Emphasises early involvement and empowerment of suppliers

The procurement department contribution involves improvements in all aspects of its activities:

- Relationships with other internal departments and service to them
- Improved service to suppliers
- Improved quality of supplies
- Improved service from suppliers
- Improvements in systems
- Improved operating procedures

People at all levels are responsible for suggesting and introducing these improvements.

Case Study: Ford

To the Ford Motor Company, continuous supplier improvement means that internal and external suppliers strive to achieve the following goals:

- Understand and improve organisational systems and processes.
- Use statistical process control in measuring performance of quality criteria.
- Establish targets for significant process and product characteristics and reduce variation around these targets.
- Obtain timely internal and external customer feedback data.
- Establish a rating system and measure customer perceptions of products and services.
- Identify principal and best-in-class competition to assess the quality of processes, products and services.
- Develop a cost of quality system.
- Educate employees in quality.
- Assist customers and suppliers, as partners, to improve the quality of their products and services.

Case Study: Dunlop Cox

In the automotive industry, vehicle manufacturers are increasingly unwilling to pay their component suppliers more their products. In other words, higher costs of wages or of materials for example, cannot be recouped from price increases. This concept of no price increases operates widely in the Japanese manufacturing industry.

As many world-class Japanese manufacturers, including the carmakers Honda, Nissan and Toyota, have invested in the UK, the approach has gathered pace. Suppliers to these Japanese organisations and other carmakers must improve their efficiency if their profit margins are to be maintained. In most organisations, this will involve continuous improvement.

Small but Continuous Improvements

The Japanese have demonstrated that to be more efficient, organisations do not necessarily have to follow the capital investment route. The Japanese way is to go for small but continuous improvements of a fraction of a% initiated by the people on the shop floor. It is a much safer alternative and the Japanese are the world's leading practitioners of continuous improvement or, as they call it, Kaizen.

At Dunlop Cox, which makes seat slides, frames and mechanisms for customers such as Nissan, Rolls Royce, Rover, Saab and Volvo, a continuous improvement programme was introduced. It followed the introduction of Cellular and Just-In-Time manufacture. The company believed then as now, that if other manufacturers had benefited from Kaizen, it would too.

Like most manufacturers, it had an intelligent workforce with a detailed knowledge of the production process. If those people could be persuaded to contribute ideas and suggestions for improvement – for eliminating waste – the process could begin.

The teams collect ideas, discuss what is to be done, implement it and every two months report to the directors. The directors' job is to disseminate good ideas across the company, not to interfere with the improvement process. Some of the results used the Japanese maxims that if it costs a lot of money, do not do it. For example, for an outlay of $11,000 in one cell, a saving of $200,000 (or 13 jobs) was achieved. The new cell layout used less space. Product flow was better, work-in-progress was reduced and quality was increased.

Benefits of Kaizen

Kaizen clearly has many benefits. It does not cost much money. The productivity gains are high and they are being delivered by many people, not just by production management. There is no resistance to Kaizen because the ideas for improvement are initiated on the shop floor and carried out there.

Shop floor involvement in Kaizen, which should be voluntary not compulsory, creates a better atmosphere in the factory.

External relationships with customers also improve. They have less to complain about because a knock on effect of increased productivity is increased reliability of the product and its delivery.

Post-Contract Award Management

After having made a fair and complete comparison, then an award is made and the contract now needs to be managed.

The worst way to 'manage' a contract is simply to leave it take its course; it will then more than likely go wrong and leave an incomplete audit trail. Let us be very clear here, control cannot be outsourced and management control must remain a core activity. Supplier Management or contract management therefore provides for the handling of contractual, commercial and collaboration aspects:

1) Contractual: Performance to a required standard and compliance with the contract conditions; for example, costs and services supplied are in accordance with the requirements of the contract and its terms and conditions. Contract control involves actively keeping the contractor's performance to the required standard. Participation by both parties is needed if this is to be successful so that any problems can be quickly identified and resolved. It is therefore important that a sound working relationship be established.

If monitoring indicates that a contractor's performance has deteriorated, action will need to be taken. The nature of the action will depend upon the level of the under-performance or complaints. If regular monitoring is effectively carried out, problems will be spotted early and the degree of any disruption from corrective action will be minimised. In most cases a discussion on the problem, will be all that is required to secure agreement on remedial action.

2) Commercial: Clear and documented records with evidence where necessary, to invoke any non-compliance procedures, for example, recording complaints received from customers of the service and recording customer satisfaction with the service. It is important for contract managers to have clear and documented evidence if contracts do not run smoothly. Records of all meeting and telephone conversations should be held on file. The contractor/supplier should be notified in writing of all instances of non-compliance, and a written timetable for rectification, should be drawn up. It is likely that the contractor will also be keeping records of the problems incurred with the contract.

If the contractor continually fails to perform, this may constitute a breach of contract. The severity of the failure and the cost to the organisation will need to be assessed. Legal advice may be required before any further action is considered. Below are examples of where default in a contract may arise from a failure to:

- Perform any part of the services

- Provide financial or management information
- Employ appropriately qualified, experienced, skilled or trained staff
- Comply with legislation
- Make payment to the contractor on time (clearly both parties must fulfil their contractual obligations)

3) Collaboration and relationships between the parties, the way they regard each other and the way in which their relationship operates, is vital to making a success of the contractual arrangement.

Although it is sometimes difficult to predict accurately where problems may arise, good contract management with regular dialogue between the contractor and customer will help to identify early, potential problems. This will enable problems to be dealt with swiftly and effectively and so prevent major disputes.

Active contract management therefore requires efficient two-way communications between both parties, which will anticipate problems, so that these are dealt with quickly and corrective action is taken to prevent similar problems from arising in future. This requires established lines of communication and an overall approach that will jointly and seamlessly manage and control change, for example making joint improvements

As identified by the OGC (2002), good contract management goes much further than ensuring that the agreed terms of the contract are being met - this is a vital step, but this contractual step is only the first of many. Whilst a successful relationship must involve the delivery of services that meet requirements and the commercial arrangement must be acceptable to both parties (such as offering value for money for the customer and adequate profit for the provider), the collaboration between the parties, the way they regard each other and the way in which their relationship operates, is what is really critical in making a success of the arrangement.

No matter what ever is the scope or the terms of the contract, there will always be some tensions between the different perspectives and perceptions of the customer/buyer and the supplier/contractor. Contract management is about resolving such tensions and to do this, there must be an effective collaboration with the supplier/contractor that is based on mutual gains, understanding, trust and open communication.

Control of change

Contract requirements are often subject to change throughout the life of the contract. We live in a fast changing world with a future of "stable turbulence" and it is not therefore always possible to predict such changes and variations in advance, or, at the specification stage.

It may therefore be decided during the course of the contract, that a slight change to the requirements are needed.

Such changes to the requirements will often affect the cost and so will need to be recorded. Changes to the contract may also affect the following:

- The initial specification can be now out of date
- The cost and service, for example, changed delivery times, locations
- The nature of the services being provided

It will normally be the role of the contract manager to ensure that any need for any contract variation is recorded and the contract changed to be line with the newly agreed procurement procedures, where the variation, is clearly tied in with the main contract so that a clear audit trail is possible. Audit trails being especially important for those organisations in the public sector who find it essential to keep records of dealings with suppliers whether written or verbal as such records are required for:

- Information if problems arise
- Reviewing meetings and re-negotiations
- Audit purposes
- Planning for any subsequent tendering processes

End of Contract/Completion Reports

It is good practice at the completion of any contract to review and place on record what went well and what lessons can be learned for any future contracts, for example with a Contractor Evaluation Report. The information on this report will be used to evaluate and monitor the effectiveness of the organisations contractors. This essentially covers the outcome and extent to which the expected benefits (deliverables) were achieved.

Best Practice Contract Management

From the above look at contracts then we can identify the following aspects of good contract management. This can be summarised as follows:

1. Good preparation. An accurate assessment of needs/requirements helps to create a clear technical and/or performance based specification. Effective evaluation procedures and selection, against the specification of requirements, will then ensure that the contract is awarded to the right contractor.

2. The right contract. The contract is the legal foundation for the relationship. It should include aspects such as allocation of risk, the quality of service required, and value for money mechanisms, as well as procedures for communication and dispute resolution and the contractual obligations of the customer/contracting organisation.

3. Empathy and understanding. Each party needs to understand the objectives and business of the other. The customer must have clear business objectives, coupled with a clear understanding of what the contract will contribute to them; the contractor must also be able to achieve their objectives, including making a reasonable profit.

4. Service delivery management and contract administration. Effective governance will ensure that the customer gets what is agreed, to the level of quality required. The performance under the contract must be monitored to ensure that the customer continues to get what they expect.

5. Collaboration and relationship management. The eventual success of a contract depends on mutual trust and understanding, openness, and excellent communications. – these being just as important (and may be more so), than the fulfilment of the legal terms and conditions.

6. Continuous improvement. Improvements in price, quality or service should be sought and, where possible, built into the contract terms and the benefits shared.

7. People, skills and continuity. There must be people with the right interpersonal and management skills to manage these relationships at all the multiple levels in the organisation. Clear roles and responsibilities should be defined, and continuity of key staff should be ensured as far as possible. A contract manager (or contract management team) should be designated early on in the procurement process.

8. Knowledge. Those involved in managing the contract must understand the business fully and know the contract documentation inside out. This is essential if they are to understand the implications of problems or opportunities over the life of the contract.

9. Flexibility. Management of contracts requires some flexibility on both sides and a willingness to adapt the terms of the contract to reflect a rapidly changing world. Problems are bound to arise that could not be foreseen when the contract was awarded.

10. Change management. Contracts should be capable of change (to terms, requirements and perhaps scope) and the relationship should be strong and flexible enough to facilitate it.

11. Proactivity. Good contract management is not reactive, but aims to anticipate and respond to business needs of the future.

Supplier Management best practice

For reference purposes, then the following is our summary of best practice:

1. If a company does not have a basic supplier performance management process in place, it is very difficult to even start to think about supplier management. The first priority must be to know how key suppliers perform against the contract. Once the basics are in place then organisations can start to think about more sophisticated supplier management processes.

2. Organisations must make sure that they prioritise and categorise carefully which suppliers to address, for examply through the Kraljic procurement positioning tool techniques. Few organisations have the resources to carry out effective supplier management with a very large number of suppliers. It is far better to succeed with that important handful of suppliers first and then latter, grow the initiative.

3. Organisations must be clear about the objectives of the supplier management process; they should clearly relate to the organisation's overall aims. For example, that might be working with the suppliers to achieve better value for money, or innovation or developing approaches to new markets. The supplier management programme must link clearly to the organisational key goals.

4. It is important to recognise the mutuality of the relationship. Organisations must consider what the supplier wants out of the relationship and position their own objectives accordingly. A supplier management programme will only succeed with supplier co-operation; there must therefore be real mutual benefits.

5. Organisations must be careful not to underestimate the resource needed to carry out supplier management effectively. As we saw, there are increasingly more involved levels of supplier development, which require additional resources to gain the additional benefits. Getting results needs detailed work with defined tools and processes, and mechanisms that may include joint working parties, detailed cost analysis, or combined development projects. Organisations must be prepared to allocate the pre-requisite resources into the process otherwise, results will be disappointing.

6. Data is important. Information must be regularly reviewed, shared and constructive feedback given. Organisations must have a clear view of their contractual relationship with their suppliers, including spend patterns and performance.

7. Organisations must involve key internal stakeholders, supplier management cannot be a purely procurement department based activity. The cross-functional side of things is important and should dominate. Organisations need to ensure that everyone is really working to the agreed supplier management agenda.

8. Organisations must consider who is best placed to handle different aspects of supplier management. For instance, there is the day-to-day collection of information in terms of the operational contract delivery, and there is the important aspect of managing the improvement over say a two-five year development horizon with the supplier.

9. Organisations can be creative; there are many different techniques, tools and processes that can be useful in this programme, such as secondments of key staff, brainstorming workshops, combined project teams and joint buyer/supplier conferences.

10. Even your closest 'partner' may not meet your needs in the future, or they may decide to become a competitor, or withdraw from your business. Therefore, organisations must

remember that relationships do not last forever and in parallel to supplier management, they also need to be thinking about alternative strategies, different suppliers and contingency plans.

Case Studies: Three Lessons from Experience

1) Bill Knittle, Global Procurement, Director, refining and marketing (R&M) BP:

BP started its SRM programme in 2003 and Knittle says he has the "battle scars" to show for it.

First, the company segmented its suppliers to decide where to concentrate its efforts. It examined assurance and compliance to check if it was getting what it should from current deals, looked at spend volume and the value of the deals it had in place, and also examined what suppliers thought. It did this with the help of Honda, Toyota and an independent survey.

"It was an eye-opener," Knittle says. Of BP's 51,000 suppliers, it discovered it had just six to eight key strategic suppliers. The next tier, "sector-critical relationships", had around 170 suppliers, and there are another 800 with whom BP has sector and/or local relationships. It is SRM and supplier performance management programme – aimed at these groups – is expected to net savings of $200 million.

Start slowly with process-based decisions around supplier performance until trust is established, is his advice: "If you've been beating them up for the past few years it will take you at least 24 to 36 months to get them to talk about relationship management."

He said buyers had to send clear and consistent messages to suppliers and set KPIs appropriate to the relationship - for example, with top targets around innovation measurement for only your tier one suppliers. "Link your SRM to shareholder value (growth of business, cost efficiency, etc) otherwise it's nice but it doesn't excite the senior manager. This has helped us."

A large number of things must be in place if an organisation is to make a success of SRM and, he suggests, those still working at a transactional level are not ready for it. KPIs should support the organisation's overall objectives and performance management, clear strategic goals, the right contracts, effective planning and capable managers should all be in place: "Relationship management skills are a totally different skill-set. Don't expect anyone trained only to be aggressive for 20 years to be good at this," he adds.

2) Joseph Youssef, director of global technology supplier management, McDonald's

"Seventy-five percent of value can be lost if we don't do proactive SRM," says Joseph Youssef.

He believes executive sponsorship has been key to the success of SRM at McDonald's and says some of its suppliers have also appointed an executive sponsor to mirror the behaviour. "Conventional project sponsorship achieves only short-term goals. They need to invest a lot of time and effort."

He says SRM helped the organisation focus on long-term relationship needs and that it enhanced communication and helped to prevent "relationship value degradation". It also creates greater visibility, access to supplier capabilities and fosters innovation.

So what lessons has he learnt?

"Prioritise and focus. Do not think big picture idea, we tried it - it does not work, it failed miserably. Try one area, achieve it and move on. We started in IT, now we are moving into facilities and other areas and its better that way.

"It's led to faster negotiations of additional services; tangible results have been achieved ($40 million a year contract over the past four years, $3.5 million savings in cost avoidance). It is also led to a better dialogue with suppliers. We did not know what their pains were and what they needed. Now we have a better understanding of what they go through when we make demands on them."

3) Paul Alexander, Head of Procurement, British Airways

Alexander says the industrial action prompted by the dismissal of Gate Gourmet catering staff in 2005 made British Airways "think about upgrading SRM for the future".

In fact, he says, it is critical in an industry that has so many monopoly suppliers and is vulnerable to all manner of disruption - including weather, strikes and terrorism. "Playing suppliers off against each other is not the way of the future. It is a particular problem for airlines but it may also be a problem for you. You need to get the supplier to internalise you as the 'customer of choice'. We are moving into a world of scarcity, particularly because of the growth of India and China. My biggest challenge is competing with other buyers, not getting suppliers to compete."

Alexander says simple things such as writing thank-you letters have helped.

"Even the language you use can drive a union between you and your suppliers.

> We say things like, 'What problem are we trying to solve?' Not too many suppliers are dependent on BA so this approach has been very successful."
> **Source: Supply Management 28 February 2008**

Corporate Social Responsibility (CSR)

The concept of Corporate Social Responsibility has several common strands:

- The degree to which a company minimises its negative impact on the communities in which it operates.
- The positive benefits it brings to the community and to society in general. This extends beyond its product/service ranges to include such areas as charities, sponsorships and education.
- As the environment is inextricably linked to perceptions of corporate citizenship, a company cannot be considered a good corporate socially responsible entity unless its activities are environmentally friendly, unless it is seen to be taking positive steps to minimize the environmental impact of its operations
- The way in which a company treats its employees and the extent to which it prevents the from harm.
- A company should have an ethics code, such as that provided by the CIPS.

As procurement is responsible for a large percentage of the total costs of an organisation, the contribution to corporate social responsibility of an ethical and green supply chain cannot be ignored.

What is CSR?

"Corporate Social Responsibility is the continuing commitment by business to behave ethically and contribute to economic development while improving the quality of life of the workforce and their families as well as of the local community and society at large." – **World Business Council for Sustainable Development).**

What is involved in CSR?

Carroll offers a four-fold obligation:

- Economic
- Legal
- Ethical
- Philanthropic

Hierarchy of CSR responsibilities

After Carroll. A.B (1996) Business and Society

What do corporations mean by Corporate Social Responsibility?

- British Airways see it as ethical behaviour within business and the environment.
- BSkyB see five distinct areas; Customers, Our employees, Community, Suppliers and Environment
- Traidcraft see three distinct areas; Economic impact, Social impact and Environmental impact
- BT, "as well as just looking at trading standards in the supply chain, it's about how they relate to their suppliers, how they manage those relationships and to work in an ethical way".

The CSR issue should just be part of the adjudication criteria and be considered as part of the whole life cost.

What CIPS says

Certainly, CIPS, which represents procurement management professionals in the UK and elsewhere, believes its members can take the social responsibility agenda further.

The institute's *"Ethical practices in purchasing and supply"* draws on various codes, including the UK government backed Ethical Trading Initiative, the core conventions of the International Labour Organisation and the UN Declaration on Human Rights.

CIPS says buyers should work with suppliers to make sure that:

- Employees are free to work for their employer or not
- Employees should be given a clear contract, including how much they will be paid
- Suppliers should not discourage or prevent employees from joining trade unions
- Wages and benefits should at least meet industry benchmarks or national legal standards
- Employees should not be expected to work more than 48 hours a week regularly
- Suppliers should not abuse or intimidate employees
- Suppliers should always work within the laws of their country
- Suppliers must uphold health and safety requirements
- They aim to eradicate child labour, but in the meantime make sure children and young people are not made to work in dangerous conditions or at night, and that they have access to education.

A Government report stated:

"Corporate Social Responsibility brings with it enormous business benefits, from enhance reputation to real cost savings, from higher staff morale to greater customer loyalty. CSR is good business"

Price is only one factor when selecting suppliers (one more time!). Reputation is vital in today's critical world. Any company that wants to stay in business in the long term must treat social issues as paramount.

CSR incorporates initiatives in the local community, the workplace and the environment. Examples are:

- Barclays Bank has a scheme to make use of business suits that it no longer needs
- Tesco has a 'Computers for schools' project
- BOC has backed the UN Global Compact, a code aimed at fostering "corporate citizenship", among organisations, based on the principles of the Universal Declaration of Human Rights, the International Labour Organisation's Declaration on Fundamental Principles and Rights at Work and the Rio

Principles on Environment and Development.

- Diageo assesses new suppliers with a questionnaire to make sure they are acting sustainably

Mini-Case Study: Top Shop

Top shop has a buying executive dedicated to sourcing ethical clothing, and has signed a deal to sell Fairtrade cotton lines.

The shift presents buyers with several challenges. They need to develop the core competences of procurement professionals to include ethical considerations in buying activities. They also need to develop the capacity of the supply base. Research shows that manufacturers often do not operate to international labour standards, so buyers need to work with suppliers to ensure improvements are made across the board.

Public accountability

Since the early 1990s, global brands and retailers have been under attack. Scandals regularly swept through supplier's overseas factories exposing child labour, low wages and horrific working conditions. Consequently, many brands have signed up to codes of conduct.

Organisations have relied on these codes and on site audits, safe in the belief they are doing the best they can to improve conditions for workers in their supply chains.

Research from the Institute of Development Studies (IDS), commissioned by the Ethical Trading Initiative (ETI) to assess the impact of its base code, used by organisations including Marks & Spencer, Tesco and Gap. The researchers interviewed more than 400 workers in 23 supplier sites across the world, as well as retailers, manufacturers, agents, managers, trade unions, and non-governmental organisations (NGOs).

On the plus side, researchers found children at work in only one of the sites visited. In addition, health and safety measures were of a higher standard in most factories as a result of the implementation of the base code. Regular and overtime working hours had also fallen.

However, in other areas, the code had made little or no impact. No increase in union membership, women were still subject to basic inequalities. There was no impact in terms of ensuring workers received a living wage. For example, some workers in some Bangladeshi factories are paid just 5p an hour to produce clothes for retailers including Tesco, Asda and Primark. All three have signed the ETI's code of labour practice.

The quality of auditing in general is very poor either because of lack of training, lack of understanding, laziness or sometimes downright corruption. Strategies comprising education, communication and support need to complement audits for more challenging issues such as freedom of association and discrimination. Buyers need to examine their price, lead-time and product cycle and 'review the impact of that on their suppliers' ability to meet their standards".

Best practice: What buyers can do to improve labour conditions

Avoid putting undue pressure on suppliers that might affect workers – for example, changing an order at the last minute or shortening lead times that could mean workers are forced to do overtime.

Think about the effect of the prices you set – insist suppliers comply with the ETI base code.

Give reasonable time scales for suppliers to address areas of non-compliance and provide support to help them improve, such as education and training.

Help your major suppliers to share good practice by developing benchmarking groups where they can get together to exchange ideas about how to overcome specific issues in their region or industry.

Mini-Case Study FTSE4GOOD

In 2004, FTSE4GOOD, part of the FTSE Group, announced the introduction of the FTSE4GOOD standards for assessing human rights in supply chains.

The standards set out a timetable for organisations to introduce a policy, a system for monitoring and a reporting methodology on issues ranging from equality and discrimination to forced and child labour and worker representation. The labour standards also consider working hours, wages and disciplinary procedures.

Procurement staff can take the lead in ensuring that their organisations and their suppliers understand what is involved in being a good corporate citizen.

Compliance

Businesses can only insist their suppliers are CSR compliant if they are willing to pay more and work with them to enable improvements.

Company buying practices and management of production schedules have a major influence on suppliers' ability to comply with CSR and labour standards. Businesses should review their own buying practices to ensure they do not put undue pressure on suppliers and workers.

Organisations work with suppliers to make realistic improvements over time, rather than demanding immediate compliance.

At M&S "We will train our buyers to further understand the part they play in helping suppliers maintain labour standards in the production of our goods".

The Co-operative Group operates a "sound sourcing code of conduct" for suppliers. "Our aim is to develop an effective working partnership with our suppliers to secure safe and decent working and living conditions for anybody involved in the production of own brand products."

The Co-op audits suppliers to check CSR compliance. It also equips them with a self-assessment workbook, which enables suppliers to carry out their own site assessment, implement action plans and provide evidence of continuous improvement. This allows the supplier to learn what issues the buyer may have, and is given the chance to raise concerns or ask for clarification.

> **Checklist: Six steps to responsible buying**
> 1. Establish good relationships with suppliers to ensure long-term, stable, risk sharing connections.
> 2. Make sure your communications are clear and timely, so suppliers know the terms of the trade, have information about expectations and are able to give feedback.
> 3. Establish sustainable pricing so the supplier, buy and those further down the chain benefit from the relationship.
> 4. Give clear lead times and payments.
> 5. Show respect for human rights in the supply chain. Buyers should give preference to suppliers who demonstrate they are improving social and environmental conditions.
> 6. Offer continued support for small-scale producers and home workers. Buyers should find out who their suppliers are and if they include smallholders, home workers and those in disadvantaged areas, they should be careful not to change that.

If you want to be sure of conditions you need to know the extended supply chain.

The Ethical Trading Initiative suggests that a sound approach has been started in which buyers are addressing the problem by developing longer term and deeper relationships with fewer suppliers.

ETI stipulated that buyers have to become much more involved and have to support their suppliers and not just look for compliance.

Mini Case Study: Tesco and CSR

Tesco monitors and assesses overall company performance towards CSR with the following range of KPIs:

- Economic – local sourcing – 7000 local products
- Environment
- Energy efficiency – year on year% reduction of usage
- Water consumption
- Vehicle efficiency
- Recycling
- Social – "computer for schools" – increase value of computers donated
- Charitable donations – 1%
- Employee retention and training
- Supply chain labour standards – training staff and suppliers (including SA8000)

Source: Tesco website www.tesco.co.uk (2004)

Anti-Corruption

Corruption and Fraud

This involves many things such as:

- Unlawful acts
- Intentional acts
- Misrepresentation
- Results in prejudice to another

There are many examples involving bribery, embezzlement, extortion, the abuse of power/privileged information, showing favouritism and also nepotism.

Corruption is widespread at all levels, in all countries, in all sectors, indeed for some it is normal business and is often not recognised or appreciated. However the risks of being involved in what is always a criminal offence has extremely serous consequences with for example, individuals jailed and organisations fined

What is corruption?

There is no international definition but generally, bribery is A offering some benefit to B, as an inducement, for B or another contact C, to act dishonesty; with dishonesty defined as "an act or omission by a person, in relation to their employer's business".

Personal bribery in this regard may then occur when asked or given (the "supply side") or demanded/received (the "buy side") without approval. Meanwhile, institutional bribery may also occur where an organisation has actually given full approval.

Bribery and facilitation payments

Facilitation payments are often minor payments made to expedite services where if they are not paid, can have serious consequences of delaying or even ignoring requests, e.g. visa applications, paying invoices etc.

They are "technically" different to bribes, which is payment to do something that should not be done, whereas facilitation payments are a payment to do, something that should actually be done. Most countries, of course, criminalise both types of payments. The following are examples:

- Government officials, to get approvals
- Specification writers, to favour that bidder
- Manipulate pre qualifications
- Conceal things in bids
- Ensure wins the bid
- Fix prices
- Inflate resources/time used on a project
- Conceal or make a payment for, defective work
- Witnesses/officials in disputes to give false evidence
- Pass false invoices

Case Study: examples of Bribery

- German court fine of Euro 201 million on Siemens over contracts in Nigeria, Libya and Russia, involving 77 cases between 2001 and 2004. *(Source: Supply Management 13 December 2007)*
- Headlines in the *Sunday Times* UK, 16 March 2008: "Sainsbury's in £3 million scandal over potato bungs" and continued, "We are the victims of an alleged crime and take it very seriously. None of the payments went through our system and we believe this was limited to one supplier." (This case, after a 4 year investigation, reported bribery amounting to £8 million, involving one person from Sainsbury and two from the supplier who all received jail sentences)

Country Corruption Perception Index (CPI)

The Transparency International CPI measures the perceived levels of public-sector corruption in a given country and is a composite index, drawing on different expert and business surveys. Using the 2008 CPI as an example, this scores 180 countries on a scale from zero (highly corrupt) to ten (highly clean).

Denmark, New Zealand and Sweden jointly share the highest score at 9.3, followed immediately by Singapore at 9.2. Bringing up the rear is Somalia at 1.0, slightly trailing Iraq and Myanmar (Burma) at 1.3 and Haiti at 1.4.

(Source: http://www.transparency.org/news_room/in_focus/2008/cpi2008)

Checklist: Ramifications of corruption

Political
The 'buying' of political candidates, the judiciary and local police forces; these monies may flow from drug traffickers, businesspersons or powerful political elites and be used to distort decisions.

Military
Unaccountable and questionable procurement processes by ministries or private contractors.

Social
The use of bribery and power by organised crime groups to facilitate, for example, human trafficking and small arms running

Economic
The theft of public monies generated from natural resource wealth to fund paramilitary groups or insurgents.

Environmental
The payment of bribes by governments and organisations to dump hazardous waste and materials in marginalised communities

The Bribe Mechanisms

Perhaps unsurprisingly, many mechanisms can be used that simply reveal attempts to disguise what is going on.

- The seller can appoint agents/intermediaries and the agent issues invoices to the seller for their services, the invoices being inflated to cover the bribe. This may involve the corrupt people being paid by foreign currency offshore and the "corrected" balance being paid normally to the agent.
- Joint Ventures can fix agency agreements, as above, by a JV partner in a country, where it is least likely to be discovered or punish any bribery.

- Subsidiaries of group organisations can also become involved to overlay a complex web of connections that disguise and make checks/audits difficult.
- Sub contractors are allowed to invoice for products/services not delivered.

The common elements are that only some parties may know that a bribe has been paid with "wilful blindness" being endemic. However, in most legal jurisdictions, this will be treated as being culpable and will often involve fraud, which is defined as a deception to gain some advantage. Associated is collusion which is cooperation to commit a fraud and regularly, money laundering which involves moving cash or other assets, from one location to another, that have been gained by criminal activity.

Extortion may be used, this being a form of blackmail, for example, "do or else" and is actually a forced bribery such as "pay me or no payment will be made". It is also a criminal offence in most jurisdictions.

The Reality

A wide range of people may be caught in both the initial offence (e.g. bribery, fraud between seller/agent/buyer), plus, the site and commercial staff, and the accounting and legal staff, and the directors and managers of all the organisations involved. Accordingly individual liability is impacted of those directly involved, those indirectly involved (e.g. complicity), those in authority (e.g. CEO to managers) and of those who aid and abet (e.g. help someone to do it).

As may have already been gathered, it is no defence for individuals to say, "I am ignorant of the law", "I was acting on instructions", "It was only a small amount", "Everyone does it".

Corporate Liability can also be involved by the acts of its employees, whatever their position, by the acts of its agents, by the acts of related organisations/partners or by "turning a blind eye" or "wilful blindness".

Avoiding corruption

These are three main elements here:
- The risk of prosecution
- The risk of financial loss
- The moral argument

The risk of prosecution seems to be growing, as there is an increased awareness of the scale of corruption and there is increased pressure to stop it. New laws are involved (for example, the UK Bribery Act) involving the increased risk of detection and the greater willingness to prosecute and punish such white-collar crimes.

The risk of financial loss to organisations can be that they are disbarred or publically branded as being unsuitable. Contracts can be voided with reputation damage to organisations and individuals. Individuals may be dismissed from employment and disciplined by professional associations with litigation to recover losses

The moral argument is overwhelming to those with morals! For example, with public sector corruption, then it is the taxpayer who pays and/or the population that loses the money stolen could have been used on hospitals, schools etc.

When it is the private sector, this can lead to increased costs and prices and at its extreme, the organisation can go out of business.

Checklist: Rules to Avoid Corruption
Individual Rules
- Do not knowingly, with wilful blindness or recklessly do any of the following, or participate in any activity which involves any of the following;
- Offer, give, demand or accept any bribe or other improper advantage.
- Participate in any dishonest or deceptive activity in relation to any pre-qualification, tender or nomination process.
- Provide, conceal, or approve work, materials, equipment or services which are not of the quality and quantity required under contract.
- Provide false, inaccurate or misleading information.
- Dishonestly withhold information.
- Make or submit false, inaccurate, misleading or exaggerated records, invoices, claims, applications for variations or extensions of time, or requests for payment.
- Dishonestly refuses or fail to approve, or delay in approving, work, materials, equipment, services, invoices, claims, applications for variations or extensions of time, or requests for payment.
- Dishonestly refuse or fail to pay, or delay in paying, sums due.
- Dishonestly abuse a position in which you are expected to safeguard, or not act against, the financial interests of another parson,
- Make, adapt, supply or offer any article for use in the course of or in connection with any fraud.
- Have in your possession or under your control any article for use in the course of or in connection with any fraud.

If you are a director or officer of, or have any management responsibility for, a company, you must act as follows:

- You must make proper enquiries regarding any suspicion of corruption of which you become aware.
- You must take reasonable preventive measures to stop corruption for which the company may be liable.
- You must not instruct, authorise or condone, expressly of impliedly, any corrupt activity.

Connection with ethics

Ethics are rules of conduct governed by the values of organisations and professions, where values are what are held to be "right" or "wrong". Accordingly, ethics originate in organisational, professional and personal values and cover the complex topics of honesty, fairness, lawfulness, motivation and integrity. Such values then work into the ethical integrity of an organisation and are found in the trading principles and the development and application of ethical policies. These should communicate and involve all the relevant stakeholders as well as providing auditing, monitoring and scrutinising procedures for the organisations ethics.

Ethics and Professionals

As the heart, this covers integrity and competences that are "translated" into a professions body of knowledge, their published "code of conduct" and their self-governing rules. Additionally questions that each procurement professional needs to ask are as follows:

- Is it always wrong for a buyer to accept a gift from a supplier?
- If an action is legal and is in the company's 'best interests', how can it ever be wrong?
- How is the interpretation dependant on the moral character of the buyer?

In practice the guidelines are as follows:

- Be alert to the dangers of becoming too familiar with suppliers
- Be aware of tricks some suppliers might play to trap a buyer
- Purchasing department standards should be discussed, such as the requirement, say, to refuse point blank any gift and favour from suppliers and to report any such offers to management

In a study by the Centre for Advanced Purchasing Studies (USA), it was found that:

- 94% of buyers are generally 'ethical'
- There are often ethical problems with non-buyers buying
- 97% of buyers accept 'favours' (e.g. lunches or souvenirs)

- 68% of sales departments give gifts
- 58% of organisations have a written policy
- Ethical standards are lower in SMEs

In repeated studies involving purchasing staff, factors that influence a high ethical stance are the personal morality code, the behaviour of management and the behaviour of other staff. Additionally the organisational policy on ethics also had a part to play. Meanwhile, influences on unethical behaviour were (again), policy, the behaviour of management and the behaviour of other staff along with the ethical climate in the industry/country and importantly, any personal financial problems.

In this later regard, indicators of fraud/corruption come from the following:

- Family pressure to succeed
- "Getting my own back" following from for example, feelings of being disadvantaged, being underpaid, receiving no recognition etc
- Maintaining certain relationships and excluding others
- Living beyond means and excessive spending (for example, in the earlier mentioned buyer corruption case at Sainsbury's, the court revealed the buyer was spending of £20 000 per month on meals, drink, entertainment etc.)

Checklist: Combating Unethical Practices

- Effective supplier selection
- Competent and professional staff
- Contract/Supplier performance measurement and procedures
- Legislation and Directives
- Discipline the violators

Principles and Standards of Ethical Supply Management Conduct: CIPS UK

These are published as below:

- Avoid the intent and appearance of unethical or compromising practice in relationships, actions and communications.
- Demonstrate loyalty to the employer by diligently following the lawful instructions of the employer, using reasonable care and granted authority.
- Avoid any personal business or professional activity that would create a conflict between personal interests and the interests of the employer.
- Avoid soliciting or accepting money, loans, credits or preferential discounts and the acceptance of gifts, entertainment, favours or services from present or

potential suppliers that might influence, or appear to influence, supply management decisions.
- Handle confidential or proprietary information with due care and proper consideration of ethical and legal ramifications and governmental regulations.
- Promote positive supplier relationships through courtesy and impartiality.
- Avoid improper reciprocal agreements.
- Know and obey the letter and spirit of laws applicable to supply management.
- Conduct supply management activities in accordance with national and international laws, customs and practices, your organization's policies and these ethical principles and standards of conduct.
- Develop and maintain professional competence.
- Enhance the stature of the supply management profession.

The US version follows:
- **Loyalty to your organisation**
- **Justice to those with whom you deal**
- **Faith in your profession**

From these principles are derived the Institute of Supply Management (ISM) standards of supply management conduct, as below:
- Demonstrate loyalty to the employer by diligently following the lawful instructions of the employer, using reasonable care and granted authority.
- Avoid any personal business or professional activity that would create a conflict between personal interests and the interests of the employer.
- Avoid soliciting or accepting money, loans, credits or preferential discounts and the acceptance of gifts, entertainment, favors or services from present or potential suppliers that might influence, or appear to influence, supply management decisions.
- Handle confidential or proprietary information with due care and proper consideration of ethical and legal ramifications and governmental regulations.
- Promote positive supplier relationships through courtesy and impartiality.
- Avoid improper reciprocal agreements.
- Know and obey the letter and spirit of laws applicable to supply management.
- Encourage support for socially diverse practices.
- Conduct supply management activities in accordance with national and international laws, customs and practices, your organization's policies and these ethical principles and standards of conduct.
- Develop and maintain professional competence.
- Enhance the stature of the supply management profession.
  – approved January 2005

The similarity will have been noted between the UK/CIPS and the USA/ISM principles. Finally, details on the recent UK Bribery legislation follow:

Case Study: Bribery and corruption legislation

Further international moves against economic crime are exemplified by the UK's Bribery Act, which is probably the most comprehensive and stringent anti-bribery legislation in the world today. The Act goes significantly further than the existing US Foreign Corrupt Practices Act (FCPA), in particular covering all bribery, whether or not it involves a public official.

The Act came into force on 1 July 2011. The impact of this legislation will be broad; it affects any company with operations in the UK, regardless of the domicile of the company or the locus of the offence. In addition, there is no limit to the amount of fine levied against a company found to be guilty. The Bribery Act contains four offences of bribery: two general (one 'active' and one 'passive') and two 'commercial':

- offering or giving a bribe (active)
- requesting or accepting a bribe (passive)
- bribing a foreign official in order to obtain a business advantage (commercial)
- failing to prevent bribery (commercial)

The last one of these is particular noted, since it includes the activities of any person acting on behalf of a company, including not just employees but also agents and subsidiaries. There is a defence to "failing to prevent bribery" if an organisation to prove that it is 'policing itself' through adequate procedures. This imposes a clear requirement for all organisations to make a risk assessment.

The other commercial offence, 'bribing a foreign official' may affect certain geographical areas of an international business, particularly where payments have previously been regarded as an essential lubricant of the wheels of business and to ensure government action.

The UK Act does not follow the US Foreign Corrupt Practices Act in allowing a defence that payment is legal in the jurisdiction concerned or is bona fide and/or reasonable. Nevertheless, the framers of the Guidance are at pains to emphasise that they live in the real world and the public interest will be considered before taking action under this head.

The Guidance has now been issued that, for example, pays some attention to corporate hospitality, analysing degrees of motive, commercial necessity and luxury emanating, for example, from visits to the Six Nations at Twickenham and conferences in New York. A few more things that are general leap out, for example enforcement will depend on reasonableness and there must be a proved connection between an offered advantage and an intention to influence.

The Guidance provides six high-level and principles-based pointers as to what will be necessary for 'adequate procedures'.

These can be summarised as:

1. Procedures should be proportionate to the risks faced and the size and complexity of the business. They also need to be 'clear, practical, accessible, effectively implemented and enforced'.

2. Top-level management commitment should be demonstrable, including fostering a zero-tolerance culture towards bribery.

3. Initial and periodic risk assessment should be performed and documented, considering both internal and external risks. Five common external risks are identified as 'country, sectoral, transaction, business opportunity and business partnership'.

4. Proportionate and risk-based due diligence should be carried out on any party performing services for or on behalf of a company to ensure effective mitigation.

5. Bribery prevention policies and procedures need to be embedded throughout a company through communication, both internally and externally, and training. While again on a risk-based approach, training may need to extend to agents and other associates.

6. Regular monitoring and review should be in place to evaluate the effectiveness of bribery prevention procedures and make improvements where necessary.

While the Guidance helps in clarifying the nature of a well-defined compliance programme that is required to mitigate the risk of violation and minimise penalties should one occur, the need is clearly there for every company with UK-based operations to re-examine carefully its approach to managing the bribery risk and ensuring that its procedures are robust.
Source: www.ttclub.com 30 May 2011

See also:
http://www.justice.gov.uk/guidance/docs/bribery-act-2010-guidance.pdf?campaignkw=Bribery-Act-2010-Guidance

It will be seen that Anti-corruption measures are wide-ranging. As always in Procurement, "Caveat Emptor" (Let the buyer beware).

Bibliography

@UK (2006) E-procurement update.

Aberdeen Group. (2001). *E-sourcing-negotiating value in a volatile economy*

Aberdeen Group. (2005). *The CPO's Agenda*

Aberdeen Group. (2011). *Spend Optimisation*

Abbiati, P. (2001). 'Virtual agreement' in *Supply Management*, March 2001.

Arminas, D. (2004). 'Corporate Social Responsibility - Supply Chain CSR criteria unveiled' in *Supply Management*, December 2004.

Berger, Gattorna. (2001.) *Supply Chain Cybermastery*. Gower

Benmaridja, M and Benmaridja, A. (1996). 'Is it interesting for a company to outsource purchasing and under what conditions?' Paper presented at *IPSERA Conference*, Eindhoven University of Technology.

Benn, I *et al.* (2003). *Strategic Outsourcing*. London: Gower.

Birchall, J. (2006). 'Corporate Responsibility' in *Financial Times*, February 2006.

Blackburn, A. (2004). 'Audits ineffective against irresponsible purchasing' in *Supply Management*, July 2004.

Blackburn, A. (2004). 'CSR Academy is open for business' in *Supply Management*, July 2004.

Bradley, A. (2006). 'Tire Giant Outsources to save a Billion' in *Supply Management*, March 2006.

Bradley, A. (2006). 'Outsourcing – Call to develop post contract skills' in *Supply Management*, May 2006.

Bradley, A. (2006). 'Complacent IT deals are fraught with error' in *Supply Management*, April 2006.

Burnett, K. (2001). 'Electronic rules' in *Supply Management*, February 2001.

Browning, J. M, Zabiskie, N.B. and Huellmantel, A.B. (1983). 'Strategic purchasing planning' in *Journal of Purchasing and Materials Management*, pp. 19 – 24.

Cardon, T and Vollman, C. (2008). *The Power of Two*. Palgrave MacMillan.

Carr, A. & Smeltzer, L. (1999). 'The relationship of strategic purchasing to supply chain management' in *European Journal of Procurement Management*, vol 5 pp 42 – 51

Carroll, A.B. and Buchholtz, A.K. (1996). *Business and Society: Ethics and Stakeholder Management*. Cengage Learning.

Clarke, E. (2007). 'Purer Source' in *Supply Management*, January 2007.

CSR Section. (2006). 'Dell considers linking buyers to new standards' in *Supply Management*, April 2006.

Chandler, A. (1962). *Strategy and Structure*. Cambridge MA, MIT Press.

Chandler, A. (2007). 'Outsourcing procurement - from the inside out' in *Supply Management*, May 2007.

Cooper, A. (2007). 'To outsource or not to outsource?' in *Supply Management,* May 2007.

Clark, L. (2011). 'Procurement helps boost Premier Profits' in *Supply Management*, February 2011.

Day, Alan. (2010). *SRM Report*, State of Flox.

Dearing, D. (2004). 'Ethical Traders' in *Supply Management,* November 2004.

Ellinor, R. (2006). 'SMEs lack skills for online business' in *Supply Management,* March 2006.

Emmett, S., and Crocker, B. (2006). *The Relationship Driven Supply Chain.* Gower.

Emmett, S., and Crocker, B. (2008). *Excellence in Procurement*, Cambridge Academic.

Emmett, S., and Crocker, B. (2009). *Excellence in Supplier Management*, Cambridge Academic.

Emmett, S., and Granville, D. (2007). *Excellence in Inventory Management*, Cambridge Academic.

Emmett, S. (2005) *Supply Chain in 90 minutes* , Management Books 2000

Emmett, S. (2011) *Quick Guide to Supplier Relationship Management* , Cambridge Academic

Emmett, S. (2011). *Quick Guide to Systems View of the Supply Chain*, Cambridge Academic.

Evans, E. (1996). 'The disappearing department' in *Supply Management*, July 1996.

Future Purchasing Alliance. (2003). *Connecting purchasing and supplier strategies to shareholder value.* FPA

Galetto. F.F., Pignatelli. A. and Varetto. M. (2003). 'Outsourcing guidelines for a structure approach' in *Benchmarking: An International Journal* Volume 10 no.3.

Gildert, P. (2012). 'We're past asking for a seat at the table' - an interview with CIPS President in *Supply Management*, November 2012.

Gluck, F.W., Kaufman, S.P. and Walleck, A.S. (1980). Strategic management for competitive advantage. *Harvard Business Review 80404*, pp 154 - 161.

Guinipero, Sawchuk. (2000). *E-purchasing plus*. JGC Enterprise.

Gilbert, H. (2006). 'Ethical Supply Chains – Sourcing Good CSR' in *Supply Management,* March 2006.

Greenwood, M. (2005). 'The nuts and bolts of CSR' in *Supply Management,* February 2005.

Gooch, F. (2003). *Socially Responsible International Purchasing: The Why and How.* Traidcraft Exchange UK CIPS Regional Event.

Heinritz, S., Farrell, P., Giunipero, L. and Kolchin, M. (1993). *Purchasing, Principles and Applications*, 8th edn. New Jersey: Prentice Hall.

Hunt, M. (2004). 'Teaming with Talent' in *Supply Management*, August 2004.

Hurst, R. (2006). 'Ethics and the Purchaser' in *Supply Management*, March 2006.

IBM. (2004). *E-procurement benefits*.

John, G. (2004). 'CSR Roundtable – Beyond the greenwash' in *Supply Management*, July 2004.

Kearney A.T. (2002). *Global survey of e-procurement*.

Matthews, J. (2004). 'Outsourcing – The Rise of the Virtual Company' in *Supply Management*, July 2004.

McIvor, R. (2000). 'A practical framework for understanding the outsourcing process' in *Supply Chain Management, an International Journal*, Volume 5, no.1.

Mukhopadhyay, T., and Sunder, K. (2002). 'Strategic and operational benefits of electronic integration in B2B procurement processes' in *Management Science*, 48 (10), October 2002.

Mosco, L, (2004). 'Lip service won't suffice' in *Supply Management*, September 2004.

Norris, M., West, S., and Gaughan, K. (2000). *E-business Essential*. John Wiley and Sons.

O'Brien, L. (2005). 'Charity case rings an ethical warning' in *Supply Management*, June 2005.

PA Consulting Group. (1996). *International Survey on Outsourcing*

Pralahad, C.K., and Hamel, G. (1990). 'The core competence of the corporation' in *Harvard Business Review*, May/June 1990.

Parker, G. (2001). 'Money for something' in *Supply Management*, March 2001.

Reason, M. and Evans, E. (2001). *Implementing E-Procurement*. Cambridge: Hawksmere.

Riley, H. (2002.) 'Yes, we have ethical bananas' in *Supply Management*, March 2002.

Schroeder, R. (1989). *Service Framework for Purchasing and Supply Management, Operations Management*. McGraw Hill International.

Sellis, M. (2006). 'Outsourcing: Getting Closer' in *Supply Management*, April 2006.

Snell, P. (2006). 'Are we getting the message' in *Supply Management*, April 2006.

Snell, P. (2007). 'Diageo cures audit fatigue' in *Supply Management*, March 2007.

Stannack, P., and Jones, M. (1996). *'The death of purchasing?'*. Paper presented at IPSERA Conference, Eindhoven University of Technology.

Stannack, P. (2005). 'The Intelligent Customer' in *Supply Management*, May 2005.

Smith, G. (1995). *Handbook of Purchasing*. Gower.

Taylor, I. (2005). 'The time for excuses is over' in *Supply Management*, March 2005.

The McKinsey Quarterly. (2007). 'McKinsey global survey of purchasing executives' in *The McKinsey Quarterly*.

Transparency International. (2007). *UK Anti Corruption Training Manual.*

Varley, P. (2000). 'Serviceable solutions to all-out chaos' in *Supply Management*, January 2000.

Weeks, M. (2012). 'Procurement and Internal Customers - connecting to your customers' in *Supply Management*, November 2012.

Wheatley, M. (2000). 'World order' in *Supply Management*, September 2000.

Wheatley, M. (2003). *How to know if e-procurement is right for you?* CIO16.

Wheatley, M. (2004). 'Outsourcing: Getting the measure of services' in *Supply Management*, September 2004.

Whitehead, M. (2002). 'Corporate Social Responsibility' in *Supply Management*, March 2003.

Wilson, D. (2002). 'A facility for friction' in *Supply Management*, October 2002.

Index

Total Quality Management (TQM) 31, 57, 63, 64, 146, 147, 148, 149, 150, 151, 154, 155, 156, 204
  Q principles 149
  quality assurance 148
  quality control 148
  quality management 148
Toyota Production System (TPS) – *see also* Quality 147, 151, 152, 153, 154, 155, 156
  rules 152–153, 154
Transfer of Undertakings Protection of Employment (TUPE) 141, 142, 146

Value added 6, 23, 63

Weighted Multi Variable Auction – *see also* Electronic Auctions (E-Auctions) 106
Whole Life Costs (WLC) 9

9 781903 499726